Reading Shakespeare with Young Adults

Reading Shakespeare with Young Adults

Mary Ellen Dakin
Revere High School
Revere, Massachusetts

National Council of Teachers of English
1111 W. Kenyon Road, Urbana, Illinois 61801-1096

Staff Editor: Carol Roehm-Stogsdill

Interior Design: Doug Burnett

Cover Design: Pat Mayer

Cover Images: A collage of iStockphoto.com images. iStockphoto.com/ Goldmund, iStockphoto.com/DaddyBit, and iStockphoto.com/Lars Brinck.

NCTE Stock Number: 39042

It is the policy of NCTE in its journals and other publications to provide a forum for the open discussion of ideas concerning the content and the teaching of English and the language arts. Publicity accorded to any particular point of view does not imply endorsement by the Executive Committee, the Board of Directors, or the membership at large, except in announcements of policy, where such endorsement is clearly specified.

Every effort has been made to provide URLs that were accurate when the text was written, but because of the rapidly changing nature of the Web, some sites and addresses may no longer be accessible.

Library of Congress Cataloging-in-Publication Data

Dakin, Mary Ellen, 1952–
    Reading Shakespeare with young adults / Mary Ellen Dakin.
        p. cm.
    Includes bibliographical references.
    ISBN 978-0-8141-3904-2 (pbk.)
    1. Shakespeare, William, 1564–1616—Study and teaching (Secondary) I. Title.
    PR2987.D35 2009
    822.3'3—dc22

                                                                      2009012384

Contents

11. Reading with Eyes and Ears 151

The act of reading Shakespeare is visual, auditory, kinesthetic, tactile, and technical. To explore the full range of Shakespeare's imagery and sound, students will draw words, read images, construct storyboards, compose film scripts, perform, record, report, and produce using early modern, modern, and new age tools.

III. Fluency: Hearing and Speaking Shakespeare 185

12. Exploring Sound, Meaning, and Expression 187

Shakespeare's text is like music—it is written to be heard. This chapter provides teachers and students with a framework for learning to speak Shakespeare's words with greater clarity and conviction by exploring the sound, the grammar, and the imagery of Shakespeare's living language.

Epilogue: Independent Reading 211

PETER: *I pray, sir, can you read?*
ROMEO: *Ay, mine own fortune in my misery.*
PETER: *Perhaps you have learned it without book. But I pray, can you read anything you see?*
ROMEO: *Ay, if I know the letters and the language.*
                              Romeo and Juliet 1.2.57–61

By almost no means can Shakespeare be considered independent reading for young adults. Within the range of reading difficulty, Shakespeare's plays fall at a level somewhere between instructional and frustration.
Since almost all of the work of reading Shakespeare with young adults outlined in this book happens in collaborative classroom groups, teachers and students may want to extend the experience of reading the plays by choosing to read independently or in literature circles a novel based upon the life, the times, and/or the works of William Shakespeare. The epilogue lists a selection of whole works for independent reading inspired by the Bard.

Permission Acknowledgments

"Adapted second-person singular familiar pronoun chart." Reprinted with the permission of Washington Square Press, a Division of Simon & Schuster, Inc. from SHAKESPEARE SET FREE: Teaching Midsummer Night's Dream by Skip Nicholson; General Editor Peggy O'Brien. Copyright © 1993 by The Folger Shakespeare Library. All rights received.

"Biopoem graphic organizer" from SUMMARIZERS: ACTIVITY STRUC-TURES TO SUPPORT INTEGRATION AND RETENTION OF LEARN-ING by Jon Saphier and Mary Ann Haley. Published by Research for Better Teaching, Acton, MA, 1993. www.RBTeach.com. Used by permission of the publisher.

"Designing a soundscape/cue sheet" from SEEING AND BELIEVING by Mary T. Christel. Published by Boynton/Cook Publishers, Inc., 2001. Permission authorized by author.

"Guide to designing our project" from THE DIRECTOR IN THE CLASS-ROOM by Nikos Theodosakis. Published by Teach4Learning, Inc., 2001. www.thedirectorintheclassroom.com. Used by permission of the author.

Millais, Sir John Everett. *Ophelia*. Courtesy of © Tate, London 2009.

O'Brien, Peggy, PhD, "Multidimensional Shakespeare," NCTE presentation, Nashville, November 1998. Used by permission of the author.

"Storyboarding Activity #1 and 2" from READING IN THE DARK by John Golden. Copyright 2001 by the National Council of Teachers of English. Reprinted with permission.

VOCABULARY CARTOONS by Sam, Max, and Bryan Burchers. Published by New Monic Books, 1997. Used by permission of the authors.

Introduction: "To the great Variety of Readers"

Reade him, therefore; and againe, and againe: And if then you doe not like him, surely you are in some manifest danger, not to understand him.

John Heminge, Henry Condell, 1623 Folio

W*hy* should we read Shakespeare, again and again, with young adults in classrooms across the country? And if we can agree upon some answers to that question, the corollary ensues— *How*?

This book began years before I wrote it with a series of questions I couldn't answer on my own. But at the core of all my interrogatives there stood a stubborn, imperative spine: Speaking Shakespeare, writing about Shakespeare, performing Shakespeare, listening to and viewing Shakespeare, all proceed from *reading* Shakespeare, and the act of reading Shakespeare is something we need to understand.

Reading Shakespeare with Young Adults celebrates the collaborative reading of Shakespeare's plays. *Collaborative* as in what we can learn from classroom teachers, adolescents, literacy researchers, Shakespearean scholars, performers, and media specialists; *reading* as in what we can do with increasing independence to construct meaning from the transaction with challenging content written in early modern English; *plays* as in what we can apply to thirty-seven of them because the reading skills and strategies outlined in this book are transferable across the collection of Shakespeare's plays.

This book is written by an English teacher who knows firsthand the complexity, the challenge, and the reward of working with apprentice readers in the secondary classroom. The students at my school bear every label the educational system can muster—advanced, at-risk, mainstream, minority, English language learner, limited English proficient, straight, gay, special needs. In the crucible that is the twenty-first-century American classroom, reading Shakespeare with all of these students has become the most rewarding transaction we share. I use the word *transaction* as Louise Rosenblatt defines it in her preface to *Literature as Exploration* to suggest the infinite ways in which meaning "'happens' during the transaction between the reader" and a word, a line, a speech, or a scene in a Shakespearean play (xvi).

So *why* should we read Shakespeare again and again, in secondary classrooms across the country? My answers, outlined briefly here and in detail throughout this book, neither begin nor end with me. In fact, I can no longer distinguish between my reasoning and the reasoning of hundreds of others—students, teachers, researchers, scholars, performers, artists—who have over time whispered answers in my ear. Pardon me then in assuming the public voice, the royal "we," to state the reasons why we should read Shakespeare with our students.

Because he never ages. His plays are continually performed and made into films that feature actors with broad adolescent appeal— Leonardo DiCaprio, Claire Danes, Laurence Fishburne, Ethan Hawke, Julia Stiles, Ian McKellan, and Denzel Washington, to name a few. He has spawned a small library of young adult literature spin-offs.

Because he includes. More than any writer in the English-speaking canon, Shakespeare transcends the isolation of human being and the barriers of time, place, gender, race, and status that divide us. His plays have been translated into more than eighty languages. "Shakespeare," writes Ralph Alan Cohen, "is not about exclusion" (17).

Because he is in the water supply. In December of 2008, as I composed the final draft of this introduction, I was struck (again) by the degree to which Shakespeare permeates our culture. Uncle Bob, voracious reader and ad hoc family archivist, had saved me his copy of the *New York Times Book Review* with a note, "See page 11," scribbled on the front. On page eleven was the review of a book I had just purchased, Marjorie Garber's *Shakespeare and Modern Culture*; the first sentence of her introduction states, "Shakespeare makes modern culture and modern culture makes Shakespeare." The night before, I had paused in my reading of the 1999 novel *Ahab's Wife*, at Chapter 93, entitled "Shakespeare and Company." These are merely the most recent random episodes in what has come to feel like a perpetual state of déjà vu: Shakespeare is cited on the nightly news and emulated in pop culture ("Is this a dagger which I see before me, or a pizza? Mmmm, pizzaaa."—*MacHomer*). He is so quotable that, as Garber points out, he is often "quoted without quotation marks" (xviii). He is one of the most frequently anthologized and most frequently taught authors in America's schools (Applebee 75, 105).

Because we still can. Nothing lasts forever, not even Shakespeare. We are lucky to be born just heartbeats away from the early modern era in which Shakespeare wrote his plays, and to read the pieces of what he left us, not in translation, but with our own hearts and minds (Rosenbaum 511). It's only a matter of time before Shakespeare, like the *Beowulf* poet, requires a translator.

Because his plays are not just literary texts, they are working scripts. They require collaboration, voice, and movement. Choral readings, comparative viewing, quartos and folios, tableaux vivant, speaking text and subtext, writing directorial commentary, blocking scenes—these and other reading, writing, and performance strategies empower students to explore language with their whole bodies.

Because his plays are not just working scripts, they are literary texts. For the past three decades, the pedagogical and scholarly emphasis on Shakespeare as script has tended to minimize Shakespeare as text. In his 1997 introduction to *King Lear*, R. A. Foakes seeks a kind of equilibrium by asserting, "Plays have a double life, in the mind as read, and on the stage as acted," and that each experience is "different but equally valid" (qtd in Erne 23). In 2003, Lukas Erne published a scholarly study that vigorously argues "that the assumption of Shakespeare's indifference to the publication of his plays is a myth" (26). Yet even if we continue to accept the claim that Shakespeare wrote his plays not for readers to pore over but for actors to perform, a mere seven years after his death they were published in a book to be read and reread—"Reade him, therefore; and againe, and againe . . . "—and they remain, as Ron Rosenbaum proclaims, the bottomless treasure of the English language (12–18). As working scripts *and* as literary texts, their exploration requires an arsenal of reading skills.

This brings us to the last, best reason why we should read Shakespeare with young adults:

Because he is the great equalizer in the literature classroom. He is new and strange to us all. His English is early modern, and perhaps most richly felt by those readers in the early stages of their own development. His language challenges us all to think twice, to look again, to doubt our eyes, and this perhaps gives our English language learners a small advantage since this is what they must do with every text they read. His characters defy easy labels, just as our too-frequently labeled students do. We need to teach the reading of Shakespeare's plays to all of our students because the very nature of the task requires that we study to the roots of what we know and think we know about the needs of novice and intermediate readers, struggling readers, and English language learners.

And *how* do we read Shakespeare with young adults?

The answers began to manifest themselves in 1994 at the Folger Shakespeare Library's Teaching Shakespeare Institute (TSI). It was here that I met Peggy O'Brien, director of education at the Folger since 1981, and her team of teacher educators—Louisa Newlin, Mike LoMonico,

Paul Sullivan, Sheri Maeda, Caleen Jennings, Michael Tolaydo—and resident scholars Russ McDonald, Stephen Booth, and Jean Addison Roberts. It was here that I made a friend for life in Janet Field-Pickering, a secondary English teacher in Pennsylvania who would take the helm at the Folger when O'Brien left for the Corporation for Public Broadcasting in 1995, and who would enlist a brilliant new team of scholars in Rob Watson, Margaret Maurer, and Stephen Dickey.

The Folger introduced me to the fundamentals of performance-based teaching outlined in the series of books that came out of the institute, Shakespeare Set Free. The methods were time-consuming, but being told that we didn't have to read the whole play and that we could provide our students with scene summaries to advance their initial comprehension of the text felt liberating. Still, I began to hear the inarticulate stirrings of something more fundamental than performance. The act of reading Shakespeare was something I needed to understand.

In 2001, I found myself sitting on the Massachusetts Department of Education's Assessment Development Committee for the Grade 10 English Language Arts exit test. (In newspeak, that's the MDOE ADC for the ELA MCAS.) In four years' tenure on this committee, I saw firsthand the need to equip students with the skills and strategies they would need to read and write on demand. In an urban district where almost 70 percent of the student population qualifies for free or reduced lunch, the sophomores at Revere High School would be expected to read excerpts from texts of varying complexity, answer multiple-choice questions about those texts, and write open responses and an essay that demonstrate their comprehension of text—on their own. And oh yes, Shakespeare would be on the test. A 2006 survey of author frequency on my state's grade 10 ELA exit test since its inception in 1998 places William Shakespeare in the lead with six appearances. The second runner-up is Sandra Cisneros, with three. Revere High School literacy coach Christina Porter conducted the survey.

So in 2003 I revised an old question and wondered where to look for the answers: *What things do accomplished readers do to understand Shakespeare's text, and how can we teach these things to our students?*

Some of the answers could be found in the performance-based teaching methods I had learned in the past. But not all. So I went looking again, and started with myself. What were the things I did to understand? What reading Shakespeare survival skills did I develop as an undergraduate, when to read a play a week, independently, was the norm? What things did I do with a Shakespeare text before I would teach it to others?

I looked to my colleagues and found a partner in Christina Porter, an English teacher with a master's degree in adolescent literacy and a passion for theater and Shakespeare's plays. Porter's encouragement and advice permeate this book. I shared ideas and lesson plans with novice teachers Ben Murphy and Althea Terenzi and with veterans Nancy Barile, Kelly Andreoni, and Allison Giordano and got back from them as much as I ever gave. Curriculum directors Ron Eydenberg and Jonathan Mitchell provided constant support and encouragement. I made frequent trips down the hall to technology teachers—David Kaufman who teaches Web design and Alec Waugh who teaches music technology—for their expertise on the newest literacy tools.

As the Shakespeare elective teacher to juniors and seniors and a teacher of sophomore English, a course whose required whole works included *Macbeth* and *Hamlet*, I began to see the classroom as a laboratory and my students as assistants. Finally, I began to read the research on adolescent and adult literacy and to incorporate this new knowledge more consciously into my practice. Four years later, in 2007, I began to write this book.

This book is what happens when a work-in-progress meets a final deadline. Its author will always have questions that go unanswered for another day; some of the activities and projects described in these pages will reshape themselves as classroom technology continues to advance. But into these pages I have unpacked a lifetime of wondering about *why* William Shakespeare's plays[*] still matter, to me, to colleagues, and to the students who wander into our classrooms every day from the mean and easy streets of America. We can't force kids to believe that Shakespeare matters. But we can teach them—with explicit skills instruction, with interdependence, with humility, with wonder, and with imagination—*how* to read Shakespeare, and they will learn the power and play of words, the frustrating complexity of meaning, and the necessity of community. Unrestricted by an omniscient narrator, untutored by an authorial presence, unburdened by descriptive stage directions and prescriptive directorial commentary, they will experience reading as active, constructive, visceral. Because reading him requires so much of them, they will take Shakespeare with them into college, into the armed forces, into jobs that pay the bills, into hospitals, cemeteries, and jails, and they will feel less alone. Shakespeare's characters have already been there.

----

[*]Unless otherwise stated, all line citations in this book are from *The Oxford Shakespeare: The Complete Works*, 2nd Edition, edited by John Jowett, William Montgomery, Gary Taylor, and Stanley Wells.

What's past is prologue.

Enter Ms. Dakin, sophomore English teacher. The year is 1990 and the curriculum mandates *Julius Caesar*. With a bachelor's degree in English and an unquenched thirst for words, words, words, I come trailing clouds of glory into a secondary school filled with urban adolescents and watch in helpless dismay as the things I love come crashing to the classroom floor.

How do I teach this stuff? And why?

This book is one teacher's attempt to answer her own questions.

I Vocabulary: Understanding Words

POLONIUS:	What do you read, my lord?
HAMLET:	Words, words, words.

Hamlet 2.2.193–195

Every time I scratch the surface of what students know about words, I throw imaginary arms up in disbelief. It is not just the English language learners who struggle with tier-two words, high-frequency mature words that occur less in conversation and more in content-area written texts (Beck et al. 16–20). The past three decades have produced a rich body of research on the necessary relationship between vocabulary instruction and comprehension, yet the gap between research and practice has barely closed (Allen 87–91). Deciding which words to teach when students seem so far from the 60,000 they are supposed to know by adulthood (Neergaard A10) is the first dilemma. Reading the research and revamping outmoded methods of instruction—word lists with dictionary definitions and multiple-choice/fill-in-the-blank assessments—is the next task. Making time in the notoriously overstuffed secondary curriculum for meaningful and frequent vocabulary instruction is the third challenge.

The lessons in this section tackle word study from two different directions. First, think of *understanding* as a verb. As a verb, you might want students to understand, for example, what a stage direction such as *exeunt* means. You might want to demystify the high-frequency archaic words—*hence, anon, knave*—that distinguish the Shakespearean vernacular from our own. Of course, there are the traditional collections of tier-two words in Shakespeare's plays provided by textbook and test-prep publishers, but if you check the word frequency lists in Michael LoMonico's *The Shakespeare Book of Lists*, you will discover that their appearance in the plays is rare. In fact, the highest-frequency words in Shakespeare's plays are basic, tier-one words.

Next, think of *understanding* as a verbal. In this sense, you want students to have a vocabulary rich enough to express a fine-grained understanding of the complexity and ambiguity of Shakespeare's characters or of the myriad tones with which words and lines can be read and spoken.

The lessons in this section support a systematic and sustained approach to word study that is crucial to understanding and enjoying Shakespeare's plays.

1 The Functional Vocabulary of Shakespeare's Stage Directions

Flourish the bell. The Kids *exeunt the classroom and descend to the cafeteria. Hautboys play in the headphones. Enter* CHORUS *of* Friends *and advance to their table. The dumb-show enters and in an aside, the* Friends *make fun of them. Within, the* Lunch Ladies *yell at some* Kid. ALEX *advances to* TESS. *She draws.* ALEX *retires to the dumb-show table. Flourish the bell.* Students *exeunt severally, attended by the* Dean.

Stage directions composed by sophomores, 2005

For too many years, I took for granted that students understand the high-frequency words that constitute the working vocabulary of Shakespeare's stage directions. After all, the most frequent stage directions are written in general, everyday language—*Enter, Exit, Dies*. With a cavalier dismissal of stage directions as sight words,[1] I failed to see the irony of my neglect: the explicit stage directions in Shakespeare are in fact sight words in that they help readers to visualize the text. For example, we read "[*Hecate retires*]" in the Dover edition of *Macbeth* 4.1. "What does *retires* mean?" I asked a roomful of sophomores one day. Blank stares, shoulder shrugs, then one response, "It's what you do when you're old." I opened my eyes a little wider that day to the little big words in italics.

Playing Peek-a-Boo

Some people do retire when they are, as one fifteen-year-old put it, "old," so I thought it would be fun to play with the multiple meanings of words. I skimmed the plays I teach most frequently for the stage directions common to each and put them in a list:

Enter

Exit

Exeunt

Flourish

Sennet

Aside

Alarum

Advances

Attends

Within

Retires

Draws

Beneath

Dies

Descends

If I showed students the entire list at once, they would probably read it immediately as stage directions so I needed a way to de-contextualize the words. I made an overhead transparency of the list but also made a cover for it using heavy paper and a precision hobby knife to cut tabs that could be peeled back to reveal just one word at a time. Then we played peek-a-boo.

Peeling back the tab for *Draws*, I asked students what this word means. They went silent the way adolescents do when the answer to your question is so obvious that it doesn't deserve a response. Someone drew pictures in the air. I tried again with *Attends*. "That's when you go to school," someone said. Then I peeled back the tab for *Retires* and they smelled a rat. Revealing the whole list to them, we started from the top, easily defining most stage directions and taking guesses at some.

Then I distributed a handout of definitions adapted from *The American Heritage Dictionary* (Figure 1.1), an odd source, one would think, for definitions of theatrical jargon but the only one I could find to guide me in the construction of a handout I needed the next day. To this day, I think it does the trick.

To practice and extend their new awareness of Shakespeare's functional vocabulary, we considered these more detailed stage directions, taken from several plays, and talked about the possibilities of meaning.

Enter, with train

Enter Chorus

Enter, attended

The dumb-show enters

Exeunt severally

Functional Vocabulary Definitions

We can understand the most common stage directions, *Enter* and *Exit*, without the help of a dictionary. Others, like *Dies* and *Descends*, are just as easily understood. Nonetheless, even these most readily understood stage directions require the reader to imagine just how, in each set of circumstances, the performance of the stage direction should look and sound.

Before we read Shakespeare's play, review the meanings of these stage directions, most of which are extracted from *The American Heritage Dictionary of the English Language*:

> *Advances:* Moves forward; moves against another.
>
> *Alarum:* Loud, frantic, or excited activity; clamor. The sounds of war or warlike activity. The movement of soldiers across stage.
>
> *Aside:* A piece of dialogue intended for the audience and supposedly not heard by the other actors on stage. A remark made in an undertone so as to be inaudible to others nearby.
>
> *Attended:* To be accompanied or waited upon as by a companion or servant.
>
> *Beneath:* In a lower place; below. Underneath the stage.
>
> *Draws:* Pulls out a weapon for use.
>
> *Exeunt:* Two or more performers leave the stage.
>
> *Flourish/Sennet:* A fanfare (of horns, trumpets, etc.) to announce the entrance or exit of a person of distinction.
>
> *Retires/Withdraws:* Seeks seclusion; moves back or away without actually exiting the stage; recedes.
>
> *Within:* An inner position, place, or area close to, but not actually on, the stage.

NOTE: Most modern editions of Shakespeare's plays follow the practice of putting into parentheses, brackets, and/or half-brackets anything that isn't in the copy text of the play. The copy text is the quarto or the First Folio used as the basis of the modern edition. In other words, brackets *almost always* alert the reader that whatever is in the brackets has been added by an editor to clarify what is implied but not stated in the original text.

Figure 1.1. Functional vocabulary definitions.

Ordnance shot off within

They retire without the door

Exit, pursued by a bear

"Think about the trains on the Blue Line," I asked them. "How could someone enter, with a different kind of *train*, like '*Enter Caesar and his train*'?"

"Should *Chorus* be a group? Does it have to be?"

"If someone is said to be deaf, dumb, and blind, what can *dumb* mean? And what might a *dumb-show* be?"

Before re-contextualizing the vocabulary of stage directions to Shakespeare's plays, I challenged my students to write their own stage directions, using people they know as characters and incorporating multiple stage directions from the list. The epigraph at the beginning of this chapter is one example. I think you will find, as I have, that adolescents are invariably delighted by the strange, new faces of familiar words.

What's Going on with Those Brackets?

"I don't know," I was forced to admit one day when a student, motivated perhaps by curiosity but more likely by the desire to stump the teacher, called attention to those funny little signals scattered throughout the pages of the play, especially in the vicinity of the stage directions. I had majored in English as an undergraduate and taken every Shakespeare course offered, and I had taught the plays for at least ten years without paying any attention to the parentheses, brackets, and half-brackets that encased Shakespearean words and lines like innocuous little warning flags, content to be ignored.

Enter Margaret Maurer, Shakespearean scholar at Colgate and faculty member of the Folger Library's TSI. It was she who first taught me to pay attention to these editorial signals, in part because so many of the explicit stage directions in Shakespeare's plays have been written by someone else. The parentheses and brackets are used by editors to indicate this textual interference in the modern editions of the plays. In the introduction to the New Folger Library text of *Othello*, for example, editors Barbara Mowat and Paul Werstine point out that there are two printed versions of this play from which editors draw, the 1622 Quarto and the 1623 Folio.[2] Mowat and Werstine explain their signals in this way:

1. All the words in this edition that are printed in the Quarto version but not in the Folio appear in pointed brackets (⟨ ⟩).

2. All full lines that are found in the Folio and not in the Quarto are printed in square brackets ([ ]).

3. Sometimes neither the Folio nor the Quarto seems to offer a satisfactory reading, and it is necessary to print a word different from what is offered by either. Such words (called "emendations" by editors) are printed within half-square brackets (⌈ ⌉) (xlvii–xlviii).

Furthermore, Mowat and Werstine assure the careful reader that "whenever we change the wording of the Folio *or add anything to its stage directions* [my italics], we mark the change" (xlvii).

Why should we care?

Because our students need to see the possibilities in Shakespeare's text, and sometimes well-meaning editors limit or confuse those possibilities. There are places in the modern editions of Shakespeare's plays where editorial interference with the stage directions manipulates the action and potential meaning in a scene. For example, in 1.2 of *Othello*, upon a torch-lit stage, an angry father named Brabantio enters with Roderigo and officers to arrest "the foul thief" Othello who has married his daughter without Brabantio's blessing and permission. Othello is onstage with his officers, Iago and Cassio. The New Folger edition of the confrontation reads:

RODERIGO: Signior, it is the Moor.

BRABANTIO: Down with him, thief! [*They draw their swords.*]

IAGO: You, Roderigo! Come, sir, I am for you.

OTHELLO: Keep up your bright swords, for the dew will
               rust them.

When I listen to my students working through these lines (72–77) in their reading companies, I hear them questioning the text and seeking to clarify whether "*They draw their swords*" means every character onstage, or every character *except* Othello. The point is even more debatable when we read from the Dover Thrift edition, whose stage direction reads, "[*They draw on both sides.*]" If Othello is included in the pronoun *They*, then students tend to read him as aggressive. Yet it is Othello who defuses the situation by telling the mob to sheathe their swords against the dew. If he is the exception in this angry crowd, then we read and see Othello differently. Whether the added stage direction is there or not, readers need to decide what Othello does in this opening confrontation, but at this moment in the play, the editors' stage direction interferes with the text in ways that can limit or confuse our students' reading of the character Othello.

There's another reason why we should care about stage directions in square and half-square brackets, but I must return to my first reason in order to state the second: our students need to see the possibilities in Shakespeare's text, with their own eyes first.

Too often, editors' emendations do the reading for us, not only by stating the obvious, as in this example from 3.1.63 of the Folger edition:

POLONIUS: I hear him coming. Let's withdraw, my lord.
             [*They withdraw.*]
. . . but also by too eagerly explaining what the dialogue implies. Even if you do not teach *Romeo and Juliet*, consider distributing this excerpt from act 3.1, in which Tybalt goes hunting for Romeo but is lured from his target by Mercutio. The scene is famous enough that some students might recall film or stage readings, but read it aloud once and then challenge students to reread it in small groups and stage it in their mind's eye. The text is the New Folger edition, lines 61–108, minus all editorial emendations:

TYBALT: Romeo, the love I bear thee can afford

             No better term than this: thou art a villain.

ROMEO: . . . Villain am I none.

             Therefore farewell. I see thou knowest me not. . . .

MERCUTIO: O calm, dishonorable, vile submission!

             Alla stoccato carries it away.

             Tybalt, you ratcatcher, will you walk?

TYBALT: What wouldst thou have with me?

MERCUTIO: Good king of cats, nothing but one of your nine lives
             . . . .

TYBALT: I am for you.

ROMEO: Gentle Mercutio, put thy rapier up.

MERCUTIO: Come, sir, your *passado*.

ROMEO: Draw, Benvolio, put down their weapons.

             Gentlemen, for shame forbear this outrage!

             Tybalt! Mercutio! The Prince expressly hath

             Forbid this bandying in Verona streets.

             Hold, Tybalt! Good Mercutio!

             Away, Tybalt!

MERCUTIO: I am hurt.

             A plague o' both houses! I am sped.

             Is he gone and hath nothing?

BENVOLIO: What, art thou hurt?

MERCUTIO: Ay, ay, a scratch, a scratch. Marry, 'tis enough.

             Where is my page?—Go, villain, fetch a surgeon.

ROMEO: Courage, man, the hurt cannot be much.

MERCUTIO: No, 'Tis not so deep as a well, nor so wide as a church door, but 'tis enough. 'Twill serve. Ask for me tomorrow, and you shall find me a grave man. . . . A plague o' both your houses! . . . Why the devil came you between us? I was hurt under your arm.

From the day I first read this scene to now, I am deeply moved by Mercutio's aggrieved, near-rhetorical question, "Why the devil came you between us?" and its devastating corollary, "I was hurt under your arm." Just how this fatal moment, in a play that sets its full gaze on fatal moments, manages to happen is something I want students to construct for themselves. When we teach them to read the dialogue as active instead of passive readers (or in the language of theater, as players instead of spectators), they will discover clues embedded by an actor's poet in the dialogue.

So I ask them, as I ask you now, to look for the weapons in this scene. Who draws first? When? Who is the aggressor, the first to strike? Does Romeo draw a weapon or is he so true to his love that he never draws yet thrusts himself unarmed between two enraged enemies? At what moment is Mercutio fatally stabbed, and how does he physically react? What happens to Tybalt?

Then I tell students they are the editors, and in groups they translate their reading of the scene into stage directions, using the vocabulary of stage directions listed in Figure 1.1.

After students have begun to see the text with their own eyes, I distribute the same lines of dialogue with the addition of stage directions composed by the Folger editors:

TYBALT: Romeo, the love I bear thee can afford

            No better term than this: thou art a villain.

ROMEO: . . . Villain am I none.

            Therefore farewell. I see thou knowest me not. . . .

MERCUTIO: O calm, dishonorable, vile submission!

            Alla stoccato carries it away.   [*He draws.*]

            Tybalt, you ratcatcher, will you walk?

TYBALT: What wouldst thou have with me?

MERCUTIO: Good king of cats, nothing but one of your nine lives. . . .

TYBALT: I am for you.   [*He draws.*]

ROMEO: Gentle Mercutio, put thy rapier up.

MERCUTIO: Come, sir, your *passado*.   [*They fight.*]

ROMEO: Draw, Benvolio, put down their weapons.

[*Romeo draws.*]

Gentlemen, for shame forbear this outrage!

Tybalt! Mercutio! The Prince expressly hath

Forbid this bandying in Verona streets.

Hold, Tybalt! Good Mercutio!

[*Romeo attempts to beat down their rapiers.*

Tybalt stabs Mercutio.]

Away, Tybalt!

[*Tybalt, Petruchio, and their followers exit.*]

MERCUTIO: I am hurt.

A plague o' both houses! I am sped.

Is he gone and hath nothing?

BENVOLIO: What, art thou hurt?

MERCUTIO: Ay, ay, a scratch, a scratch. Marry, 'tis enough.

Where is my page?—Go, villain, fetch a surgeon.

[*Page exits.*]

ROMEO: Courage, man, the hurt cannot be much.

MERCUTIO: No, 'Tis not so deep as a well, nor so wide as a church
door, but 'tis enough. 'Twill serve. Ask for me tomorrow, and you shall find me a grave man. . . . A plague o'
both your houses! . . . Why the devil came you between
us? I was hurt under your arm.

Though some students are pleased to learn that what the editors
saw embedded in the dialogue they saw too, others are ready to disagree
with the professionals. To well-meaning editors everywhere I would ask
in the name of Shakespeare's youngest readers and their teachers, *Why
the devil come you between us and the text*? One of the reasons why we so
need Shakespeare is because he so needs us. More than three centuries
before a literary critic would insist that "The literary work exists in the
live circuit set up between reader and text" (Rosenblatt 24), and more
than three centuries before a biologist would claim that language is "like
nest-building or hive-making, the universal and biologically specific activity of human beings" (Thomas 89), this poet-playwright understood
that language and meaning must be under constant construction.

Seeing Implicit Stage Directions

There's another way to look at this: whenever editors change, omit, or add to the stage directions, they are reading what's not there, and often, what's not there is what we want our students to read.

When Macbeth says, "I drink to the general joy of the whole table," I stand stiff and motionless at the front of the room (with a water bottle strategically situated within reach on my desk) and challenge them to read a stage direction that's not written on the page. I say the line again, in a party-hostess voice, with arms glued stubbornly to my side. "It's a toast!" some young veteran of a family wedding always cries out, "Raise the water bottle and say it again!" At a moment such as this one, tell students that Shakespeare's plays are filled with invisible stage directions, that those stage directions are call *implicit* stage directions because they are implied, not stated, and that in order to read Shakespeare, we need to read the cues for gesture, action, line delivery, and props embedded in the lines.

The next time your students arrive at a dramatic, action-filled scene in Shakespeare, copy it, white out all the stage directions (or at least the bracketed ones), and distribute the text to your students as Shakespeare most likely would have written it and distributed it to his company, entrusting the players to read the page onto the stage. Review the terms *explicit* and *implicit stage directions,* and let them work in groups at writing their own stage directions, as editors do, for the places where a particular gesture, action, or prop illuminates a word or line. For some wonderful classroom activities that address Shakespeare's explicit and implicit stage directions, see Rex Gibson and Janet Field-Pickering's *Discovering Shakespeare's Language,* pages 127–131.

One of my favorite scenes for reading implicit stage directions is act 3.4 in *Macbeth* in which the bloody ghost of Banquo appears at a banquet. After we have read the scene once for initial comprehension, I tell students to close their books and put them away—they are not students in an English classroom anymore but players in Shakespeare's company, and he has written a scene for them filled with dialogue and ripe for action. In small groups they look for the clues to action embedded in the dialogue, and then I ask for volunteers to show us what they found. Reading for what's *not* on the page is required reading in Shakespeare.

Parsing Explicit Stage Directions

ex·plic·it *adj.* Fully and clearly expressed; leaving nothing implied.

Earlier in this chapter I acknowledged *The American Heritage Dictionary* as my source for definitions of the most common explicit stage directions. But lo and behold, when I looked up the word *explicit*, the second half of the definition rang an alarum bell in my head. When it comes to Shakespeare's stage directions, and for that matter to almost any word or phrase of consequence in literature or life, ambiguity is not only desirable but also essential. In an essay entitled "Information," biologist Lewis Thomas points out that, "It is often necessary, for meaning to come through, that there be an almost vague sense of strangeness and askewness" in the language we use to inform (94). In other words, *explicit* doesn't mean there's only one way to get the job done.

Take *Hamlet*'s "*Enter* GHOST," for example.

How can a Ghost enter a theater, a stage? How should it enter? In a play echoing with questions of heaven, hell, and purgatory, if the Ghost enters from above, what does that imply about its nature? If it enters through the trap door of the stage floor, what does that imply? If it walks on level ground as you and I, what implications are there? If you had a million-dollar budget, how would your Ghost enter? If your *Hamlet* were set in present-day New York City as opposed to seventeenth-century London or twelfth-century Denmark, how might the Ghost enter? If you were filming *Hamlet* instead of staging it, how could technology be made to serve art? Keep asking your students to question the explicit stage directions. Leave nothing clear.

Enter. Exit. Retires. Dies. No two are alike.

2 Archaic Words

'Tis still a dream, or else such stuff as madmen
Tongue, and brain not; either both, or nothing,
Or senseless speaking, or a speaking such
As sense cannot untie.

Cymbeline 5.5.239–242

O, but it can, most of the time. And when sense cannot completely untie an archaic word or phrase, it can borrow understanding from the neighbors, 98 percent of which are current, modern English words (Cohen 108). And if that fails, sense can loosen its collar and have a little fun. Though I cannot smoothly tongue *honorificabilitudinitatibus*, I can brain it by the first two syllables. And simply saying such words out loud makes me smile. Alongside the puns and the oxymorons, Shakespeare's archaic words are the stuff of wordplay.

So why bother writing or reading a chapter that addresses 2 percent of Shakespeare's words? My first reason for writing this chapter is to challenge the stereotype that Shakespeare's language is "too hard" because it's "old"—it's not old English; it's early modern English. My second reason is to acknowledge that Shakespeare's high-frequency archaic words can be a needless distraction, especially but not exclusively for the intermediate, transitioning, and mainstreamed English language learners in our classrooms, but one that is quickly and easily addressed. In 2007, when literacy coach Christina Porter collaborated with ELL instructor Judy Shea and me on lessons for an abridged script of *The Tempest*, Porter found that when she charted and defined the frequently repeated archaic words in this play, Shea's students' fluency improved. My third reason is to defy the trend toward modernized Shakespeare by encouraging students to play with the "weird words," as Michael LoMonico calls them (59), and to rediscover the joy of word-making that every human child inherits. Consider Shakespeare's archaic words the baby talk of his mother tongue. No wonder they remain such fun.

High-Frequency Archaic Words

Alack, wherefore should a harried teacher, perforce driven to dispatch an overwrought curriculum and to attend the diverse needs of every babe in Christendom, resolve the call to teach in Shakespeare's tongue? How will this fadge?

Start with some of the most frequently occurring archaic words. I display these words on an overhead transparency and ask students to guess at their meanings:

adieu

anon

dost, doth

hark

ho

list

ne'er

perchance

sirrah

thee

wench

woo

Students will guess at some, especially if they have already read one of Shakespeare's plays. At the very least, you will have captured their attention.

The complete list, Figure 2.1, is a handout composed from a combination of sources. First, I made a list of high-frequency archaic words common to the plays I usually teach. I shared this list with literacy coach Christina Porter and she confirmed that these little words were a constant distraction to the intermediate and transitioning English language learners with whom she was working. Then I consulted LoMonico's *The Shakespeare Book of Lists*. Chapter 3 of LoMonico's book is a treasure trove of "some of the most common, most curious, most confusing, and most coarse" words in the plays (57). Finally, I vetted the list using an online Shakespeare concordance to confirm that the words occur frequently throughout the plays. Word frequencies range from thirty-two appearances for *resolve* to thousands for *thee, thy, thou,* and *thine;* the majority of words on the list appear somewhere between one hundred and three hundred times. The short definitions hale from Schmidt's *Lexicon* and *The American Heritage Dictionary.*

Figure 2.1 lists thirty-five high-frequency archaic words and forms of a word (*alas, alack*) that span the plays, but since Porter was working with a group of ELL students and their only Shakespearean text was *The Tempest,* she decided to abridge the list but leave room for troublesome

---

High-Frequency Archaic Sight Words

high-frequency: words that occur often in the text
archaic: words no longer in use, or used differently
sight: words to know automatically

These archaic words appear frequently in Shakespeare's plays. Since we will be tripping all over them as we read the plays of William Shakespeare, it's worth knowing them automatically.

Adieu: good-bye; farewell	Oft: often
Alas, alack: expresses sorrow	Passing: surprisingly, exceedingly
Anon: soon, immediately after	Perchance: maybe
Art: are	Perforce: of necessity
Attend: to wait upon; to pay attention	Prithee: I pray thee; please
Cousin: any close relative	Resolve: to answer; to reply
Dost, doth: do, does	Sirrah: a lowly person
Ere: before	Thee, thy, thou, thine: you, your, yours
Fie: a curse	Thence: from that place; from there
Hark: listen	'Tis: it is
Hast, hath: have, has	Troth: belief
Hence: from this place	'Twere, 'Twas: it were, it was
Ho: an exclamation that calls to attention, mocks, or celebrates	Want: lack
Knave: a villain	Wench: a female person; varies in tone from tenderness to contempt
List: listen	Wherefore: why
Morrow: day	Woo: to seek and gain
Nay: no	Yea: yes
Ne'er: never	

Figure 2.1. High-frequency archaic sight words.

archaic words that she and her students might encounter and add to the chart as they read through the play (Figure 2.2). Before distributing any definitions to students, we both decided to begin with lines from Shakespeare that contain the archaic words and to have students use context clues to guess at their possible meanings. For this work, we went back to the online Shakespeare concordances, she to harvest lines from *The Tempest* and me to collect lines from a broad spectrum of the plays for each of the thirty-five high-frequency archaic words on my list. Figure 2.3 is a list of thirty-five short sentences from the plays, one for each of the high-frequency archaic words.

High-Frequency Archaic Vocabulary in *The Tempest* Use this organizer to keep track of the archaic vocabulary we come across in this play.	
1. 'Tis	14. Pray
2. Prithee	15. Mine
3. Hence	16.
4. Thence	17.
5. Thee	18.
6. Thy	19.
7. Thou	20.
8. Thine	21.
9. Hast	22.
10. Hath	23.
11. Art	24.
12. Dost	25.
13. Didst	26.

Figure 2.2. High-frequency archaic vocabulary in *The Tempest*.

High-Frequency Archaic Sight Words in Context

1. **Adieu, adieu, adieu**. Remember me.
2. **Alas**, then she is drown'd.
3. You shall see **anon** how the murderer gets the love of Gonzago's wife.
4. O Romeo, Romeo, wherefore **art thou** Romeo?
5. Well, sir, I'll bring you to our master Lear, And leave you to **attend** him.
6. We hear our bloody **cousins** are bestow'd In England and in Ireland.
7. O, she **doth** teach the torches to burn bright!
8. O coward conscience, how **dost thou** afflict me!
9. **Ere** the bat **hath** flown His cloister'd flight . . . there shall be done A deed of dreadful note.
10. **Fie** on't! ah **fie**! 'Tis an unweeded garden That grows to seed.
11. **Hark!** I hear horses.
12. For **thou hast** been As one, in suffering all, that suffers nothing.
13. **Hence,** horrible shadow! Unreal mockery, **hence!**
14. Stand **ho!** Who's there?
15. There's **ne'er** a villain dwelling in all Denmark But he's an arrant **knave**.
16. **List, list,** O **list!** If ever **thou** didst thy dear father love—Revenge his foul and most unnatural murder!
17. O, never Shall sun that **morrow** see.
18. **Nay**, press not so upon me; stand far off.
19. For I **ne'er** saw true beauty till this night.
20. The evil that men do lives after them; The good is **oft** interred with their bones.
21. She swore, in faith, **'twas** strange, **'twas passing** strange.
22. **Perchance** she weeps because they killed her husband, **Perchance** because she knows them innocent.
23. To take't again, **perforce!** Monster ingratitude!
24. I **prithee**, take **thy** fingers from my throat.
25. **Resolve** me, with all modest haste.
26. Peace, **sirrah!** You beastly **knave**, know you no reverence?
27. Get **thee** to a nunnery.
28. There is the playhouse now, there must you sit; And **thence** to France shall we convey you safe, and bring you back.
29. Three thousand ducats; **'tis** a good round sum.
30. By my **troth**, Nerissa, my little body is aweary of this great world.
31. You are dull, Casca, and those sparks of life That should be in a Roman you do **want**.
32. Now, by the world, it is a lusty **wench**. O, how I long to have some chat with her!
33. Say, why is this? **wherefore?** what should we do?
34. But **woo** her, gentle Paris, get her heart.
35. Did I not tell **thee yea?** . . . Why **dost thou** ask again?

Figure 2.3. High-frequency archaic sight words in context.

Again, Porter modified this activity for ELL students by writing each *Tempest* high-frequency archaic word and three lines of dialogue from that play onto index cards, and the ELL students worked in small groups to figure out the meanings of the words:

(1)**'Tis**
'Tis time I should inform thee farther. Lend thy hand,
And pluck my magic garment from me. *Prospero*

'Tis far off
And rather like a dream than an assurance. *Miranda*

'Tis a villain, sir,
I do not love to look on. *Miranda*

Some they decoded easily (*thee, thy, thou*) but others were more difficult (*prithee*). In addition to distributing the chart in Figure 2.2 for students to record definitions and keep in their notebooks, Porter copied the chart onto a large poster and displayed it on the wall of the classroom for quick daily reference.

In the Shakespeare class, I distribute Figure 2.3 to the whole group with every fifth line highlighted (in other words, some students work with lines 1, 5, 15, etc., while some students work with lines 2, 6, 16, etc.) so that every word and every line is examined by at least two different students, who then get together to compare notes. Only after students grapple with the possible meanings of these high-frequency archaic words in context do I distribute definitions. As a summarizer, cut the thirty-five lines of dialogue into strips, distribute them to students, and challenge them to arrange their lines into dramatic mini-scenes.

Better than telling students that Shakespeare's early modern English is accessible to them, these activities show students that the small percentage of Shakespeare's archaic words is surrounded by recognizable, modern words and that context clues and vocal inflection are natural tools for understanding them. ELL students survive this way, hungrily gleaning the page for sound and context clues, but as Porter points out, "Too many adolescent readers for whom English is their first language simply skip words they don't know and fail to use context clues to solve for meaning." It is one of the fundamental arguments of this book that Shakespeare is the great equalizer in the language arts classroom in that his text is new and strange to all of our students. Instead of skipping over the "hard stuff," we should encourage our students to embrace it.

Low-Frequency "Weird" Words

Weird words are low-frequency archaic words that appear not at all today and very infrequently even in Shakespeare's plays. Still, they are wild and whirling words that often contain clues—recognizable word parts, imagery, and/or sounds—that suggest their meaning. Bringing them into a twenty-first century classroom is like giving students an opportunity to resurrect an extinct species. The short list of weird words I distribute to students (Figure 2.4) is a compilation made from materials in two lengthier sources, *The Book of Lists* and *Discovering Shakespeare's Language*. Students have fun guessing the meanings of these words, and often come away from this activity less troubled by their perceived limitations of Shakespeare's language and more troubled by the limitations of our own. When we spend some time exploring Shakespeare's archaic words with students, writes Ralph Cohen in *ShakesFear and How to Cure It*, we "show them some of the treasures our language has lost" (125).

Several excellent resources for classroom activities that get students having fun with archaic English include *Shakespeare Set Free: Teaching* Romeo and Juliet, which includes a "Shakespearean Insult Sheet." You don't have to teach *Romeo and Juliet* to enjoy this activity. In *Discovering Shakespeare's Language*, Rex Gibson and Janet Field-Pickering offer a variety of creative approaches to archaic language, including excerpts of scenes from *King Lear* and *Henry IV Part 1* that are rich in Elizabethan insults (135–137) as well as activities for inventing words and dialogue that draw upon Shakespeare's fluid inventiveness with words (64–66). In Chapter 5 of his book, Cohen outlines a comprehensive approach to what he calls "Student Complaint #1: Shakespeare's Too Hard" by tackling the issue of Shakespeare's language in a series of "general approaches" (106–109).

Synthesis: Shakespearean Sentences and Dialogue

Each spring in Massachusetts, all grade 10 students take an exit exam in English Language Arts. Each spring at my school, all grade 10 students read *Hamlet*. So in the spring of 2004, to settle my nerves, I built a syntax chart using Shakespeare's language. The exit test is bad enough, but every year in the nights before beginning *Hamlet* I am seized by a kind of stage fright (*This play is so hard to teach!* half my brain shouts; *But I love teaching it!* the other half rejoins). The best cure for a runaway brain, I always say, is a little grammar in the night, so I finished a first draft

Weird Words

Contrary to popular opinion, most of the words in Shakespeare's plays are still common to **modern English**. His plays also include **high-frequency archaic words**. Finally, there are the low-frequency **"weird words."** These words appear not at all today and very infrequently even in Shakespeare's plays.

Directions: *Fold the paper so that the definitions in the third column are hidden. Then "translate" the weird words by looking closely at the parts within a word, by imagining the imagery, or by noting the sounds of the word. Finally, compare your weird definitions to the ones Shakespeare would have known in the third column.*

Shakespeare's weird word:	Your weird definition:	Definitions
1. Ambuscado (noun)		
2. Brabbler (noun)		
3. Dotard (noun)		
4. Englut (verb)		
5. Flirt-gill (noun)		
6. Hie (verb)		
7. Honorificabilitudinitatibus (adj.)		
8. Lewdster (noun)		
9. Maltworm (noun)		
10. Onion-eyed (adj.)		
11. Slug-a-bed (noun)		
12. Smilet (noun)		
13. Thwack (verb)		
14. Unhaired (adj.)		
15. Yare (adj.)		

1. ambush 2. quarreler 3. old fool 4. gulp down 5. loose woman 6. hurry, hasten 7. loaded with honors 8. a lecher 9. heavy drinker 10. weepy 11. sleepyhead 12. little smile 13. drive away 14. beardless 15. ready, nimble

Figure 2.4. Weird words.

syntax chart and lugged it into school for the purpose of breaking the Shakespearean ice that may have formed over the winter, reviewing the essentials of a sentence and building some pre-test and pre-play confidence. Much to my surprise, students loved it right from the start, and with each passing year I have tinkered with the chart and ways to use it.

Figure 2.5 is a condensed and simplified version of the original seven-column chart I made on legal-size paper, but it does the trick. In 2004, I asked students to write Shakespearean sentences, underline and label the grammatical constructions (subject, predicate, direct/indirect object, phrase, clause) and as many parts of speech as they could (adverb, adjective, preposition, interjection). All of my students were successful in writing vivid sentences, and most of them could label the subject, predicate, and modifiers in their sentences. For the most part, though, only some of the students in an honors class could distinguish between phrases and clauses, adjectives and adverbs. Nonetheless, no matter their background knowledge of grammar, this exercise does cause students to look more closely at Shakespeare's language and the ways in which we (and he) construct sentences.

The classroom was alive with questions about words (*What's an apothecary? What does "to dew her orbs" mean?*) and though some of the words on the Shakespearean sentences chart are defined on the handouts I later made for archaic and "weird" words, many are not. Since the classroom dictionaries might be of limited value for the archaic expressions and since even with modern English words a dictionary often only adds to students' frustration, I decided to bypass the dictionaries and ask students to draw what they think the words in their sentences mean. To do this, I encouraged them to look closely at the words for word parts, imagery, and sound, habits worth nurturing in the days before beginning a play by Shakespeare. Figure 2.6 is a collection of illustrated Shakespearean sentences composed by student Shaina Cohen.

Recently, when I brought the Shakespearean sentences chart into the Shakespeare elective class, the students (mostly seniors) weren't satisfied with writing sentences. They wanted to construct dialogue in small groups but struggled with how to begin. After fitful starts, we made a serendipitous discovery—brainstorm for Shakespearean scenarios and the dialogue almost writes itself. Since in all my years of reading *Macbeth* I have wondered if the connection between Lady Macbeth and the Witches is anything more than psychic, I imagined a Lady Macbeth plotting with First Witch against Lady Macduff, and so I began:

Figure 2.5. Constructing Shakespearean sentences.

Constructing Shakespearean Sentences

Directions: Select words and phrases from each column, in any order. Weave the words into sentences! Compose Shakespearean dialogue! Write a sonnet! Add words of your own where you need them. Try varying your sentences—start some with a prepositional phrase or an interjection. Experiment with ways of showing your work, by drawing or performing the words.

What kind? Which one? How many? How much? Compound Adjectives	Who? or What? Subjects and Objects	Does what? Predicates	How? When? Where? Why? Modifiers, Phrases, and Clauses	Whoa!? Interjections
puppy-headed	witch	burn and bubble	oft	hark
hag-born	the Weird Sisters	bid	anon	alas
wide-chopped	gravedigger	sup	ne'er	alack
sea-swallowed	cousin	wander	when the hurly-burly's done	'Swounds
birth-strangled	clodpole	equivocate	in the morrow	O
marble-hearted	soothsayer	despise	when we have shuffled off this mortal	fie
ill-composed	ghost	woo	coil	ah
tempest-tost	wench	knowest	when the blast of war blows	aye
up-staring	poor apothecary	englut	at some hour in the night	yea
wasp-stung	valiant Moor	dispatch	on his wedding day at night	nay
mad-headed	Spartan dog	unseam	within a month	ho
lack-brained	smiling villain	o'erleap	hence	prithee
outward-sainted	tedious old fool	shriek	thence	fo
lily-livered	monster	laugh	through the fog and filthy air	holla
logger-headed	queen	croak	in fair Verona	hail
foul-spoken	mother	defend	upon the heath	'Sblood
stretch-mouthed	king	tear	to a nunnery	zounds
long-tongued	father	burn	in Arthur's bosom	fo
iron-witted		*Helping verbs:*	in my mind's eye	illo ho ho
cream-faced	slug-a-bed	art (are)	in the dark backward and abysm of time	woe
glass-gazing	lunatic, lover, and poet	dost/doth (do/ does)	to dew her orbs	well-a-day
nimble-footed	henchman	hast/hath (have/	to sweep the dust behind the door	
frosty-spirited	boatswain	has)	to suffer slings and arrows	
star-crossed	cobbler		for fear / for love / for sorrow	
pale-hearted	sirrah		for Harry, England, and Saint George!	

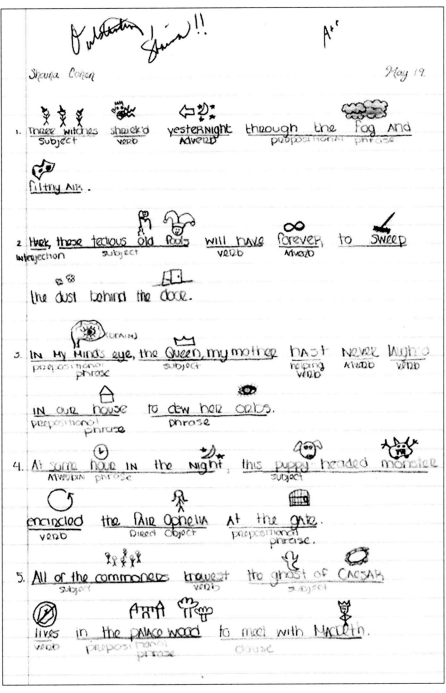

Figure 2.6. Student illustrations of Shakespearean sentences.

| LADY MACBETH: | Yea, but I despise that pale-hearted, lily-livered wench! |
| FIRST WITCH: | Nay, that outward-sainted mother hast ne'er hurt thee! |

Two students put a modern spin on a timeless love story, refashioning their names into Shakespearean characters and imagining a conflict over a bachelor party in fair Verona.

Amandeo & Juliette
By Amanda Todisco and Julieth Jaramillo-Rodriguez

AMANDEO:	O, Juliette! I bid thee to frolick through the fog and filthy air in fair Verona, then shall we be wed!
JULIETTE:	By my troth, for love upon the heath, I will be there.
AMANDEO:	Anon, sirrah! (*To servant*) Bid for Harry, England, and Saint George! We must get to a nunnery at some hour in the night for a bachelor party!
JULIETTE:	What, ho! On his wedding day at night? You birth-strangled lewdster!
AMANDEO:	Hark, Juliette! "The Weird Sisters" shall be dancing at some hour in the night.
JULIETTE:	O fie to heaven or to hell, ne'er to the nunnery will thou attend!
AMANDEO:	O, thou hast a problem? Well, get thee to a nunnery, long-tongued wench, for once I saw through yonder window *thee* performing the Weird Sisters' routine! Now, to sweep the dust behind the door!
JULIETTE:	Nay!
AMANDEO:	Aye and anon! I bid thee good morrow.
JULIETTE:	O woe!

Needless to say, my students renamed this activity "Shakespearean Trash Talk." Perfect.

The 2 Percent Solution

I once attended a middle school production of *Romeo and Juliet* in which the students performed a modernized version of the script. The student performers were well-rehearsed and wonderful, the production was rich, the teacher-directors creative and dedicated, and the parents enthusiastic and supportive. My disappointment was not so much in the script itself, which retained perhaps 10 percent of Shakespeare's language, as in some dialogue written for two narrators who sat with the audience in the front row and occasionally stood up to explain what already had been explained by way of a modernized script. The two narrators were entertaining, but their dialogue reinforced the myth that Shakespeare's language is hard and old, especially when they spoke lines like, "What Miss Smarty-Pants just tried to say was . . . " Ouch. This hurt my ears.

It would be false to assert that Shakespeare is easy reading. He is a writer of rare complexity. Scholars, directors, performers, and readers whose first, best love is Shakespeare will spend their lives in pursuit of his Grail. But if our students are to attempt this journey, their first few steps must be sure and steady and fun. Bypass the Globe Theater, postpone Aristotle's unities, and avoid like the plague modernized scripts and thirty-minute biographical videocassettes of the Bard. Begin with the most archaic 2 percent of Shakespeare's words, the very words that have earned Shakespeare a bad rap (and while you're at it, try looking up the word *rap* in a comprehensive dictionary just to be reminded of the ways in which words change over time), then ask your students to do the math. The 2 percent that is old in Shakespeare will be new to them, and the remaining 98 percent will be the most eye-opening new they have ever read or spoken in an English class.

3 Generating Character Vocabulary

Macbeth is evil.
Lady Macbeth is evil.
The Witches are, well, evil.
> Topic sentences, sophomore character analysis papers

S omewhere in the middle of that stack of drafts, something snapped. I stopped reading, stopped writing comments, and stopped trying to believe that I was a good teacher. I couldn't blame the assignment; it was adapted from an excellent project in *Shakespeare Set Free: Teaching* Hamlet that begins with students meeting in character committees and tracing what their character says and does throughout the play. I wouldn't blame *Macbeth*, because up until the writing of their first drafts, our informal classroom readings and discussions had gone well. Once I put away the blame game, I began to understand something about my students, their writing, and my teaching. What I came to understand then, and what I should have understood long before, is that one of the reasons students struggle with Shakespeare's language is because their own is so limited.

Shakespeare's characters are as rich and complex as the language they speak, but too many students lack a personal vocabulary equal to the task of describing and analyzing such complexity. This approach to vocabulary instruction begins with words not necessarily found in the text but necessary for a deeper understanding and expression of the complex and ambiguous nature of Shakespeare's characters. This approach will help students to develop a rich and useful vocabulary for describing Shakespeare's characters; to know, through frequent and varied use, a collection of mature, high-frequency words; and to make inferences about complex and ambiguous characters and support those inferences with evidence from the text.

Generating a Play-Specific List

Fold a paper in half lengthwise and in the left column list the important and interesting characters in the play your students are about to read. In Shakespeare's plays, even characters that appear in only one or two scenes, like the Porter in *Macbeth* or Fortinbras in *Hamlet*, often contribute to the play's mood and meaning. In the right column, brainstorm for words you as a teacher and expert reader might use to describe the characters you have listed, words that take into account their dynamic and often contradictory natures. In this chapter, I will refer to the character vocabulary list I constructed for *Macbeth* (Figure 3.1) with definitions from *The American Heritage Dictionary*.

After generating a random list of twenty-seven modifiers, I narrowed it down to what felt like a manageable twenty and decided to order the words not alphabetically but in order of appearance of the characters. Since the Witches appear first, my list begins with *equivocating* and *weird*. This is not to suggest that these two words can only be used to describe the Witches: in fact, I encourage students to explore the extent to which each word on the list describes all or most of the characters at some point in the play. During our reading of act 1.5, when Lady Macbeth and Macbeth discuss King Duncan's imminent arrival under their battlements, one student observed that the Macbeths are *equivocating* because "Lady Macbeth uses other words to say what she really feels. It's like as if they talk in code, because they don't say 'I want to kill him' but they do."

Arranging a character vocabulary list by order of appearance helps students see immediate and apparent applications for the words as they begin to read the play.

Varied Applications, Multiple Contexts

Definitions are only the starting point, and for some students, definitions can be deadly. Students are more apt to learn and remember new words when they are useful and used repeatedly in a variety of contexts. In fact, students need at least seven exposures to a new word in context to learn it. Consider the following instructional activities adapted from an excellent book on vocabulary instruction entitled *Bringing Words to Life*:

- Beyond definitions, create student-friendly explanations for words in both conversational and written form. On the day that I hand out the character vocabulary list, I also display it on the overhead projector and we read aloud and talk about each word. "Where have you seen or heard this word *paranoid* before?" "Do you recognize a word inside this word *irrational*? What does *rational* mean?" "*Equivocate*: Does anyone know what *equi* might mean in Latin? What about *vox* and *voc*? What does the expression mean *to speak out of both sides of your mouth*?" For some of my sophomores, this is the first time they've taken part in a conversation not so much with as about words.

Character Vocabulary for Macbeth	
Characters	**Modifiers**
King Duncan Malcolm Donalbain	**e·quiv·o·cat·ing** 1. Using ambiguous language intentionally. 2. To avoid making an explicit statement. See Synonym, *lying*.
Macbeth Lady Macbeth Banquo Fleance	**weird** 1. Of, relating to, or suggestive of the preternatural or supernatural. 2. Of a strikingly odd or unusual character; strange. 3. *Archaic:* Of or relating to fate or the Fates.
Macduff Lady Macduff Ross Lennox	**no·ble** 1. Possessing hereditary rank in a political system or social class derived from a feudalistic stage of a country's development. 2. Having or showing qualities of high moral character, such as courage, generosity, or honor: *a noble spirit*. 3. Grand and stately in appearance; majestic.

Porter
 	
Witches
Hecate
	na·ive or **na·ïve**
	1. Lacking worldly experience and understanding, especially:
	    a. Simple and guileless; artless: *a child with a naive charm*.
	    b. Unsuspecting or credulous.
	2. Showing a lack of sophistication and critical judgment.

	loy·al 1. Steadfast in allegiance to one's homeland, government, or sovereign. 2. Faithful to a person, ideal, custom, cause, or duty. 3. Of, relating to, or marked by loyalty. See Synonyms, *faithful*.
	val·iant 1. Possessing valor; brave; courageous.
	am·bi·tious 1. Greatly desirous; eager. 2. Requiring or showing much effort; challenging.
	de·ceit·ful 1. Given to cheating or deceiving. 2. Deliberately misleading; deceptive. See Synonyms, *dishonest*.
	ma·nip·u·la·tive Serving, tending, or having the power to influence, exploit, maneuver, or control to one's advantage by artful or indirect means.
	cun·ning 1. Marked by or given to artful subtlety and deceptiveness. 2. Executed with or exhibiting ingenuity. 3. Skilled in deception and guile.
	continued on next page

Figure 3.1. Character vocabulary list.

Figure 3.1 continued

treach·er·ous
1. Marked by betrayal of fidelity, confidence, or trust; perfidious. See Synonyms, *faithless*.
2. Not to be relied on; not dependable or trustworthy.
3. Marked by unforeseen hazards; dangerous or deceptive: *treacherous waters*.

per·verse
1. Directed away from what is right or good; perverted.
2. Obstinately persisting in an error or fault; wrongly self-willed or stubborn.
3. Marked by a disposition to oppose and contradict.

ir·ra·tion·al
1. a. Not endowed with reason.
   b. Affected by loss of usual or normal mental clarity; incoherent, as from shock.
   c. Marked by a lack of accord with reason or sound judgment: *an irrational dislike*.

anx·ious
1. Uneasy and apprehensive about an uncertain event or matter; worried; *spent an anxious night waiting for the test results*.

par·a·noid
2. Exhibiting or characterized by extreme and irrational fear or distrust of others: *a paranoid suspicion that the phone might be bugged*.

ty·ran·ni·cal
1. Of or relating to a tyrant or tyranny: *a tyrannical government*.
2. Despotic and oppressive: *a tyrannical supervisor*.

skep·ti·cal also **scep·ti·cal**
1. Marked by or given to doubt; questioning: *a skeptical attitude; skeptical of political promises*.

com·pul·sive
1. Having the capacity to compel: *a frightening, compulsive novel*.
2. *Psychology* Obsessive.

cal·lous
1. Having calluses; toughened: *callous skin on the elbow*.
2. Emotionally hardened; unfeeling: *a callous indifference to the suffering of others*.

cyn·i·cal
1. Believing or showing the belief that people are motivated chiefly by base or selfish concerns; skeptical of the motives of others.
2. Selfishly or callously calculating: *showed a cynical disregard for the safety of his troops in his efforts to advance his reputation*.
3. Negative or pessimistic, as from world-weariness: *a cynical view of the average voter's intelligence*.

- Help students to build word relationships. For example, before students use the words to describe characters in a play, have them respond to this prompt, using a variety of words from your list: "Describe someone you know who is *naïve.*"

- Create character webs and have students select words from your list that describe one or more characters. Encourage students to consider words with both positive and negative connotations as they build their character descriptions. See Figure 3.2.

- Create sentence stems for students to complete. I created a bank of sentence stems by assigning three classes of sophomores (about 75 students) to use any ten words from our *Macbeth* list in sentences with context clues. From those I culled the most effective sentences and removed the students' context clues, then typed the stems into the handout you see in Figure 3.3.

- Try these activities as quick, daily warm-ups at the overhead projector: (A) Write word questions for students to complete: "When do you feel *anxious?*" "Can a *cynical* person be *naïve?*" "Could you remain *loyal* to a *deceitful* person?" (B) Challenge students to explain how pairs of words on their list are alike and/or different: *skeptical* and *cynical, ambitious* and *treacherous.* (C) Make true/false statements: *Naïve* people are difficult to deceive: True? False?

- As a culminating activity, have students arrange the words on a connotation continuum from, for example, positive to negative. This can be especially fun when you write each word on 8½-inch by 11-inch paper, distribute the words to students, and have them post their word on a giant continuum across the walls or chalkboards of the classroom. This activity generates constructive noise; I enjoyed watching students jostle one another for what they considered the "right" place for their word on the wall. After they finished and sat down to admire their work, there were smiles and a few good-natured debates about whether it's more evil (there goes that word again!) to be *treacherous* or *tyrannical.*

In addition to these applications, colleague and first-year teacher Ben Murphy devised a chart with the character traits listed vertically and the character names listed horizontally (Figure 3.4). His original intention was to pause at the end of each scene in *Macbeth* and have students check off the traits that each character demonstrates. But he quickly realized that what he thought would be a straightforward checklist actually requires group conversations and inspires interesting debates. So he and his students work together on the checklist, and he established ground rules: If students want to check off a square, they have to double-check

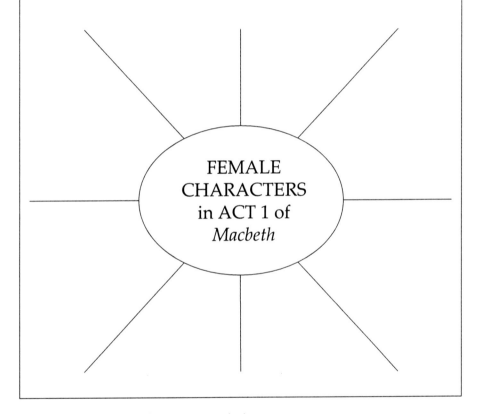

Figure 3.2. *Macbeth* character vocabulary.

the definition and convincingly support their opinion with lines from the play. "They've proven me wrong a few times," Murphy admits, "but it's a nice side effect."

Macbeth Character Vocabulary
Sentence Stems

Directions: *Complete these sentences by adding words and phrases that vividly explain the meaning of the bold vocabulary words.*

1. Some consumers are so gullible and **naïve** that they

2. I will always remain **loyal** to _____ because

3. Sometimes the news media can be very **manipulative**; for example,

4. In history, _____ is remembered as a **treacherous** dictator because

5. The general hatched an **irrational** plan to

6. The **anxious** family pleaded with the doctors to

7. Many people are **skeptical** of _____ because

8. The athlete was so **compulsive** about her health that she

9. She was a **cynical** person who didn't believe that

10. Because he is an **ambitious** employee,

11. Throughout the investigation into corruption, the **equivocating** senator

12. The **deceitful** athlete was thrown off the team after

13. In the story of Eden, the **perverse** serpent succeeds in

14. His **callous** reaction to the news of their tragic loss

15. My mother has **noble ambitions**; she wants to

16. One of the **weird**est things I've ever seen was in a cemetery where

17. The man began to feel **paranoid** when he realized

18. Alcoholism is a **cunning** disease because it

19. One of the most **valiant** characters in all of literature is _____ because

20. Some teachers are **tyrannical** when it comes to

Figure 3.3. Sentence stems.

	King Duncan	Malcolm	Donalbain	Macbeth	Lady Macbeth	Banquo	Fleance	Macduff	Lady Macduff	Ross	Lennox	Porter	Witches	Hecate
Equivocating														
Weird														
Noble														
Naïve														
Loyal														
Valiant														
Ambitious														
Deceitful														
Manipulative														
Cunning														
Treacherous														
Perverse														
Irrational														
Anxious														
Paranoid														
Tyrannical														
Skeptical														
Compulsive														
Callous														
Cynical														

Figure 3.4. Character trait chart.

Say Why

Beyond the trite reliance on *evil* as a modifier for just about every character in *Macbeth*, too many students struggle to say, both in their classroom talk and in their writing, why they think a certain character is a certain way at a certain point in a play. As they become more familiar with the character vocabulary list, my students use more specific and appropriate words to describe the characters in *Macbeth*, but breakdowns sometimes occur when I ask them why they chose a particular word to describe a particular character. Their textual evidence is often vague and confused.

Because students must learn to pay close attention to the narrative fragments (*what characters say, what they do, what others say about them*) that support their conclusions, I constructed a handout with a provocative image, sketched by student Jennifer Pollard, of Lady Macbeth in the center and three sentence stems along the two sides and the bottom of the page. Students worked in pairs to select three different modifiers from the list that they would use to describe Lady Macbeth in act 1, and to say why each modifier describes her. In other words, they needed to support their opinions (the modifiers they used to describe her) with literary evidence (narrative fragments). As they worked, I circulated to listen and to prod their thinking. Figure 3.5 displays the handout with the written work of students Kristina Gravellese and Kerri Roach.

When Bobby and John wrote this sentence about Lady Macbeth, "Lady Macbeth is *ambitious* because she will do anything to crown her husband," I asked them what "anything" is in act 1. When they said, "She wants to kill Duncan," I asked them where she says that. With lots of page-turning (which is exactly what I wanted them to do) they found places where she talks about her "keen knife" and "when Duncan is asleep . . . " and multiple references to "it," but they were surprised that she never flat-out says what "it" is. Together, we wondered why. Until that brief conversation with Bobby and John, I had never caught a glimpse in act 1 of the Lady Macbeth of act 5, sleepwalking and haunted by guilt.

BioPoems

Several years ago, as part of a course called "Understanding Teaching," I learned of a wonderful graphic organizer called the BioPoem, and added it to our study of the characters in this play and many other literary works. I assign BioPoems for *Macbeth* as a summarizing activity because students can draw on the full and often contradictory range of traits their chosen character has displayed (Figure 3.6). I don't limit students to the modifiers from the character vocabulary list, though most students use some of them. Note the dreaded modifier "evil" in line 3 of Michael's BioPoem; still, his poem conveys a much fuller understanding of Macbeth's complexity than I had seen before working with students on their character vocabulary.

Macbeth, A BioPoem

Macbeth
Backstabber, valiant, cynical, brave
Husband of the evil Lady Macbeth
Lover of power, wealth, luxury
Who feels paranoid, callous, angry
Who needs a new wife, better decision making, anger management
   classes

Characterizing Lady Macbeth in Act I

1) Lady Macbeth is ___ambitious___ because:
She wants more than anything to become queen. She wants her husband to come home so she can talk to him about working hard to become king. She believes that he can become king because she says, "Which, fate and metaphysical aid doth seem to have thee crown'd withal." (pg. 12)

2) Lady Macbeth is ___deceitful___ because:
Instead of being loyal to the king and honoring him like she is supposed to, she is letting herself plot his murder. By welcoming Duncan into her home nicely, she is tricking him so that there will be no suspicion of murder. she says, "that my keen knife see not the wound it makes." (pg. 13)

3) Lady Macbeth is ___manipulative___ because:
She is trying her hardest to persuade MacBeth into letting her kill Duncan, even if she must do it herself she says, "Look like the innocent flower, but be the serpent under't... "... leave all the rest to me." (pg. 13)

Figure 3.5. Lady Macbeth handout.

Describing Characters in a BioPoem
Reproduced from "Summarizing with Biopoems" by Research for Better Teaching, Inc.

Directions: *Select precise language to fit the form of this poem and of your character. Begin on this sheet, but write your final draft on loose-leaf.*

Form:

Line 1   Your character's first name

Line 2   Four traits that describe your literary character

Line 3   Relative (parent, brother, sister, child, grandchild, etc.) of

Line 4   Lover of_____, _____, and_____(3 things or people)

Line 5   Who feels_____, _____, and_____(3 emotions)

Line 6   Who needs_____, _____, and_____(3 items)

Line 7   Who fears_____, _____, and_____(3 items)

Line 8   Who gives_____, _____, and_____(3 items)

Line 9   Who would like to see_____, _____, and_____(3 items)

Line 10   Resident of_____

Line 11   Your character's last name

Figure 3.6. Describing characters in a BioPoem.

Who fears everyone and everything
Who gives to no one but himself
Who would like to see the killing stop
Resident of Hell Gate
Macbeth

—Michael Palleschi

Illustrated Dictionaries

Across the country, many school districts have witnessed a shift in student demographics with sometimes overwhelming gains in students whose native language is not English. A course I took in the fall of 2006, Sheltering Content for English Language Learners, helped me to understand that there are fundamental things teachers can do to guide all our students, from native speakers to limited English proficient speakers, toward greater understanding of the content we teach.

Show beats tell: use objects, pictures, videos, and physicalization to help students see words and ideas. That made me think of a set of vocabulary workbooks entitled *Vocabulary Cartoons* that I had used with much success in the past. I found a way to fuse the two by having students work in small, cooperative groups to construct an illustrated dictionary (Figure 3.7). Though it took longer than I had originally anticipated, at the end of a highly constructive and enjoyable school week, my sophomores had "published" more than twenty mini-dictionaries, complete with clever sentences, creative illustrations, and witty captions for any ten of the twenty words their groups had chosen from the *Macbeth* character vocabulary list. In the spirit of differentiated instruction, groups of three to four students parceled out the work of writing, drawing, and producing their own dictionaries.

Though my sophomores do this vocabulary work in the second quarter while reading *Macbeth*, many students continue to use these twenty modifiers later in the year and in different literary contexts. With each year, I adopt these strategies for a different whole work, and students keep a growing collection of useful, mature, high-frequency modifiers that empower them to say with fine-grained specificity what they think about the complexity of human and literary beings.

***Macbeth* Character Vocabulary: An Illustrated Dictionary**
Adapted from *Vocabulary Cartoons* by Sam, Max, and Bryan Burchers

You will work in small groups to construct an illustrated dictionary that demonstrates your understanding of the vocabulary words we are studying as we read this play. For each of the twenty words on the list, follow these directions:

1) Print the word, spelling it correctly.
2) Write a short, accurate definition for the meaning(s) of the word.
3) Create an illustration that shows the meaning of the word.
4) Write a clever caption for the illustration.
5) Write 2-3 sentences that use the word correctly and provide a context clue.

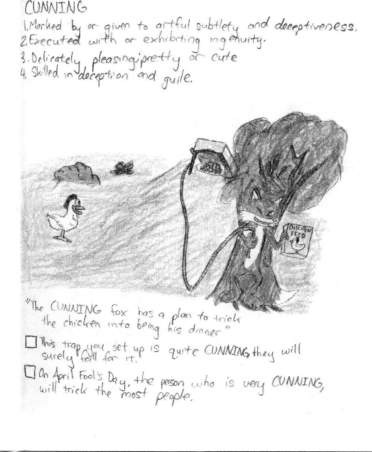

Figure 3.7. "Cunning" illustration, caption, and sentences by Mona, Ariel, and Victor.

4 HeartSpeak: A Tone Vocabulary

LEAR: No eyes in your head . . . yet you see how this world goes.
GLOUCESTER: I see it feelingly.

King Lear 4.5.141–145

In one of the most searing scenes in all of Shakespeare, in a play with more than one hundred references to eyes and the act of seeing, the new-blinded Gloucester joins the cast of Shakespearean characters driven to speak the vernacular of the human heart. In Shakespeare's plays, characters literally speak themselves into existence, and the act of speaking not only to be heard but to *be* requires an ear for the cadence of tone. Getting our students to see Shakespeare's words feelingly, to read and speak them not just from the head but from the heart, is perhaps our greatest challenge.

Tone can be a notoriously difficult literary concept for students to grasp, yet it is critical to the reading of Shakespeare's dialogue. Our students hear and speak in tones of voice, but their reading is too often tone-deaf. This chapter outlines a series of activities that will attune students to the ways in which the emotions of the speaker affect the meaning of the speaker's words.

Speaking in Tongues

I know how a symphony conductor feels. In 1998 at the annual NCTE convention, Peggy O'Brien chaired a presentation on what she called "Multidimensional Shakespeare." O'Brien's purpose was to get teachers looking at the words in a scene from *King Lear* through three different lenses simultaneously, the lens of the reader, the stage actor/director, and the film director, as sketched in Figure 4.1.

She selected a speech from act 2.2, the scene in which Lear, divested of his knights by his daughters, rushes into the storm; the members of her team would lead participants through a series of activities layering the lenses of reader, stage actor, and filmmaker. Following O'Brien's introductory remarks, I began with one line and more than 250 readers:

I prithee, daughter, do not make me mad. (2.2.391)

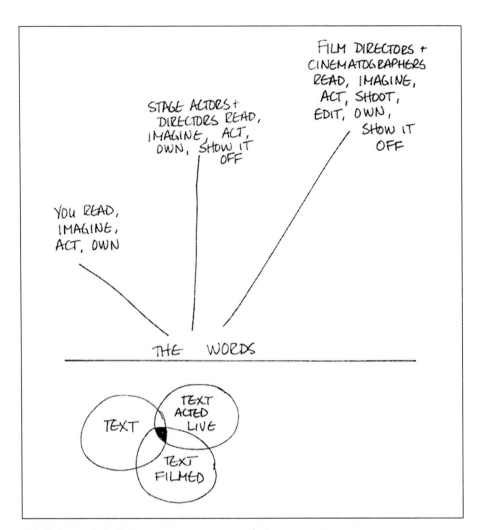

Figure 4.1. O'Brien's diagram.

I read the line in a monotone. Then I asked the room full of English teachers to speak the line, " . . . as if you are MAD!" In near-unison and with remarkably consistent pitch, 250 voices threatened, and then broke into self-surprised laughter at the power of our voice. "Now speak the same line as if you are PLEADING!" The sound of their single voice nearly broke our hearts. "Now speak the line as if you don't take your daughter seriously, as if you are MOCKING her!" The room rang with ridicule.

Students need to study the book of the human heart if they are to appreciate the ways in which text (the words on the page) is affected by subtext (the speaker's thoughts and feelings as he or she speaks the words). There are wonderful exercises on text and subtext in the Folger's three volumes of *Shakespeare Set Free*. One of my favorites is in Lesson 9 of *A Midsummer Night's Dream* and begins with the sentence: "Don't go!"

Then students receive cards with these sentences written on them:

"I command you to stay!"

"Please stay around if you care for me."

"It's not safe out there."

"I warn you—you'll be sorry if you go."

Students take turns speaking "Don't go!" according to the subtext on their cards while the rest of us guess which card they have. With this simple activity, students become more conscious of the ways in which the tones of the human voice affect meaning.

For the students in Advanced Placement English Language and Composition, I developed a lengthy tone vocabulary list as a reference tool and sets of tone-free, base sentences that students rewrite in a variety of tones. This is one example:

An Exercise in Tone

Directions: *Write variations of the base sentence that retain the basic information but express different, even contradictory, tones.*

BASE sentence: As the sun rose, the workers harvested the crops.

TONE: *optimistic*
As the sun combed its golden fingers through endless acres of New World wheat, the immigrants rose from their beds, dressed, ate, and prayed, then took to the fields to harvest their first crop.

TONE: *apprehensive*

TONE: *scornful*

After asking students what they did to the base sentence to craft variations in tone, they begin to develop a sharper eye for the ways in which writers employ diction and the elements of syntax to convey tone.

Still, I never figured out how to refine the daunting AP tone vocabulary list for students of all ability levels, and I relied solely on the text and subtext exercises to teach tone in Shakespeare classes. It was colleague Christina Porter who figured out how to merge text and subtext activities with a manageable tone vocabulary, and to bring these concepts into a classroom filled with intermediate and transitioning English language learners who were reading, of all things, abridged Shakespeare.

What follows is Porter's work with a Shakespearean tone vocabulary, written in her own words.

Words of Love, Hate, and Everything in Between

Christina Porter: Literacy Coach, Revere High School

In the spring of 2007, I was invited into the classroom of Judith Shea, an English language learner (ELL) teacher at Revere High School, to co-teach a play by William Shakespeare. Together, we have taught abridged versions of *The Tempest* and *A Midsummer Night's Dream* in Shea's ELL reading and writing classes. Prior to this collaboration I had worked extensively with ELL students, tutoring them to pass the state-mandated graduation exam in English. However, I had never attempted to teach the works of an author with all the wonder and complexity of Shakespeare; in the beginning, this was indeed a brave new world to me.

An ELL classroom is a world of language, quite literally. In Shea's classroom over the past two years, we have worked with students whose first languages include Spanish, French, Arabic, Portuguese, Khmer, Chinese, and Vietnamese. This rich cacophony of language seems a fitting home for the master of words.

Early in our reading of the first play, Judy and I realized that it is essential in working with diverse students from so many language backgrounds to explicitly teach students how to speak Shakespeare. Since using tones of voice to communicate is a concept that transcends language and is essential to speaking Shakespeare, we begin with tone. To introduce this concept to students, I use an activity that I first saw done by Mike LoMonico at the Folger Shakespeare Library's Teaching Shakespeare Institute when I was a participant in 2006.

I give students a handout containing one sentence, "He did not kick his neighbor's dog," reformatted seven times. Each time, a different word in the sentence is underlined. I ask for volunteers to read the sentences aloud, instructing them to really stress the underlined word. After each reading, we pause to talk about how making one word stand out can change the meaning of the sentence. For example, in emphasizing the word *kick* (He did not <u>kick</u> his neighbor's dog), it is left to the listener's imagination to decipher what exactly he *did* do to this poor animal. Once students have an understanding of how tone, conveyed in this instance by stressing a word, can affect meaning, it is time to transfer this to Shakespeare.

I was familiar with the work Mary Ellen had done with her AP students to examine the construction of tone in writing. I had also seen her tone vocabulary list and was inspired to modify it and make it

Basic Emotions (Front of card)	Synonyms (Back of card)
Anger	hostility, indignation, irateness
Fear	alarm, apprehension, dread, horror, panic, terror
Hatred	abhorrence, detestation, horror, loathing, repulsion
Joy	bliss, cheerfulness, delight, excitement, wonder
Love	adoration, affection, devotion, passion
Sorrow	grief, heartache, heartbreak, regret

Figure 4.2. Porter's tone chart.

work for the ELL students in speaking Shakespeare. I wanted them to explore how using different tones of their voices affects the meaning of Shakespeare's language. I also wanted them to have an opportunity to discuss with their peers why they chose to speak a given line or sentence in a certain way. Speaking and listening in English are essential skills in the ELL classroom. To help them experiment with tone, I constructed a Shakespearean tone vocabulary activity.

I begin by focusing on the most basic human emotions: anger, fear, hatred, joy, love, and sorrow. On index cards, I write one emotion on the front of each card and synonym sets for each emotion in alphabetical order on the back. Including synonyms provides an opportunity to teach ELL students complex vocabulary in word families. The following chart in Figure 4.2 can be modified to include fewer or more synonyms:

As a class, we go through each card, pronouncing, discussing, and defining unfamiliar words and experimenting with the ways in which these emotions can affect the sounds of our voice. To clarify the emotional overtones of the words within families, I sometimes have students rearrange the words into a continuum based on degrees of intensity. For example, synonyms for *fear* may be arranged as *apprehension, dread, alarm, panic, horror,* and finally *terror*.

As we go through each index card, it is useful to have a line from the play we are studying on the board so that we can speak it in each tone. Students find it really amusing to speak lines in mismatched tones, such as "The course of true love never did run smooth" in a tone of horror.

When students understand the meaning of all the tone vocabulary words, I put them into groups no larger than three and give them another set of index cards with lines from a scene or act we have already read as a class. Based on their knowledge of the characters and events at that moment in the play, students match the lines with the most appropriate tones and practice speaking them in those tones. If students are comfortable, I ask for volunteers to speak their lines to the class and then discuss why they chose the tone or tones that they did. It is exciting when students in different groups choose similar tones for the same line, and even more interesting when they disagree about which tones to use. *"Prospero wouldn't say it like that; he would say it like this...!"* In the ELL classroom, exploring tone allows students a meaningful opportunity to explore language.

Reading in Tongues

Porter's approach to teaching tone to ELL students in the context of William Shakespeare's plays is immediately transferable to the mainstream English classroom into which former ELL students transition. In fact, most teachers have students in various stages of English language acquisition. According to a 2009 article in *NEA Today*, the number of ELL students in America's schools "has grown by 57 percent" since 1995 "to a staggering 5.1 million students," and 64 percent of these students are born here (Flannery 24). As stated by Deborah Horan at the Boston College Lynch School of Education, "Teaching ELLs is every educator's responsibility."

Even students in Advanced Placement English have much to learn about how we read tone and speak it.

When I take Porter's lesson into the mainstream class, I still begin with the Folger's "Don't go!" exercise, but instead of using it to introduce the concept of text and subtext, I use it as an introduction to tone. At the overhead, I display the base sentence "Don't go!" and the list of secondary sentences and ask students to speak the base sentence chorally in tones appropriate to each secondary sentence. Then we brainstorm for tone words to describe each of the secondary sentences—*commanding, pleading, fearful, threatening*. We talk about what tone is in speaking and writing and come up with definitions like *attitude* and *emotion*. Since this is an introductory lesson to an important literary and rhetorical concept, I display two essential questions that I tell them we will explore throughout our study of the English language:

How do we read tone? How do we speak tone?

"What things did you just do with your voice and your facial expressions to convey a certain attitude?" I ask. In this way, we begin to think about the sounds of meaning.

Then I ask students to generate a list of the most basic human emotions. On a September morning in 2008, my students offered these: happiness, sorrow, fear, anger, love, hate, pride, and curiosity. Alongside their words, I display a list of twelve fundamental human emotions (there are many sources for such lists but my favorite comes from a brilliant tone "color chart" that I recently discovered in Chapter 5 of Mason and Nims's poetry textbook, *Western Wind*). Each emotion is coupled with its complement—Love and Hate, Pride and Fear, Joy and Sorrow, Wonder and Apathy, Hope and Despair, Pity and Anger.

As a whole group, we brainstorm for a synonym for each emotion, then I divide the class into small groups and assign each group a pair of complements—there is the Love and Hate group, the Pride and Fear group, and so on. I distribute a tone chart that synthesizes Porter's format with the contents of Mason and Nims's color chart (Figure 4.3).

We share all our words at the overhead and discuss which of the synonyms best express the least and most intense form of each emotion. Finally, I use an online concordance to find lines from the play we are about to read, list each line by basic emotion, and challenge the small groups to read their single line for tone, to agree upon its intensity, and to speak their line aloud to the whole group. With the tone chart displayed at the overhead, filled in with all of our tone words, we try to guess which tone they have tried to speak. These are some of the sentences I chose from *A Midsummer Night's Dream*:

Anger
Full of **vexation** come I, with complaint
Against my child, my daughter Hermia. (1.1.22–23)

Fear
Lysander, look how I do quake with **fear**.
Methought a serpent ate my heart away . . . (2.2.154–55)

Hate
What, should I hurt her, strike her, kill her dead?
Although I **hate** her, I'll not harm her so. (3.2.270–71)

Joy
Joy, gentle friends—**joy** and fresh days of love
Accompany your hearts. (5.1.28–29)

Love
The more I **love**, the more he hateth me. (1.1.199)

TONE CHART		
Degrees of Emotion: *Less*	EMOTION:	Degrees of Emotion: *More*
admiring, affectionate, caring, flirtatious, lustful	Love	devoted, passionate, obsessed
	Hate	
	Pride	
	Fear	
	Joy	
	Sorrow	
	Wonder	
	Apathy	
	Hope	
	Despair	
	Pity	
	Anger	
Essential questions: *How do we read tone? How do we speak tone?*		

Figure 4.3. Tone chart.

The speaking of a single line in several degrees of emotion helps students to hear which tones are more and less appropriate to the line. It can also cause us to add new synonyms to the chart. For example, the students who spoke the "angry" line, "Full of vexation come I," were working with this list of tone words for anger: *aggravated, flustered, upset, resentful, mad, enraged, furious.* They tried their best to speak the line in an "upset" tone, but what we all heard as a class was something different. When I asked students to describe the tone we had just heard, we added a new word to the anger line—*stern.* After students spoke the love line, "The more I love, the more he hateth me," they too expressed some frustration with the tone words we had generated for love: *admiration, affection, caring, lust, devotion, passion, obsession.* "You actually sounded confused," I said, and suddenly a roomful of young adults and one no-longer-young adult smiled to think that love is the most confusing emotion.

Finally, speaking Shakespearean lines in various tones causes students to engage in some pretty sophisticated reading. When I asked students at the end of the exercise what they were doing to read tone, they mentioned things like punctuation and the meanings of specific words. Since they hadn't read this play yet, they didn't know the speaker or the context, but still they were able to read and speak in tones.

You can follow this whole group activity with a full speech. In small groups, students mark a speech for line delivery, with particular emphasis on the shifts in tone. It helps students to know, early in the reading of a play, that Shakespeare's speakers frequently begin long speeches with some emotional restraint and pick up verbal and emotional momentum in the middle or end. Of course, there are exceptions to this pattern. In the Cambridge School edition of *Henry V*, actor Robert Hardy characterizes Henry's speech in 3.1 to his troops at the siege of Harfleur, "Once more unto the breach, dear friends, once more," using the language of an engine:

> You are in full armour, apparently shouting at thousands . . . the speech starts at the top, then you have to change down to first, then up to second, to third, to fourth, to overdrive, and at the end still have trumpet and clarion left. (80)

When students read for tone, they are reading for meaning that is both literal (*what is the speaker saying?*) and analytical (*what is the speaker's emotional state, and when and to what degree does it shift?*). They read for clues visible in the lines—the choice of words, sentence structure, punctuation—as well as for clues that hover between and around the lines—the emotional intensity of the situation and their tentative understanding of the speaker.

When students speak for tone, they explore the relationship between meaning and sound. In Porter's lesson, ELL students begin the exploration of tone by speaking aloud the same line, "He did not kick his neighbor's dog," seven times, each time stressing one of the seven words. They immediately learn that stress is one of the audible clues speakers employ to convey emotion. But how do we stress a word? "Think of all the different ways there are," write the authors of *How to Speak Shakespeare*, "to make a word stand out" (35).

In the mainstream classroom, I extend Porter's lesson by asking a summary question: *How does the human voice convey meaning? What are the vocal tools of speaking?* Remind students of the ways in which they have used their voices throughout this lesson. What have they done to convey emotion? Play an audio recording of a speech that the students marked for tone, focusing their listening on the actor's voice. Then brainstorm for the things people do with their voices when they speak. The list your students generate will probably include:

- Volume (from whisper to shout; even silence can be a vocal tool)
- Pitch (from low to high)
- Pace (from slow to fast)
- Pause (hesitating before a word)

Tone is much more than a literary and rhetorical concept; it is a fundamental tool of human expression. Students are more likely to own words when they experience them "in body, breathe, voice, . . . mind and heart" (Rodenburg 355).

This chapter focuses on the vocabulary of tone. For a fuller discussion of tone as a speaking device, see Part III of this book. Two excellent resources are Patsy Rodenburg's *Speaking Shakespeare* and Cal Pritner and Louis Colaianni's *How to Speak Shakespeare*.

Speaking in Full Voice

Patsy Rodenburg, director of voice at London's Royal National Theater and author of *Speaking Shakespeare*, observes that ours is a world "full of noise, imprecision, and stress, where it's a struggle to hear or be heard." By contrast, "Shakespeare's world is a world of speakers . . . a place full of vocal colour, definition, and silence, where speaking is an art" (40–41). In every English classroom, from ELL to AP, students need to connect with words in ways that are meaningful not only to the text but to them. This demands creative reading and writing strategies, but it also begs instruction in speaking words aloud with clarity and conviction.

In Shakespeare's plays, characters speak to survive. ELL students know this feeling; all of our students deserve to know it. When they practice speaking Shakespeare out loud in our classrooms, our students are preparing for those moments in life when how they say words will matter as much as the words they say. Speak in full voice, from the mind and the heart, and you will be heard. This is a lesson every hero in Shakespeare knows; it is a lesson every despot has abandoned.

5 Problematical Pronouns

HAMLET: I did love you once.

OPHELIA: Indeed, my lord, you made me believe so.

HAMLET: You should not have believed me . . . I loved you not.

OPHELIA: I was the more deceived.

HAMLET: Get thee to a nunnery.

Hamlet 3.1.117–123

What just happened to the second-person pronouns in this famous exchange between Prince Hamlet and Ophelia? Why does *you* become *thee*? Too often in Shakespeare's dialogue, subtle pronoun shifts shoot like beacons from another world and we, their distant receivers, fail to detect or understand them.

When a Shakespearean speaker adopts the second-person singular familiar—*thou, thee, thy, thine*—or exchanges the singular *I* for the plural *we*, the dynamics of a relationship or an event change. It isn't difficult for most readers to identify pronouns on the page; what's difficult is simply noticing them in the first place. And what's truly fun is wondering what the pronouns actually say.

The Royal *We*

"Who's *we*?" a student asked long ago.

"Pardon me?" was my dumb reply. We were reading King Claudius's lengthy speech in *Hamlet* 1.2, focusing on the four big ideas: the funeral-wedding, young Fortinbras's threat, Laertes's request to return to France, and finally, the delicate matter of his new "son," Hamlet. I wasn't prepared to think about the little things like pronouns.

"He keeps saying *our* and *we*," the student persisted. I looked more closely at the first sentence and there it was, plain as pie:

Though yet of Hamlet **our** dear brother's death
The memory be green, and that it **us** befitted
To bear **our** hearts in grief and **our** whole kingdom
To be contracted in one brow of woe,
Yet so far hath discretion fought with nature
That **we** with wisest sorrow think on him
Together with remembrance of **ourselves**. (1.2.1–7)

And then my American brain remembered that sometimes kings, queens, and popes speak of themselves in the plural to convey their status as the embodiment of large and powerful institutions. "I think it's the royal *we*," I deduced. Interesting, though it didn't seem very significant, since Claudius was Denmark's new king and this was his first speech as head of state.

But when we got to the fourth big idea in the speech, the part about his new role as Hamlet's father, one little line and two little pronouns flashed across the radar screen of our brains like first contact from another planet:

But now, **my** cousin Hamlet, and **my** son. (1.2.64)

What just happened? Why did *our* become *my*? And what might that little shift reveal about Claudius, Hamlet, and the public/private dynamics of this scene?

That day long ago marked the first time in one of my classes when a Shakespearean shift in pronouns would spark wonder, discovery, and debate. We were none of us actors but we talked that day about how the volume and tone of Claudius's voice might shift with his pronouns from public to private. Students wondered if Claudius deserved Hamlet's scathing reply, "A little more than kin and less than kind," since Claudius seemed to have dropped his big-shot voice for the voice of an ordinary man who loves his grieving stepson. Or maybe he was just going through the motions of being Hamlet's new dad.

Weeks later in our reading of the play, at the point where both "father" and "son" fully understand the threat each one poses to the other, a student noticed that King Claudius asks Queen Gertrude,

Where is **your** son? (4.1.3)

A seismic shift, registered in the movement of pronouns.

Most of Shakespeare's plays list at least one monarch in the cast. Though the histories are infrequently taught in American schools, some are ripe for the taking. The *Henriad*, for example, is filled with sweeping action, great speeches, and memorable characters, most notably the enigmatic Prince-to-King Hal. Whether *Henry V* is part of the curriculum or not, there is a speech in act 1.2 that can be part of a self-contained lesson on the pronouns a king uses to name himself (Figure 5.1).

Context is everything to this speech, so readers need to know that the speaker is a young and inexperienced king with lots of baggage. His father Henry IV usurped the English crown and plummeted England into civil war, and Prince Henry rebelled against his father by

---

Problematical Pronouns: *Henry V 1.2.259–297*

Read King Henry's speech to the French Ambassador. The speech is formatted to advance our literal comprehension. Our task is to circle the **pronouns** Henry uses to name himself and to draw some conclusions about what the pronouns might reveal about the speaker.

In response to a mocking gift of tennis balls, Henry compares the game of tennis to an invasion of France.	We are glad the Dauphin is so pleasant with us. His present and your pains we thank you for. When we have matched our rackets to these balls, We will in France, by God's grace, play a set Shall strike his father's crown into the hazard. Tell him he hath made a match with such a wrangler That all the courts of France will be disturbed With chases.	**Dauphin:** eldest son of a French king **hazard:** a hole in the wall of a royal tennis court **wrangler:** one who quarrels **chases:** 1) winning strokes in tennis 2) routs in battle
Henry acknowledges that he was wild in his youth.	And we understand him well, How he comes o'er us with our wilder days, Not measuring what use we made of them. We never valued this poor seat of England, And therefore, living hence, did give ourself To barbarous license—as 'tis ever common That men are merriest when they are from home.	**license:** lack of restraint; excessive freedom
Henry asserts that he has changed into a powerful king.	But tell the Dauphin I will keep my state, Be like a king, and show my sail of greatness When I do rouse me in my throne of France. For that have I laid by my majesty And plodded like a man for working days, But I will rise there with so full a glory That I will dazzle all the eyes of France, Yea strike the Dauphin blind to look on us.	
Henry returns to the tennis metaphor to describe the effects of the French Prince's mockery.	And tell the pleasant Prince this mock of his Hath turned his balls to gunstones, and his soul Shall stand sore charged for the wasteful vengeance That shall fly from them—for many a thousand widows Shall this his mock mock out of their dear husbands, Mock mothers from their sons, mock castles down; Ay, some are yet ungotten and unborn That shall have cause to curse the Dauphin's scorn.	
Henry asserts his divine right to the French throne.	But this lies all within the will of God, To whom I do appeal, and in whose name Tell you the Dauphin I am coming on To venge me as I may, and to put forth My rightful hand in a well-hallowed cause.	**well-hallowed:** holy, sanctified **savor:** smell or taste **convey:** transport
Henry dismisses the French Ambassador.	So get you hence in peace. And tell the Dauphin His jest will savor but of shallow wit When thousands weep more than did laugh at it.— Convey them with safe conduct.—Fare you well.	

Figure 5.1. Problematical pronouns.

spending his youth in reckless company. As the new King of England, he has resolved to assert his legal right to the French throne and to lead his army into France, but Henry's reputation as a leader and a man is in question. In this scene, King Henry has just received a "treasure" of tennis balls from the Prince of France (the Dauphin), a taunting reminder of his prodigal past and a blatant mockery of his coronation.

After introducing students to the royal *we* and to the dramatic and historical context of this speech, read the speech aloud, then open the floor to debate. In this forty-line speech, why does Henry begin with the royal *we* and shift in line 15 to the personal pronoun *I*? The authors of *Speak the Speech! Shakespeare's Monologues Illuminated* believe that with the dozen repetitions of *we*, *us*, and *our* in the beginning of the speech, Henry establishes his superiority over "that little smart aleck of a Dauphin" and that he then shifts intentionally and manipulatively to the pronoun *I* to assert "his personal power" (125–126). Though students don't always see the shift in this speech from *we* to *I* as an intentional, rhetorical choice on the speaker's part, they feel it as a very human response to humiliation. "It's like he's saying, 'this is more than politics, this is personal,'" one of my students observed. The character of Henry V evokes an extreme and contradictory range of readings, from heroic to Machiavellian, but my students are usually sympathetic to the speaker of this speech. Adolescents are particularly sensitive to the sting of public humiliation.

Finally, it was a student who pointed to another set of pronouns at work in the lines. Though King Henry delivers the speech to an inferior (the French ambassador), he never employs the patronizing *thee* of the archaic second-person familiar. "He might sound like he's mad," this student observed, "but he's in control."

Sometimes, the little words say a lot.

The Second-Person Familiar

If there is one set of archaic words that students associate with Shakespeare, it is the second-person singular familiar pronouns *thou*, *thee*, *thy*, and *thine*, and their tagalong verb inflections ending in *-est*. The chart in Figure 5.2 is adapted with minor modifications from one developed by teacher Skip Nicholson and published in *Shakespeare Set Free: A Midsummer Night's Dream*.

Though modern English has dropped the second-person familiar, Rex Gibson and Janet Field-Pickering explain that Elizabethans engaged in a kind of code-switching, "one to the other depending on the social context." *You*, *your*, and *yours* were "usually the more formal, distant, respectful form of address" when used in the singular while *thou*, *thee*,

---

The Second-Person Singular Familiar Pronouns
Chart adapted from Shakespeare Set Free/MND, p. 54

Pronoun Case	1st Person	2nd Person	3rd Person
Subject case	*I*	*you* becomes *thou*	*he/she/it*
Object case	*me*	*you* becomes *thee*	*him/her/it*
Possessive case: Adjective	*my mine**	*your* becomes *thy thine**	*his/her/its*
Possessive case: Noun	*mine*	*yours* becomes *thine*	*his/hers/its*

*Used before a noun beginning with a vowel

Second-Person Singular Familiar Verb Inflections

Add the ending *-est, -'st,* or *st*
Example: *thou givest, thou sing'st*

Examples, with indications of status:

Spoken by a gentleman to a soldier in *Othello*:
>*You* told me *you* did hold him in *your* hate
>becomes
>"*Thou* told'st me *thou* didst hold him in *thy* hate."

Spoken by a father to a son in *Hamlet*:
>This above all, to *your* own self be true
>becomes
>"This above all, to *thine* own self be true."

Written by a prince to a commoner in *Hamlet*:
>*Yours* evermore, my dear lady
>becomes
>"*Thine* evermore, my dear lady."

Spoken by a queen to an ass in *MND*:
>I pray *you*, gentle mortal, sing again
>becomes
>"I pray *thee*, gentle mortal, sing again . . ."

Figure 5.2. Second-person familiar pronouns.

thy, and *thine* "could be friendly and familiar, but could also signify contempt for a social inferior" (61). The most fascinating thing about the second-person singular familiar is its duality; when speakers of *thou* are addressing a social inferior, the tones can range from intimate and affectionate to patronizing, contemptuous, and even hostile. In roughly that range, consider the following exchanges. (Italics are added for emphasis.)

- Romeo immediately addresses Juliet at the Capulet's ball in the second-person familiar ("Let lips do what hands do; They pray, grant *thou* . . ."); and while she retains the more formal *you*, in the orchard scene that follows, Juliet too adopts the intimate tones of the second-person familiar: "O Romeo, Romeo, wherefore art *thou* Romeo?" (2.1.75).

- In *Hamlet*, father Polonius says with seeming affection to son Laertes, "This above all—to *thine* own self be true" (1.3.78).

- In *Twelfth Night*, the bankrupt drunkard Sir Toby Belch addresses his solvent but simple-minded dupe, Sir Andrew Aguecheek, in patronizing tones throughout the play: "Let's to bed, knight. *Thou* hadst need send for more money" (2.3.176–77). Yet when Sir Toby coaches Sir Andrew in the art of insulting others, he instructs him to use the second-person familiar: "If *thou* 'thou'st' him some thrice, it shall not be amiss" (3.2.42–43). True to form, Sir Andrew never detects the irony.

- In the first exchange between the merchant Antonio and the Jewish moneylender Shylock in act 1.3.104–133 of *The Merchant of Venice*, Shylock addresses his Christian "superiors" with the formal and technically respectful *you*, and Antonio is careful to return the favor: "Well, Shylock, shall we be beholden to *you*?" But when Shylock replies with a long list of grievances against Antonio's abuses—"*You* call me misbeliever, cut-throat, dog, And spit upon my Jewish gaberdine . . ."—Antonio drops all pretence of respect and lashes back contemptuously, "I am as like to call *thee* so again, To spit on *thee* again, to spurn *thee* too. If *thou* wilt lend this money, lend it not As to *thy* friends . . . But lend it rather to *thine* enemy. . . . "

- In the nunnery scene in *Hamlet* (3.1.90–191), six lines of which are cited in the epigraph to this chapter, Hamlet's tone fluctuates with his choice of pronouns from seeming affection (or is it sarcasm?) at the beginning of the scene—"Nymph, in *thy* orisons Be all my sins remembered"—to blatant hostility before he exits: "If *thou* dost marry, I'll give *thee* this plague for *thy* dowry . . . " Still, if we scan this scene looking for Hamlet's heart in his pronouns, we find no logical degeneration from love to hate but only turmoil. Throughout the scene, he addresses Ophelia erratically in both the second person and the second-person familiar.

In these and all of Shakespeare's scenes, the pronouns are only one piece of a great puzzle, but a fascinating piece. While I remain skeptical of lists that claim to "crack the code" of Shakespeare's text, if I were to write one, the royal *we* and the second-person familiar would be on the list.

Though students are usually interested in the wordplay of *you* to *thou*, they are easily intimidated by the grammatical gobbledygook of the pronoun chart in Figure 5.2. If you reproduce it for students, practice reading aloud and comparatively the lines from *Othello, Hamlet,* and *A Midsummer Night's Dream,* experimenting with the ways in which the pronouns can impact the line delivery.

You can also reverse the process by having students convert lines with modern second-person singular pronouns into the archaic second-person familiar. In each of these lines from *Romeo and Juliet,* the speaker has chosen the more formal, public, and respectful *you, your,* and *yours* in addressing a single character. Let students try their hand at translation, both in writing and speaking the lines:

> Good pilgrim, you do wrong your hand too much (1.5.96).
>
> Why the devil came you between us? I was hurt under your arm (3.1.102–03).
>
> Here, sir, a ring she bid me give you, sir.
> Hie you, make haste, for it grows very late (3.3.162–63).

It is worth noting that there is no plural form of the second-person familiar; *thou, thee, thy,* and *thine* are singular. Therefore, when *you, your,* or *yours* refer to more than one person, as they do when Prince Escalus castigates the mob, the speaker's only option is the formal *you*:

> If ever you disturb our streets again
> Your lives shall pay the forfeit of the peace. (1.1.93–94)

Students thoroughly enjoy writing dialogue using the second-person familiar, though they are notoriously inept at distinguishing between cases ("I shalt go to the Dean." "Nay, not by thou lonesome. I shalt accompany thee."). Still, I don't fuss over the grammar, but let them play with this new old toy of language. In the twenty-first century classroom, everything old can be new again.

Confusion and Clarity

Beyond the shifts of meaning that occur in transitions from *I* to *we* and *me* to *thee,* pronouns with uncertain antecedents can be problematical in Shakespeare. Consider the opening lines in *Othello*:

>   1.1 *Enter Iago and Roderigo*
> RODERIGO: Tush, never tell **me**! I take it much unkindly
>   That **thou**, Iago, who hast had **my** purse
>   As if the strings were **thine**, shouldst know of this.
> IAGO: 'Sblood, but **you** will not hear **me**!
>   If ever **I** did dream of such a matter, abhor **me**.

RODERIGO:	**Thou** toldst **me thou** didst hold **him** in **thy** hate.
IAGO:	Despise **me**

Despise **me**
If **I** do not. Three great ones of the city,
In personal suit to make **me his** lieutenant,
Off-capped to **him**; and by the faith of man
I know **my** price, **I** am worth no worse a place.
But **he**, as loving **his** own pride and purposes,
Evades **them** with a bombast circumstance
Horribly stuffed with epithets of war,
Nonsuits **my** mediators; for 'Certes,' says **he**,
'I have already chose **my** officer.'
And what was **he**? . . .

Good question, Iago. Beyond the obvious fact established by the contrast in second-person pronouns that Iago is socially inferior to Roderigo, nothing else is clear because we are bombarded by a relentless series of third-person pronouns cast far afield of their noun antecedents. What *him* does Iago hate? Who is *he* that required a lieutenant, loves *his* own pride and purposes, and evades *them*? And who is *them*?

Short of summarizing the first forty lines of this play and starting with Iago's second speech, "O, sir, content you. I follow him to serve my turn upon him," we can injure this play on day one by belaboring the opening speech, or we can arrange volunteers at the front of the classroom with signs in their hands that read "Othello, the Moor," "Three Great Ones of the City of Venice" (three volunteers needed to hold this sign), and "Michael Cassio, a Florentine." We can ask for two volunteers to read, very slowly, for Roderigo and Iago, and the rest of us can function like directors—every time we hear a personal pronoun, we tell the volunteers where to point. The first three lines would look like this as in Figure 5.3.

As it gets more complicated, it gets more fun. I learned this approach to Shakespeare's problematical pronouns and noun antecedents from Janet Field-Pickering. On pages 61–63 of the book they coauthored, she and Rex Gibson provide several activities for confusing pronouns.

Sometimes Shakespeare's pronouns lend unexpected clarity to a play. In all my readings of *The Tempest*, the airy spirit Ariel was unmistakably female. Until, that is, a group of students politely pointed out that I was wrong.

"Ariel's a *he*, Ms. Dakin," one of them gently asserted after I wondered out loud whether Ariel's question in 4.1.48, "Do you love me,

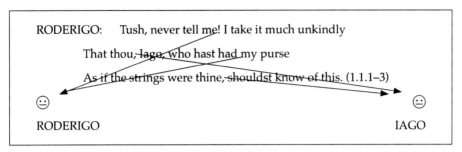

Figure 5.3. Personal pronouns.

master? No?" was an indication that her feelings for Prospero were no longer platonic. They took me back to 1.2.190–94, to Ariel's first lines:

> All hail, great master, grave sir, hail. I come
> To answer thy best pleasure . . .
> Ariel and all his quality.

"*His.* This has to be a mistake," I claimed, and promised to check the other editions I kept at home. "Ariel is delicate. Ariel is dainty. Ariel is even a harpy in the banquet scene. Aren't harpies mythological female birds?" Shock, denial, anger, guilt—that day I went through all the stages of grief for female Ariel and my students seemed genuinely sympathetic. Still, though there's no arguing with a personal pronoun, in my mind's eye this *he* will always be a *she*.

Early in the reading of a Shakespearean play, attune students' eyes and ears to the pronouns. The significance of any shift to or from the royal *we* or from *you* to *thee* will depend upon the speaker and the context, but each shift is an opportunity for Shakespeare's readers to derive fascinating inferences from the premise of the pronouns.

II Comprehension: Making Meaning

Gentle breath of yours my sails
Must fill, or else my project fails . . .

Epilogue, spoken by Prospero, *The Tempest*

The poem or the novel or the play exists in the transaction that goes on
between reader and text. (27)

Louise Rosenblatt, *Literature as Exploration*

In every great reader, William Shakespeare is reborn. Perhaps no writer, dead or alive, depends on the living as profoundly as he does. Though there is disagreement, many scholars believe that he paid little attention to the publishing of his plays, handing them over as working scripts to the very actors whose physical and psychic attributes may have been the clay with which he shaped their working parts. He neglected almost entirely the writing of stage directions, through which he could have asserted some directorial control. And as Stephen Orgel wistfully reminds us, "What we have of the Shakespeare text, all we have ever had, is a set of versions with no original" (xiv).

The chapters in this section develop a series of prereading, reading, rereading, and postreading strategies, many of which are not unique to the act of reading Shakespeare but are indispensable to it. The methods outlined in these chapters unfold from teacher-directed to student-centered. The objective in each chapter is handoff from expert to novice readers. With frequent modeling, scaffolding, and practice, Shakespeare's young readers will learn to navigate the undiscovered country that lies between them and Shakespeare's text, that place from whose bourn few readers return unchanged.

6 Prereading the Play

First, good Peter Quince, say what the play treats on; then read the names of the actors; and so grow to a point.

A Midsummer Night's Dream 1.2.8–10

The chapters in Part I build a foundation of word knowledge for comprehending and expressing the layers of meaning in Shakespeare's text. This chapter places students at the doorstep of the specific play they are about to read and hands them a set of keys—key stage directions, key lines, cast lists, and summarizers.

Flourish. Enter the KING

Stage directions specific to a play can prepare students for the dramatic world they are about to enter. When arranged in sequence, these telegraphic phrases can suggest the storyline and mood of the play. Figure 6.1, a collection of dramatic stage directions for *Macbeth*, is one way to enter the dark world of this play. At a glance, students learn that the play they are about to read has witches, murderers, apparitions, and soldiers. They need to know what *exeunt* and *exeunt severally* mean. And they need to play with the possibilities—how might Witches enter and Murderers exit? Finally, the stage directions I selected from the Dover Thrift edition that we use in class are strange enough to whet the curiosity of most students.

Julius Caesar, one of the most frequently taught of Shakespeare's plays, can be a challenge for novice readers. At its surface, it is speechy, political, and male-bound. Guiding students not past these things but more deeply into them is an immediate necessity. Inspired by the work of Paul Sullivan, a master teacher at the Folger Library's Teaching Shakespeare Institute (TSI) in 1994, I incorporated the language of stage directions into a prereading "silent scene" for the assassination of Caesar (Figure 6.2). This activity usually takes at least one full period to plan and perform, but the payback is worth it. Not only do students get to physicalize the stage directions, but they also begin to know and participate in the factions that vie for power in this play. After the silent scene is planned and performed, students need to talk about the implications of a Good Man (GdM) not only refusing to help his Boss (BM) but participating in his murder.

Figure 6.1. Explicit stage directions.

Sketching Shakespeare's Explicit Stage Directions

Use your understanding of Shakespearean explicit stage directions to sketch ways of showing these stage directions for *Macbeth*:

Enter three Witches.	*Alarum within. Enter a bleeding* Sergeant.	*Flourish. Enter King Duncan.*	*Exeunt three* Murderers, *severally.*
Witches retire.	*Third Apparition, a Child crowned, with a tree in his hand. Descends.*	*A show of eight Kings, the last with a glass in his hand.*	*Enter with drum and colours* Malcolm, *other* Thanes, *and* Soldiers.

SILENT SCENE
For use with *Julius Caesar*, act 3.1

(1) A Friendly Crowd (FC) *enters* and waits for the Boss Man (BM). A group of about 7 Grumpy Guys (GrGs) *enter* and *ascend* to the base of a statue, apart from the FC. A Good Man (GdM) *advances* to them.

(2) *Flourish. Enter* Boss Man (BM), *attended* by Servants. BM walks through the Friendly Crowd (FC), waving and shaking hands. He *advances* to GrGs when a Strange Man (SM), in an *aside*, tries to warn BM about the GrGs, but BM brushes him off and continues to *advance* toward the GrGs.

(3) BM stands before the statue, looking very important. GrGs *advance* to him one by one, some with requests, some on their knees. BM brushes them aside.

(4) One by one, the GrGs *draw* their weapons and attack BM. He turns for help to GdM. GdM *draws* his weapon and stabs BM. Embracing GdM, the bleeding BM, incredulous, *dies*.

(5) GdM withdraws from the dying BM's arms, then instructs the GrGs to smear BM's blood on their hands and arms. GdM does this too.

(6) GdM and GrGs *advance* toward FC (which now stands for Frightened Crowd) waving their arms in triumph. The body of BM is left unattended. *Exeunt all, severally.* In the distance, an *alarum* sounds.

This activity is adapted from an idea by Paul Sullivan, TSI 1994 Master Teacher at the Folger Teaching Shakespeare institute in Washington, D.C.

Figure 6.2. Silent scene.

As an extension of the activities outlined in Chapter 1, I begin *Hamlet* with a prereading lesson on the stage directions. On the day before I distribute the books, I display this stage direction on an overhead projector:

> *Hamlet.* By William Shakespeare. Ed. Shane Weller. New York: Dover Thrift, 1992.

> *Flourish. Enter the* KING, QUEEN, HAMLET, POLONIUS, LAERTES, VOLTIMAND, CORNELIUS, Lords, *and* Attendants.

To reinforce that all reading, but perhaps most especially reading Shakespeare, is seeing and hearing words, and to review what we've learned about explicit and implicit stage directions, we imagine the possibilities. What might this "flourish" sound like? This entrance seems formal. What might a formal entrance look like? We talk briefly about film scripts and the degree of detail that film script writers include in their directions (referred to as *directorial commentary*). Then I show them how director Kenneth Branagh chose to read this stage direction:

> Branagh, Kenneth, and William Shakespeare. *Hamlet.* New York: W. W. Norton, 1996.

> **Interior / State Hall / Day**

> A glorious procession of the new KING CLAUDIUS and his QUEEN GERTRUDE. We move with them into a packed gathering of smiling Courtiers and Commoners. The men are crisp, sexy. The military cut—all dashing clothes and hair. The women's clothes colourful, gloriously textured, shapely, and flesh-revealing.
>
> They walk from the enormous doors through rows of bleachers. It's like the House of Commons. Everyone stands. The guard of honour salutes. CLAUDIUS in full military regalia. Severe, cropped hair, brushed back, standing to attention atop a striking face that bears a crisp beard. GERTRUDE, complete with veil and generous bosom on show, also trim and vigorous. This irresistibly sexy, confident couple reach the throne. They face their AUDIENCE of bright festive colours and supportive faces.
>
> The King begins to speak . . . As the AUDIENCE applauds, the Camera tracks slowly past them and comes to a halt under the right hand balcony. There at the other end of the hall is a black silhouette of a man. . . . (11–14)

Before showing the brief but dramatic film clip of this entrance, I ask, "Who do you think the 'black silhouette of a man' might be?" They can usually guess. One stage direction goes a long way in Shakespeare.

Figure 6.3 is a good follow-up, but it can also stand on its own as a prereading activity for *Hamlet*. These five stage directions never fail to produce rich classroom conversations about the performance potential of commands like *Enter* and *Exit* GHOST. Student ideas range from dramatically simple—"Okay, for stage, my *Enter* GHOST is a pitch-black stage, the audience can't see anything, and then one spotlight suddenly lights on a tall guy with white hair and gray makeup standing in the middle of the stage!"—to cinematically complex—"For a movie, there's this painting hanging on a wall in a dark castle and the camera is just looking at it and slowly the face in the painting starts to come off the painting and form into a GHOST that looks like a dead version of the face that was in the painting, and then it walks into the camera and it's gone and we still see the painting, but there's no one in it!" Perhaps a little Harry (Potter) in the night here, but this student joins the rank of directors who borrow from great filmmakers of the past.

Finally, with a play like *Hamlet*, it's difficult to resist Shakespeare's longest stage direction, from the Dover edition of act 3.2:

> Enter a KING and a QUEEN, (very lovingly), the QUEEN embracing him and he her. (She kneels and makes show of protestation unto him.) He takes her up and declines his head upon her neck. He lies him down upon a bank of flowers. She, seeing him asleep, leaves him. Anon comes in another man, takes off his crown, kisses it, pours poison in the sleeper's ears, and leaves him. The Queen returns, finds the King dead, makes passionate action. The poisoner with some three or four come in again, seem to condole with her. The dead body is carried away. The poisoner woos the Queen with gifts. She seems harsh awhile but in the end accepts his love.

Read it aloud, ask for volunteers to stand in for King, Queen, another man/poisoner, and some three or four, and let the class direct. The implications of this prereading activity will stay with students throughout the reading of a play in which the Queen's degree of guilt is questionable.

Students enjoy collaborating on ideas for the stage directions to a play they haven't read yet. By this time tomorrow, they will be ready to begin reading:

> *Elsinore. A platform before the castle.* FRANCISCO *at his post. Enter to him* BERNARDO.
>
> BERNARDO: Who's there?

Cast Lists

Many years ago, as part of our district's professional development plan, a special needs specialist from the Boston College Graduate School of

---

Stage Directions in *Hamlet*

Brainstorm for how you would direct or perform each of these explicit stage directions, all of which are in the play we are about to read. Have dramatic and creative ideas for both a stage and film production.

(1) *Enter* GHOST.
Production ideas for stage: Production ideas for film:

(2) *Exit* GHOST.
Production ideas for stage: For film:

(3) GHOST *beckons* HAMLET.
Production ideas for stage: For film:

(4) *Enter two* GRAVEDIGGERS.
Production ideas for stage: For film:

(5) HAMLET *leaps into the grave.*
Production ideas for stage: For film:

Figure 6.3. Stage directions.

Education presented a series of reading and writing strategies we could incorporate into our classes that benefit all students, from at-risk to advanced. At the time, I was about to teach *Macbeth* to three sections of sophomores in three tracks—honors, college prep standard, and college prep basic. I was listening.

"Before you read a novel with your students," she said, "what do you do to introduce them to the main characters?" Not much, I thought.

"Why not make character bookmarks for your students that list and briefly describe them?" she suggested. "Then they can read the novel with their character bookmarks on their desks, and this will help them to keep the characters straight."

The cast lists in some paperback editions of the plays, notably the Folger and Cambridge School editions, are very helpful to students, but in many editions the characters in Shakespeare's plays are listed with minimal information about named characters and in order by males, then females, supernaturals, and unnamed generics (Lords, Gentlemen, Officers, Soldiers, Attendants, etc.). With a little improvising, I came up with a plan—distribute blank index cards to my students, tell them to work the card vertically, distribute the play or a copy of the cast list, and begin to read and reread the list looking for two fundamental social relationships among these characters they do not yet know, relationships of social status and family.

The chart in Figure 6.4 lists most of the named characters in *Macbeth*. The first column is reproduced from the edition of the play that we distribute to students, while the second column is an example of how rearranging the cast list by power and family can help students begin to construct an understanding of the status and relationships that will fuel the dynamics of the play.

This activity can spark some astute observations and raise significant questions about status and family. For example, in terms of power, once students are aware that Hecate is a goddess, queen of the underworld, and protector of witches, they begin to wonder just how powerful the supernatural characters in this play will be, a question that is fundamental to an understanding of Macbeth and free will. Though both Macbeth and Banquo are generals, students conclude from the title of the play that Macbeth has an edge in the power department. And when the families in this play are reunited, students can see, in the most traditional sense of what "family" means, three incomplete families: there is no QUEEN for King Duncan, the Macbeths have no children, and Banquo has no wife. These missing characters can account in part

Macbeth Dramatis Personae	*Macbeth* Character Bookmark
DUNCAN, king of Scotland.	? HECATE, 3 Witches, Apparitions?

MALCOLM,
DONALBAIN, his sons.
	DUNCAN, king of Scotland
	    MALCOLM, 1st son
	    DONALBAIN, 2nd son

MACBETH, BANQUO, generals of the King's army.	MACBETH, general Lady MACBETH

MACDUFF,
LENNOX,
ROSS,
MENTEITH,
ANGUS,
CAITHNESS, noblemen of Scotland.
	BANQUO, general
	    FLEANCE, son
	
	MACDUFF
	Lady MACDUFF
	    BOY, son

FLEANCE, son to Banquo.	LENNOX ROSS
BOY, son to Macduff.	MENTEITH
Lady MACBETH. Lady MACDUFF.	ANGUS, CAITHNESS
HECATE. Three Witches. Apparitions.	

Figure 6.4. Character bookmark.

for the choices their family members will make in this play about loyalty, survival, and royal accession.

Throughout the years, my students have created character bookmarks for more than a dozen of Shakespeare's plays, and each time, the process provokes interest and insight into a play they have not yet begun to read. When we reassemble the Dover edition's Dramatis Personae, the royal family of Denmark usually looks like this (Figure 6.5).

Invariably, a communal "Hmmph," arises from the floor when students prune this family tree. "Wait a minute," some sophomore always says, "Hamlet's mother married Hamlet's uncle? She married her dead husband's brother?"

"How would you feel," I ask them, "if you loved your father, your father died, and soon after the funeral, your mother remarried your father's younger brother?" Welcome to Elsinore, kids.

Sometimes, when we read and reread a cast list looking for relationships of social status and family, the discoveries can be quite unexpected. For example, to help my students understand the stratifications

CLAUDIUS, King of Denmark.

GERTRUDE, Queen of Denmark, mother to Hamlet.

HAMLET, son to the late, and nephew to the present king.

GHOST of Hamlet's Father.

Figure 6.5. Royal family chart.

of society in *Othello*, I list four types of social status in this play: political, military, ethnic/racial, and domestic. Knowing what they do not yet know, that Othello is one of Shakespeare's great "others," I have always expected that when my students sift through the Dramatis Personae for *Othello*, they will discover that the tragic hero they are about to meet is an outsider in fundamental and significant ways, and that he will not top the list of the powerful in this play. But as my students and I worked on this activity in November of 2008, on a whim I decided to assign numeric values to each title. I projected the categories and rankings of status in this play at the overhead and we started to assign point values and add up the numbers (Figure 6.6).

This whole process may be more complicated than necessary, but it helped us to discover something surprising. Focusing on the Duke of Venice, Senator Brabantio, and Othello, we found that the Duke earns five points for his political status, five for his ethnic status, and five for his domestic status as someone's husband and/or father, for a total of fifteen points. Senator Brabantio earns four for his political status, five for his ethnic status, and five for his status as Desdemona's father, for a total of fourteen points. Othello's lineage is noble, so he earns two points for his political status, five for his military status of general, two for his racial status as a Moor, and five for his status as Desdemona's husband. At fourteen points, he appears equal to Senator Brabantio. But when I tell students that Othello has been assigned to replace Montano as governor of Cyprus, he becomes the Duke's numeric equal. What this activity revealed to both me and my students is that while Othello's race and religion are real issues in this play, we cannot impose the American experience upon the Shakespearean one and expect an instant understanding of the social forces at work in his plays. Nonetheless, another effect of examining cast lists for the political, military, ethnic, and domestic status of characters is to reveal the glaring limitations imposed

Status in *Othello* – The Cast List		
Status	*Dramatis Personae* **Dover Thrift Edition**	*Cast List* **Rearranged by Status**
<u>Political Status</u> 5 Duke 4 Senator 3 Governor 2 Gentleman 1 Gentlewoman	DUKE of Venice BRABANTIO, a senator GRATIANO, brother to Brabantio LODOVICO, kin to Brabantio	
<u>Military Status</u> 5 General 4 Lieutenant 3 Ancient (Ensign)	OTHELLO, a noble Moor in service of Venice CASSIO, his lieutenant IAGO, his ancient RODERIGO, a Venetian gentleman	
<u>Ethnic/Racial Status</u> 5 Venetians 4 Florentines 3 Cypriots 2 Moors 1 Turks	MONTANO, Othello's predecessor in the government of Cyprus	
<u>Domestic Status</u> 5 Husband / Father 4 Wife / Mother 3 Son 2 Daughter 1 Mistress	DESDEMONA, daughter to Brabantio and wife to Othello EMILIA, wife to Iago BIANCA, mistress to Cassio	

Figure 6.6. Cast status list.

upon females in Shakespeare's world. An activity such as this is not only a window into the world of *Othello*, it is an opportunity to look in upon ourselves. In class, we talk about status at school and in our culture. We consider the ways in which things have changed and failed to change.

Key Lines

Another way to preread a play is to select key lines from act 1 and to guide students through a process of inferential thinking that not only gets them reading, speaking, and hearing Shakespeare in small, manageable doses, but also begins to paint the "big picture" of the play without the teacher doing any of the brushwork. The list of key lines from act 1 of *Macbeth* (Figure 6.7) never fails to elicit fun and fascinating interpretations and predictions in a whole group follow-up discussion.

Summarizers

Of the thirty-seven plays ascribed to Shakespeare, it remains unclear how many of the plots are thought to be original to him. Joseph Papp and Elizabeth Kirkland report in *Shakespeare Alive!* that "not a single one of the stories in his plays was his own creation" (153); Shakespearean scholar Russ McDonald advises that when we consider the sources of Shakespeare's plots, we expand our notion of what a source is to include such "noncanonical forms . . . as pamphlets and ballads," as well as "non-printed texts" (146–147). Certainly, when it comes to plot, Shakespeare was not a lender but a borrower. In his list of "The Shakespeare Teacher's Seven Deadly Preconceptions," Ralph Cohen identifies the pursuit of plot as number three. Though Cohen acknowledges that most teachers prefer to focus, and rightly so, on Shakespeare's language and characters, "in America too frequently the story line is what matters most" (35). To liberate ourselves and our students from the daily grind of reading Shakespeare to understand "what happens," Cohen recommends that students read, yes, the Cliff Notes "or some other plot summary" on their own (35). That will free them and us for the real work at hand.

In both its editions of the plays and in its treasure trove of teacher-support materials, the Folger Shakespeare Library offers a variety of prereading summarizers. Beyond the scene summaries in each Folger edition of every Shakespearean play, the three volumes of *Shakespeare Set Free* edited by Peggy O'Brien include summaries of what O'Brien calls "Play Sections." These are chunks of lines *within* each scene that are summarized; furthermore, each speaker in each section is named along

---

Significant Quotations from *Macbeth*

Directions: *Read these key lines from the Oxford edition of the play. Imagine what they might mean and who might be speaking them (someone young or old, male or female, powerful or subservient, good or evil?). Underneath each quote, write your ideas. The first one is done.*

Fair is foul, and foul is fair . . . (1.1.10)
So foul and fair a day I have not seen. (1.3.36)

> I think this means that things that look good on the outside are rotten on the inside. The second line seems to say that the weather on that day is changeable, going from bad to good. The two lines both contain the same idea about good and evil coexisting. The speaker might be someone who is struggling to choose between good and evil.

If chance will have me king, why, chance may crown me
Without my stir. (1.3.143–44)

Stars, hide your fires,
Let not light see my black and deep desires; (1.4.50–51)

Yet I do fear thy nature.
It is too full o' th' milk of human kindness . . . (1.5.15–16)

Come, you spirits
That tend on mortal thoughts, unsex me here . . . (1.5.39–40)

. . . look like th' innocent flower,
But be the serpent under 't. (1.5.64–65)

If it were done when 'tis done, then 'twere well
It were done quickly. (1.7.1–2)

Figure 6.7. Key lines from *Macbeth*.

with the number of lines each speaker has within each section. Furthermore, and of particular use as prereading artifacts, each volume of *Set Free* includes a variety of play summarizers in the form of graphic play maps (*A Midsummer Night's Dream*, p. 43; *Othello*, p. 139), improvisations (*Macbeth*, p. 204), summary scripts with a narrator and lines from the play (*Henry IV, Part 1*, p. 135–137), and clever summary poems (*Twelfth Night*, p. 68–69). Visit the Folger website and skim the collection of the latest teacher-written lesson plans for more ways to begin specific plays.

Rehearsal is the necessary prologue to performance in the Shakespeare classroom as well as the theater. Practice with the stage directions, cast lists, key lines, and summarizers, and then let the play begin.

7 Writing between the Lines

I will write all down.
He writes in his tables
Such and such pictures, there the window, such
Th'adornment of her bed, the arras, figures,
Why, such and such; and the contents o' th' story.

Cymbeline 2.2.24–27

One of the most striking memories of my early years as a teacher is highlighted, literally, in yellow. The first-year students in the reading and study skills classes at St. Dominic Savio High School in East Boston were struggling to identify the main ideas in a workbook of informational passages entitled *Six-Way Paragraphs*, so I purchased enough highlighters for each student to have his own, modeled the strategy of highlighting the main idea in a paragraph, and set them to work.

Confident that this hands-on approach to teaching reading would empower them to break through the impasse in comprehension, I circulated. To this day I'm not sure if what I witnessed was universal proof that each reader shared the same problem—a complete inability to differentiate between main ideas and supporting details—or just the domino effect of students doing what the student next to them does, but after a few minutes of awkward hesitation, they started highlighting. Everything. They highlighted every sentence with such dogged earnestness that I eliminated the possibility that this was a joke on the teacher. When I asked individual students what they thought was most important in each paragraph, their responses went something like, "It's all important." And then as an afterthought, "Or else it wouldn't be there."

Several years later, when I was assigned to teach seniors in an honors class at this private school, I saw something different. I saw a roomful of accomplished and motivated young men who owned their books both literally and inferentially. Beyond the tuition they paid to be there, they also paid a hefty book fee, and though some students resisted the urge to scribble on the pages because it affected a book's resale value, some did not and by their senior year of high school, they had developed sophisticated codes for tracking their thinking as they read and reread text. Their books almost looked like mine.

For ten years I taught at this school where students could be encouraged to write in their books, and I fell into teaching habits that were predicated on this luxury. I could focus the first or second reading of a challenging text by telling students to highlight every word, phrase, or sentence that helped them to see and hear a poem. We could read Dylan Thomas's "Do Not Go Gentle into That Good Night" and highlight the repeated commands, *Do not go gentle . . . Rage, rage . . . .* We could circle the kinds of men this poem describes, *wise men, good men, wild men, grave men,* and *you, my father.* We could letter the rhyme scheme, *a-b-a, a-b-a,* and scan the meter and number the lines in each stanza and count out the bones of the poem on the page.

Some readers, from novice to expert, will argue that annotating literary text minimizes the aesthetic experience of imaginative literature, but experience has taught me that when students can add their marks to the page, they make the words "live twice" (Sonnet 17). Using the diagram of a bird whose myriad body parts are labeled (*nape, mantle, scapulars . . .*), the authors of the poetry text *Western Wind* assert, "There are people who think that knowledge destroys their spontaneous reaction to anything beautiful. They are seldom right; generally, the more we know, the more we see to appreciate" (xxxix). Questioning, clarifying, commenting, connecting—this is the dialogue that active readers engage in with text. Annotation is the "visible record" of that dialogue (O'Donnell 82).

I would not begin to codify the whys, the whats, and the hows of teaching annotation until it became a reading and teaching strategy denied. One of the series of small shocks that ran through me in my first year of teaching at a public secondary school was the simple, everyday fact that students are not allowed to write in their books because they do not own them. I remain convinced that the habit of reading without hands hinders comprehension and handicaps the reader's ability to interact with the text, construct meaning, and own ideas. Tell me to read Shakespeare with my eyes only and you will need to tie my hands behind the mast, Odysseus-like.

Why Teach Annotation? A Brief Rationale

It sounds so old school. Even the title of this chapter is borrowed from a sentence in an article by Mortimer Adler that was first published in 1940 in *The Saturday Review*. In "How to Mark a Book," Adler points out that everyone knows you have to "read between the lines," but only the most active readers "write between the lines" (qtd. in Fielding and Schoenbach 179). Not all reading need be active; there is much to be said about reading for pleasure. But linger for a moment on the word *active* and then leap from 1940 to 2007, to the National Endowment for the Arts (NEA) report, *To Read or Not to Read: A Question of National Consequence*. Beyond the predictable negative correlations noted in this study between nonreaders and academic and economic failure are the positive correlations between readers and action. In short, readers not only do better in school and at work, they also live more active social and civic lives. In the preface, NEA Chair Dana Goioa characterizes the report "not as an elegy for the bygone days of print culture, but instead . . . a call to action." We are teaching adolescents to read in a nation that is suffering a "simple, consistent, and alarming" decline in reading among adolescents and adults, and that decline has civic and social consequences.

Teach annotation and save the world? No. But teach annotation and nurture active readers. Teach adolescents to grapple with text, to talk back to the author, to interrogate ideas and wonder over words and question and argue and leave a record of their passing and you teach them a life skill with implications that go beyond the page.

These are Adler's reasons for teaching annotation, and by adoption, my own:

1. Annotation keeps you awake. Wide awake.
2. Active reading is thinking, and thinking expresses itself in words and symbols.
3. Writing helps you remember. An annotated page is a reader's chronicle.
4. Annotation slows you down (qtd. in Fielding 181–184).

To Adler's list of reasons, I would add one more:

5. Annotation encourages rereading.

As Richard Beach and David O'Brien note in Chapter 11 of *Secondary School Literacy*, rereading reveals the limitations of first impressions, generates discussion and debate, and fosters the ability to "formulate new, alternative interpretations" of text, a skill that with practice can transfer to students' revising their own written texts (233).

"In the case of good books," Adler concludes, and here I insert Shakespeare's plays, "the point is not to see how many of them you can get through, but rather how many can get through you—how many you can make your own" (184).

How to Teach Annotation in the Shakespeare Classroom

In this section, I move between two *English Journal* articles written about annotating text by Carol Porter-O'Donnell and Matthew D. Brown because the methods I use to teach students how to write between the lines of Shakespeare's text form a sort of hybrid. Years before I read either article, I was haphazardly teaching annotation skills, especially as we read from Shakespeare, but the recent influence of Porter-O'Donnell and Brown on my practice is significant. Still, neither author specifically addresses the act of annotating Shakespeare, and the sheer complexity of his text requires its own approach. There is so much going on in a single page of Shakespeare's text that the most I can ask of my adolescent readers is to use the annotation bookmark on page 80 like a menu, choosing from it to mark what stands out as they read and reread a sentence, a speech, a page, or a scene.

Before we begin teaching students to annotate Shakespeare, it's helpful to ask students what they do when they can write on the pages. I make an overhead transparency of a page or two of the scene we have just read, covered with my annotations, talk briefly about the things I marked in the text and wrote in the margins, and distribute the survey in Figure 7.1. Students in the Shakespeare elective report that they annotate the text "sometimes" in other classes but "frequently" in their Shakespeare class (though what they consider "frequent" and what I consider "frequent" are usually two different things). The fact that we most often use the Dover editions of Shakespeare's plays with their bargain-basement prices means students can own their books, and ownership is a significant, though not a necessary, first step. Before I collect the survey, we talk as a whole group about the things on a page that students mark and the methods they use to mark them; we talk about their reasons for marking or not marking the page. This preliminary activity usually yields generalities, but it's a way to get students thinking more closely about active reading.

In her *EJ* article, Porter-O'Donnell explains how she and her colleagues Janell Cleland and Tom O'Donnell begin the process of teaching annotation in the English classroom, not with a survey but with students' written responses to a short literary work. How do you think about text *after* reading it, they ask. Students categorize the ways in which they "react or respond to a text" by generating a list that typically includes predictions, questions, opinions, analyses of the author's craft, connections, and reflections on the content and/or their own reading of the text (82). The teachers use these categories as the framework for teaching annotation.

The next step in Porter-O'Donnell's methodology is to distribute student copies of a short story, make overhead transparencies of the short story, and display the list of the reactions and responses to text

---

Annotating Text: Talking to the Page

an·no·ta·tion *n.* A writing-to-learn strategy for use while reading or rereading; a visible record of thoughts that emerge while making sense of reading. *Carol Porter-O'Donnell*

(1) When you read silently or aloud, independently or in groups, how often do you annotate the text? *Circle one:*

Always   Frequently   Sometimes   Never

(2) Are there certain kinds of text that you are more likely to annotate?
☑ *Check all that apply:*

Handouts

Books you own

Textbooks, using sticky notes

Scripts (for plays, speeches, presentations)

Something else? Explain:

(3) How do you annotate text? What methods do you use?
☑ *Check all that apply:*

Yellow highlighters

Multicolored markers (highlighters, Sharpies)

Written comments and questions

Metacognitive codes (question marks, exclamation points, numbers, symbols)

Something else? Explain:

(4) When you read Shakespeare, what things do you commonly annotate (mark in the text and/or write in the margins):

(5) Why do you (or don't you) annotate text? How does it impact your reading?

Figure 7.1. Annotation survey.

that students generated in the previous lesson. The lesson proceeds, page-by-page, in this manner:

1. The teacher, or a student, reads one page aloud.
2. The group is given time to mark their pages independently.
3. The teacher leads a whole-group discussion, recording student annotations on the transparency.
4. Before moving to the next page, the teacher asks questions that address anything overlooked—are there any predictions? Any questions? Any connections?
5. Each student writes at least one marginal comment on the page.

This process continues until the short story has been read aloud and annotated. Before the class ends, students receive an "annotating text" bookmark to guide them.

Throughout the unit, the teachers share models of annotated texts done by themselves and former students so students can see that there is no single "right" way to annotate. The marks will vary depending on "the demands of the text, the purpose for the reading, and the background experiences of the reader" (83–85).

Though Porter-O'Donnell begins with students' written responses to text and I begin with an annotation survey, we both arrive at the construction of an annotation bookmark (Figure 7.2), and we both rely on read-alouds and overhead transparencies of pages for sharing what and how we write between the lines. In the Shakespeare class, I usually begin to teach annotation when we have finished the second act of the first play we read, and conduct whole-group read-alouds and annotation shares modeled on Porter-O'Donnell's method several times a week until the first play is completed. As the year progresses, with increasing independence, students annotate the pages of their books together in their reading companies and independently, though I continue to review and model the process periodically throughout the year.

In my sophomore English classes, however, I begin modeling annotation immediately. Our first reading of act 1.1 of *Macbeth* is done together and on two planes—with the book in their hands (or a copy of the scene) and a transparency of the scene at the overhead, which I pre-mark to focus our reading on setting (*Where are we?*), mood (*What sort of a place is this?*), motive (*What do the Witches want?*), foreshadowing and vivid lines (*What does* fair *mean? What does* foul *mean? How can* fair *be* foul*? What might this play be about?*). After reading this short scene aloud, we go back and mark the text for the places in the lines that sug-

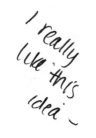

Annotating Shakespeare

When you read and reread Shakespeare, what things do you annotate (mark, comment on, explain)? This reader's bookmark contains our answers.

Mark in the text:
> ➤ Setting words for when, where, and whether
> ➤ Character lines for *direct* statements of appearance, age, reputation, motive, or actions
> ➤ Character lines for *indirect* statements of motive, values, beliefs
> ➤ Plot lines for statements of action and intention
> ➤ Soliloquies
> ➤ Scene chunks
> ➤ Speech chunks
> ➤ Lists of things
> ➤ Punctuation
> ➤ Q's & A's
> ➤ Repetitions
> ➤ Word families
> ➤ Figures of speech
> ➤ Shifts from blank verse to rhyme
> ➤ Shifts from *you* to *thee*
> ➤ Shifts from *I* to the royal *we*
> ➤ Vivid lines

Write in the margins:
> ➤ Character IDs above a character's name
> ➤ Definitions
> ➤ Questions
> ➤ Noun antecedents for vague pronouns
> ➤ Tone words
> ➤ Mood words
> ➤ Summaries
> ➤ Personal reactions
> ➤ Predictions
> ➤ Connections
> ➤ Comments
> ➤ Ratings (1 to 10)

Figure 7.2. Annotating Shakespeare bookmark.

gest answers to these questions, and we write in the margins our words for mood and meaning.

Arming fifteen-year-olds with pencils and highlighters and encouraging them to talk back to and mark up the pages of their books is a novelty for them that never gets old. Year after year with group after group, I find students universally eager to annotate Shakespeare and proud at the end of a play at how much of their thinking survives. "Save that book. Don't lose it," I tell them. Most years at graduation, and sometimes years after that, a former student will tell me, "Ms. Dakin, I still have my books!" I know exactly which books they mean.

Connecting through Annotation

Though Porter-O'Donnell's methods of teaching annotation closely align with my own, it is Matthew Brown's *EJ* article that helped me to see what was missing from my approach. I was troubled by an observation made by a student in the Shakespeare class who wrote on her annotation survey, "I feel sometimes we over analyze literature . . . we pry and dig into things that I feel our [sic] sacred and aren't meant to be pried into. In some situations annotating makes me lose meaning . . . and takes away from reading." In a follow-up conversation with this student, I learned that she was okay with annotating so long as it didn't start to feel clinical, "like brain surgery."

Though Brown begins to teach annotation in a more formal vein by distributing copies of a page or two of text that has been professionally (and heavily) annotated by scholars, he quickly shifts the focus from academia to adolescents. After they analyze what professional editors do to address their audience, achieve their purpose, and demonstrate their expertise, Brown's students grapple with an essential question: *What does it mean to connect to text?* To arrive at this question for his students, Brown first had to question himself, question us all: *What makes us love the books, plays, and poems that we love? What connections are vital?*

I remembered memorizing bits of Shakespeare long before I understood it as a scholar might, because I loved the sounds it made and I loved that it made me feel more human, more alive. I remembered chanting snatches of lines in my head just to get through some awful moment. I remembered caring about characters as if they were family and friends. So I reread my Annotating Shakespeare bookmark looking for the answers to Brown's questions with a critical eye, ready to revise an incomplete list.

I remember reading lines of Shakespeare - identifying lines but not understanding #

To make annotating not only textually but personally meaningful, Brown allows his students to select a short literary passage of their own choosing, one that appeals to them, and to mark it for the usual things like difficult vocabulary, main idea, and historical and literary context. But he places equal emphasis on connections: "Make [the vocabulary] real for us; Make connections to other parts of the book; Make connections to other visual and graphic material . . . that you have read and seen; Make connections to your life" (75). Their project is to create, in the manner of "the professional model," their own footnoted pages of annotated text, rich not only in literary detail but in personal and social connections.

So I transformed the Annotating Shakespeare bookmark into an overhead transparency with Brown's essential question at the top (Figure 7.3). I pointed to an item close to the bottom of the list, "connections," and observed that most of the things on our bookmark help us to comprehend the text and to connect to it with our minds. Then I asked them, "What about our hearts?" Their answers surprised me.

I thought the first answer would be "personal reactions" but that came at the end of our discussion, almost as an afterthought. The first response was "soliloquies." This made me think my directions were unclear. "How do the soliloquies help you connect in a personal, emotional way?" I asked.

"It's the way a character acts when he's alone and torn up that makes me care about him," Lena said. "I talk to myself all the time. That kind of talk is very personal."

Other students claimed that "character lines for direct and indirect statements . . ." made the reading more personal for them. "Why?" I asked.

"Because we start to care about them, like they're real. They make me think of people I know. Sometimes, the more real they become, the more they seem like me," said Haley.

"Plotlines for statements of action and intention," Francisco said. "You're kidding me," I almost replied, but he could read the incredulity on my face.

"Yeah, situations in a story, experiences like our own. Maybe not exactly, but when you know how it feels to be stepped on or messed up, and this character is messed up like you and has to do something about it, it can feel personal," he explained.

Lena added, "Interpreting a character's intentions, figuring out what motivates them, gets me personally involved. We all want to know why people do what they do."

What does it mean to connect to a text?

Annotating Shakespeare
When you read Shakespeare, what things do you annotate (mark, comment on, and/or explain)? This reader's bookmark contains our answers.

Mark in the text:
- Setting words for when, where, and weather
- Character lines for direct statements of appearance, age, reputation, motive, or actions
- Character lines for indirect statements of motive, values, beliefs
- Plotlines for statements of action and intention
- Soliloquies
- Scene chunks
- Speech chunks
- Lists of things
- Punctuation
- Q's and A's
- Repetitions
- Word families
- Figures of speech
- Shifts from blank verse to rhyme
- Shifts from *you* to *thee*
- Shifts from *I* to the royal *we*
- Vivid lines

Write in the margins:
- Character IDs above a character's name
- Definitions
- Questions
- Noun antecedent for vague pronouns
- Tone words
- Mood words
- Summaries
- Personal reactions
- Predictions
- Connections
- Comments
- Ratings (1 to 10)

Most of the things on this annotation list help us to comprehend the text—to connect to it intellectually.

What things on this list help you to better comprehend yourself, your world, and others as you read Shakespeare? What things help you to connect personally and emotionally with Shakespeare's text?

Figure 7.3. Connecting with the text.

Renee pointed to "shifts from blank verse to rhyme" and explained that when characters rhyme, "it sticks out more. I pay closer attention, like to music."

"How about 'vivid lines?'" I asked. "Lines that we want to keep in our head and our hearts because they are so beautiful and so smart?" On this, the whole group seemed to agree.

That day, I told my students a story about a time when I unexpectedly connected to a Shakespearean speech I did not like. Since at the time we were approaching the final act of *Othello*, I brought students to Othello's last words before he kills himself, "Soft you. A word or two before you go . . . " (5.2.347–365). We read it once, aloud. Then I displayed the speech on an overhead with my original annotations, a sparse record of this reader's emotional distance from the speaker and the words. I had underlined the line I hated most, "Of one that loved not wisely, but too well" and written "give me a break" in the margins. I'd boxed it off and labeled it a speech about "reputation" in a play where men seem obsessed with their public image.

Then I told them a story.

In 2002, I had admitted to my friend and director of education at the Folger Shakespeare Library, Janet Field-Pickering, that Othello's final speech always leaves me cold; that I could only read it as a rationale for domestic violence and a self-pitying excuse for the killing of a wife. At the time, I was a master teacher at the Folger's summer institute. Janet asked me to read it again, and again, and to transcribe the modern adaptation of the speech written for the Tim Blake Nelson film *O*. She believed that there was something in those two versions of the speech worth taking into a high school classroom.

Much later that night, I finished the first draft of a lesson plan that, among other things, asks students to treat Othello's speech not as an attempt to restore his reputation but as a suicide note. I knew it could become a powerful lesson but I worried about taking it into a high school classroom. It wasn't a "safe" lesson. It asked students to explore a difficult topic with their minds, their bodies, and their hearts. That's when she told me, "Keep it real—what we do should matter. Sometimes, it *should* hurt. But what hurts can also heal."

At this point in the story, I told my students there was something I didn't know then, that my friend's cancer, in remission for a decade, had returned and that her doctors had given her two or three years to live. Now I think I know why she wanted me to reconsider the last words of a being who knows when and how he will die. So I asked them to read Othello's last words again, not as a speech about reputation but as a suicide note.

I displayed a fresh, unmarked copy of the speech at the overhead and my students and I read it to mark the bones and open the heart. We looked at the sentences and counted seven in our edition, noting sentence six as the longest. In spite of Othello's formal politeness, we heard almost every sentence as a command. Then we looked at the words and noticed that the pronouns in the first line, "Soft you, a word or two before you go," indicate that Othello is not going with them, as they requested, so he has already made up his mind to kill himself. We wondered when and how he would produce his hidden weapon. We noticed patterns in the verb tenses—the speech begins in the present ("Soft you, a word or two before you go . . . "), shifts to the future (" . . . in your letters, When you shall these unlucky deeds relate . . . "), and ends in the past ("I took by the throat the circumcised dog, And smote him—thus."). We noted repeated expressions of regret. We found in the proper nouns cultural references to an Indian, a Turk, and a Venetian (who would be a Christian). Though the final sentence is syntactically confusing, we thought that the "circumcised dog" could refer to the "turbaned Turk," a Muslim like himself that he killed in Aleppo, but we also thought it could be the last, shocking name Othello gives himself. If it is, then this speech ends on a note of intense self-loathing.

Figure 7.4 is the handout I constructed after this lesson. It codifies the connections a roomful of students and their teacher made one winter day when we annotated Shakespeare. Janet was right—reading Othello's final speech still hurts, but it also heals.

I'm not sure of the connection between love and understanding, but I believe that we remain indifferent to the things we can't or won't understand, and too many of our students are indifferent to literature. So I continue to teach my students to annotate Shakespeare, to read and write between the lines, but I am careful to keep it personal.

Before, After, While

As Carol Porter-O'Donnell notes in the *EJ* article, "Beyond the Yellow Highlighter," most teachers employ a host of pre- and post-reading strategies to enhance and assess reading comprehension. Before students read a challenging text, we tap prior knowledge, introduce background knowledge, skim informational passages for titles, subtitles, illustrations and captions, introduce key vocabulary words, and reflect on themes we

Othello's Last Words
Oxford Edition, 5.2.347–365

Soft you, a word or two before you go.
I have done the state some service, and they know't.
No more of that. I pray you, in your letters,
When you shall these unlucky deeds relate,
Speak of me as I am. Nothing extenuate,
Nor set down aught in malice. Then must you speak
Of one that loved not wisely but too well,
Of one not easily jealous but, being wrought,
Perplexed in the extreme; of one whose hand,
Like the base Indian, threw a pearl away
Richer than all his tribe; of one whose subdued eyes,
Albeit unused to the melting mood,
Drops tears as fast as the Arabian trees
Their medicinable gum. Set you down this,
And say besides that in Aleppo once,
Where a malignant and a turbaned Turk
Beat a Venetian and traduced the state,
I took by th' throat the circumcised dog,
And smote him thus.   [*He stabs himself.*]

Reading and Writing between the Lines
In what ways is this speech Othello's suicide note?

Mark the speech for **tones** of:	Mark also any **pleas** for:
Sorrow	Forgiveness
Anger	Understanding
Regret	Remembrance
Urgency	
Self-loathing	
Determination	

Note the **sentences**—how many are there? Which sentence is longest? Sentences are usually declarative: are these sentences declarative?

Mark the **proper nouns**: what people are important enough to be named here?

Chunk the speech into a **beginning, middle,** and **end**. What patterns emerge?

Speaking the Speech
Rewrite Othello's last words into modern speech. Practice speaking it aloud. Synthesize everything you now understand about this speech into a dramatic reading.

Figure 7.4. Othello's last words.

will meet in the text. After students read, we assign questions for writing and discussion and we design projects for students to demonstrate what they have learned. Annotating the text is a strategy that can "help readers *while* they're reading" (89).

The great irony of active reading is that it slows the reader down. Adolescents have, I hope, a lifetime to return to Shakespeare in some form, if only in films future and past. While they sojourn with us, let's find the time to read and write between the lines.

8 Reading behind the Scenes

How many ages hence
Shall this our lofty scene be acted over,
In states unborn and accents yet unknown!

Julius Caesar 3.1.112–114

Shakespeare's plays are divided into five acts. These divisions, however, were not made by him but by editors after his death. Shakespeare's unit of construction, as pointed out by Douglas Brode, is the scene, not the act (Costanzo 165). Plot is what happens— some event happens, and it causes other events to happen, "and so the events tumble like dominoes until the last domino falls" (Hunt 1578). Combining these two concepts creates a tempting conclusion, that each scene in a Shakespearean play develops one event, one domino that tumbles at the end of the scene into the next. But history intervenes. "*Scene*, in Elizabethan usage," notes Russ McDonald, "refers not so much to a unit of dramatic organization as to a location." With few exceptions, McDonald concludes, "when the place changes, the scene changes" (110).

Still, the scene is our ground zero, the place where characters meet, conflict, and change. It is the place where Shakespeare's readers dwell, where we make meaning one sentence and one page at a time. As we read a scene in Shakespeare with our students, especially the scenes in the first and second acts, two modifiers should repeatedly describe the reading we do together—*guided* and *focused*.

Guided Reading

Guided reading provides students with an outline of a scene in advance of their reading. The outline breaks the scene into smaller units of sense, most often the main events or actions in a scene. Sometimes, that can mean page (or line) headings, especially in long and eventful scenes like act 2.2 of *Hamlet*. This outline, inspired by act 2 review activities from page 98 of the Cambridge School edition of the play, includes the page numbers from the Dover edition as well as the line numbers from the Oxford edition and my mini-summaries of each line set:

Guided Reading: *Hamlet* **act 2.2**
A new action begins at:

1. Page 33 / Lines 1–57, Claudius and Gertrude greet R&G
2. Page 35 / Lines 58–85, Voltimand reports that Fortinbras will attack Poland
3. Page 36 / Lines 86–172, Polonius reports the "cause" of Hamlet's madness
4. Page 38 / Lines 173–221, Hamlet calls Polonius a "fishmonger"
5. Page 40 / Lines 222–423, Hamlet "greets" R&G
6. Page 45 / Lines 424–536, Hamlet welcomes the players
7. Page 48–49 / Lines 537–551, Hamlet requests a performance for tomorrow night
8. Page 49 / Lines 551–end, Hamlet speaks his second soliloquy

Even if students can write these mini-summaries in their books, I still display them on an overhead projector because each one functions as a marker for us to pause and monitor our initial understanding of the lines and ultimately of the scene.

As a summarizer, students go back through the eight subdivisions, or chunks, of this long scene looking for one line or complete sentence that seems to express the main idea. Then we argue, negotiate, and finally assemble the most significant lines at the board and find that we have constructed a summary script using Shakespeare's very words (Figure 8.1):

Guided Reading, *Hamlet* 2.2	*Hamlet* in a Hurry, 2.2
Claudius and Gertrude greet R&G	KING: Welcome, dear Rosencrantz and Guildenstern.
Voltimand reports that Fortinbras will attack Poland	KING: Say, Voltimand, what from our brother Norway?
Polonius reports the "cause" of Hamlet's madness	POL: I will be brief. Your noble son is mad.
Hamlet calls Polonius a "fishmonger"	HAM: Excellent well. You are a fishmonger.
Hamlet "greets" R&G	GUIL: My lord, we were sent for.
Hamlet welcomes the players	HAM: Come, a passionate speech.
Hamlet requests a performance for tomorrow night	HAM: Can you play *The Murder of Gonzago?*
Hamlet speaks his second soliloquy	HAM: The play's the thing Wherein I'll catch the conscience of the King.

Figure 8.1. Guided reading/*Hamlet* in a hurry.

When we provide students with the bones of what happens in a scene, we free them to focus on other things like the patterns of language, the significance of certain lines, the purposes (spoken and unspoken) that motivate complex characters. In one stroke, students are better able to construct meaning on more than a literal level.

Dividing a long scene into such subdivisions also allows us to jump over some parts. We don't have to read every line (or every scene or act, for that matter) in Shakespeare's plays in order to construct meaning. It has been said that the high school curriculum is a mile wide and an inch deep; we have all felt the pressure to "cover" a list of authors and titles in an unrealistically short time. But time is a stern teacher and it has taught me that if I must sacrifice something in Shakespeare, it will be plot.

I first came across the word "chunking" as it relates to reading comprehension in an article by E. D. Hirsch. In a comparison between experts and novices, Hirsch notes that practiced readers and many experts in fields such as chess "are able to perform remarkable feats of comprehension and memory" in part because of their ability to break large units of information into smaller, more manageable units, or chunks (13). In that explanation I recognized a reading-Shakespeare "survival strategy" I had been modeling with students for several years. Glad that I finally had a word for it, and as a bonus a word that might appeal to the adolescent imagination ("It sounds like puke!"), I began to use the word *chunking* in the classroom.

Short scenes can be chunked into line divisions. Act 1.2 of *Macbeth*, for example, naturally divides itself into three smaller units of exposition, each one centered on the actions of four characters. Before we begin reading the scene, I display three chunks:

> **Guided Reading:** *Macbeth* **act 1.2**
>
> Three enemies . . .
>
> Lines 1–25: Macdonwald
>
> Lines 26–46: Norweyan Lord
>
> Lines 47–63: Thane of Cawdor

As we read this short scene aloud, I instruct students to draw lines between the three chunks and label them in their books. We pause within each chunk to question, clarify, comment, and predict, and students mark their books with highlighters and notes penciled in the margins. At the end of the scene, I reveal a fourth chunk:

> . . . and a hero
>
> Lines 18–25, 36–43, 59–73: Macbeth

We reread these lines in the text, focusing on the characterization of Macbeth. Finally, I post a summarizer question:

> Macbeth is not in scene 1 or scene 2, but we are already learning about him. What words are used to describe Macbeth in this scene? What words would you use to describe him?

Each time I bring this lesson into a classroom filled with sophomores of every ability level, some students begin to question not only the text ("What does this word mean?") but the ambiguous character of Macbeth himself. Once they understand that "brave Macbeth" cut his way ("carved out his passage") through the flanks of Irish foot soldiers ("kerns and gallowglasses") to execute "the merciless Macdonwald," and that he sliced him open from the bellybutton to the jaws ("unseam'd him from the nave to the chaps"), beheaded him, and spiked his head upon a post, there are mixed feelings for the "hero." Some students defend Macbeth as a great warrior while others begin to question his capacity for overkill. In approaching Shakespeare's text this way, students begin to get the conversation of comprehension into their heads.

Chunking scenes into page or line divisions can be made more challenging, either later in a play with novice readers or sooner in a play with more advanced readers, by focusing the reading of each chunk on a specific aspect of the language, the characterization, the conflict, or a theme. When the juniors and seniors in the Shakespeare elective begin *Othello*, I chunk act 1.2 into four line divisions for them:

Guided Reading: *Othello* 1.2

Chunk the text into four parts:

1. Lines 1–31: Iago alerts Othello
2. Lines 32–55: Cassio alerts Othello
3. Lines 56–94: Brabantio confronts Othello
4. Lines 95–117: Othello responds

Before they begin to read in their companies, they demarcate the scene. Then I display these instructions:

First Reading
As you read each chunk, focus on **Othello's character traits**. Highlight key lines and write character traits in the margins near the lines. In your companies, be prepared to share and explain your reasoning.

Example: First Chunk, lines 1–31
Othello's character trait = confidence
Lines that reveal this = "Let him do his spite. My services which I have done the signiory / Shall out-tongue his complaints."

My reasoning = In spite of Iago's lengthy description of Brabantio's threatening attitude, Othello seems sure that he will weather this storm.

To accomplish this, they will have to read the scene once for basic comprehension and in effect reread it to focus on the narrative fragments that reveal glimpses of character. As a summarizer, I turn their attention from Othello to Iago with a final prompt:

Iago's Two Faces
Reread/scan 1.2 for lines that reveal Iago's two faces, the one he wears in front of Othello and the one he wears behind Othello's back. Label or color-code what you find.

All compositions have a beginning, a middle, and an end. Though this structure can be the basis of scene-chunking, it is particularly useful with speeches and soliloquies. Therefore, a third method of breaking Shakespeare's text into smaller, more manageable units of meaning is to divide it into a B-M-E, looking for the sequence of thought that underpins the language. Patterns emerge, often in some combination of past-present-future or question-argument-conclusion. One of the structural patterns my students and I discovered when we set about chunking Henry V's Saint Crispin's Day speech for its B-M-E is that Henry's thoughts before the battle of Agincourt move from death to life to eternal life. In Chapter 10, I note the patterns teachers discovered when they chunked Bottom's dream speech in 4.1 of *A Midsummer Night's Dream*. Even the mother of all soliloquies, Hamlet's third, can be readily chunked into:

A beginning . . .
The "To Be" Debate

To be, or not to be; that is the question:
Whether 'tis nobler in the mind to suffer
The slings and arrows of outrageous fortune,
Or to take arms against a sea of troubles,
And, by opposing, end them.

A middle . . .

To die, to sleep—
No more, and by a sleep to say we end
The heartache and the thousand natural shocks
That flesh is heir to—'tis a consummation
Devoutly to be wished. To die, to sleep.
To sleep, perchance to dream. Ay, there's the rub,
For in that sleep of death what dreams may come
When we have shuffled off this mortal coil
Must give us pause. There's the respect
That makes calamity of so long life,
For who would bear the whips and scorns of time,
Th'oppressor's wrong, the proud man's contumely,
The pangs of disprized love, the law's delay,
The insolence of office, and the spurns
That patient merit of th'unworthy takes,
When he himself might his quietus make
With a bare bodkin? Who would fardels bear,
To grunt and sweat under a weary life,
But that the dread of something after death,
The undiscovered country from whose bourn
No traveler returns, puzzles the will,
And makes us rather bear those ills we have
Than fly to others we know not of?

And an end . . .

Thus conscience does make cowards of us all,
And thus the native hue of resolution
Is sicklied o'er with the pale cast of thought,
And enterprises of great pith and moment
With this regard their currents turn awry,
And lose the name of action. (3.1.58–90)

If students listen at least once to the reading of this intimidating monologue in the voice of an expressive reader, while reading from a handout
that illustrates its organizational structure and defines its most arcane
vocabulary, they will be on their way to understanding one of the most
famous passages in all of literature, one chunk at a time.

One of my favorite writing assignments as a teacher of Shakespeare's plays can be seen in Figure 8.2, "Writing Emulation." Though
students can emulate almost any of Shakespeare's soliloquies, asking
students to write about a dilemma of their own in the rhetorical and syn-
tactical form of Hamlet's requires them to pose a question, consider both
sides, and come to a conclusion. Preparing a double- or triple-spaced

Writing Emulation: Modeling Structure, Making New Meaning

Writers and artists crave originality; however, they often want to be like a successful or admired predecessor. You may know that the traditional way artists study painting is to imitate the masters. Many writers, too, either consciously or unconsciously spend their early writing days in a kind of apprenticeship, modeling their work on that of writers they admire.

In this activity, you will be asked to borrow the form of a Shakespearean soliloquy, but to change it into something that is about you. You will reproduce the pattern of Shakespeare's writing, but will use your own ideas and words to replace those of the Shakespearean speaker.

Directions for Writing an Emulation
Most soliloquies are internal debates in which the speaker faces a dilemma and must choose between equally difficult options. Unsure at first, the speaker argues the pros and cons of each choice, then makes a decision.

1. Select a soliloquy that appeals to you in a personal way. What dilemma does the speaker face? What decision does he or she make? What similar dilemma have you faced? What decision did you make? As the focus of your emulated passage, you will describe an actual choice or dilemma that you are facing, or have faced in the past.

2. Type the soliloquy (or cut and paste it from an electronic source) on a piece of plain paper. Double or triple space each line. Check your work for accurate spelling and punctuation. Check your work for word and line omissions.

3. Replace almost every word of the original with a word of your own that serves the same grammatical purpose. You will replace nouns with nouns, verbs with verbs, adjectives with adjectives, etc.

There will be places where you can use Shakespeare's words if you want to—conjunctions such as *and, but, or* may be kept. Prepositions, such as *in, out, above, through, with,* etc. may be kept or replaced, and any form of the verb *to be (am, is, are, was, were, being, been)* may be used as in the original. Most of what you change will be nouns, action verbs, adjectives and adverbs.

4. Retain Shakespeare's rhythm and style. Create meaning that is true for you.

For your first draft, write in the white space above the text. Then copy your final draft onto clean paper, without Shakespeare's text, and sign your name.

Shakespeare's soliloquy now belongs to you.

Figure 8.2. Writing emulation.

template of Hamlet's soliloquy for students' early drafts is essential; without one, most students will wander almost immediately astray from the text. After students have generated the personal dilemma they wish to explore, their engagement is high but the frustration level can be daunting: some students really struggle with Hamlet's syntax, which is far more intricate than their own. Still, when they find ways to work with the text and some internal conflict of their own, their sense of accomplishment is immense.

Over the years, sophomores have written some unforgettable soliloquies on topics ranging from light-hearted ("To snooze or not to snooze") to heartrending ("To report my sister for abusing her baby or not to report her, that is the question"). After one student, an English language learner who had transitioned to the mainstream classroom, completed the final draft of her emulation—"To live with my mother or return to my father, that is the question"—she told me that this assignment helped her to confront the anguish of life with her mother in Massachusetts and to return to her father, who lived in Florida. Before the school year ended, she left and did not return in September. I still wonder where she is, and if she is okay.

The full lesson, complete with student Colleen Myers' emulation, "To snooze or not to snooze," is published at the Folger Shakespeare Library website in the lesson plans archive for *Hamlet*.

Focused Reading

The difference between guided and focused reading is the difference between craft and art. Guided reading helps students to understand the sequence of events or ideas in a scene or speech; focused reading, often done in combination with guided reading, challenges students to see and feel the language.

Before launching into a guided reading of act 1.1 of *Hamlet* with students, I prefer to begin the reading of this play in which questions abound and seeing and not seeing matter a great deal with a focused reading of the first page (Figure 8.3). My notes for this part of the lesson plan read:

Focused Reading: Act 1.1, Page 1

Objective: Inferring conflict and mood from punctuation and imagery

Step One:
Display page 1 on the overhead projector. Distribute books.
Volunteers read page 1 aloud.

Students highlight every question mark and exclamation point; review at the overhead.
DISCUSS: What does the punctuation convey about the mood? Brainstorm for mood words.

Step Two:
Scan page 1 for lines that contain imagery. Circle/underline imagery at the overhead.
DISCUSS: How does the imagery convey mood? Record additional mood words on the page.

Step Three:
DISCUSS: How can the stage set, the actors, the costumes and props all contribute to the mood embedded in the dialogue?

Before we have turned one page, students have imagined what it might be like to stand shivering on a platform before Elsinore castle on a cold, black night. They have counted in our edition six question marks and three exclamations and considered the emotional implications of these. They have noted that the imagery appeals not only to sight, or rather sightlessness (though Francisco is already onstage when Bernardo enters, Bernardo can't see him—"Who's there?"), but to sound ("Have you had quiet guard?" / "Not a mouse stirring.") and to feeling ("'tis bitter cold, / And I am sick at heart.") They have generated a list of mood words: *dark, mysterious, gloomy.* They know that something is rotten in the state of Denmark when a pageful of soldiers is spooked.

I can't offer a comprehensive list of what to focus on in a Shakespearean scene or speech. It will depend on the scene or speech. But after one or two rereadings, your list will probably include some combination of the following: conflict, characterization, theme, tone, mood, purpose, staging. What draws your attention to any one of these will be the details of figurative and rhetorical language, the nondeclarative sentences, the shifts from blank verse to rhyme or verse to prose, from *I* to *we* or *you* to *thee*, the long stretches of dialogue with few or no stage directions, the lines so haunting that you need to know why they catch in your throat and make you remember what it means to be human.

The goal of guided and focused reading is handoff. Eventually, students assume the task of chunking Shakespeare's text and discussing the reasons for their page and line divisions. Eventually, students notice shifts within scenes and language patterns and they explore the connections between language and meaning.

If Shakespeare constructed scenes according to shifts in location, the subdivisions within scenes are often the result of a different sort of shift, one that occurs at the points within a scene where characters exit

---

Hamlet Act 1.1.1–16

Enter Barnardo and Francisco, two sentinels, at several doors

BARNARDO: Who's there?

FRANCISCO: Nay, answer me. Stand and unfold yourself.

BARNARDO: Long live the king!

FRANCISCO: Barnardo?

BARNARDO: He.

FRANCISCO: You come most carefully upon your hour.

BARNARDO: 'Tis now struck twelve. Get thee to bed, Francisco.

FRANCISCO: For this relief much thanks. 'Tis bitter cold

And I am sick at heart.

BARNARDO: Have you had quiet guard?

FRANCISCO: Not a mouse stirring.

BARNARDO: Well, good night.

If you do meet Horatio and Marcellus,

The rivals of my watch, bid them make haste.

Enter Horatio and Marcellus

FRANCISCO: I think I hear them.—Stand! Who's there?

HORATIO: Friends to this ground.

MARCELLUS: And liegemen to the Dane.

FRANCISCO: Give you good night.

MARCELLUS: O farewell, honest soldier. Who hath relieved you?

FRANCISCO: Barnardo has my place. Give you goodnight.   *Exit*

MARCELLUS: Holla, Barnardo!

BARNARDO: Say—what, is Horatio there?

Figure 8.3. *Hamlet* act 1.1.1–16.

and enter. This movement of characters within scenes triggers reaction and new action. But the changes that occur within Shakespeare's scenes are not limited to entrances and exits. Indeed, the shifts can be subtle and detecting them can be critical to understanding the dynamics of a conflict or relationship. Every strategy described in this chapter on making sense of Shakespeare's most fundamental unit of construction comes together in the quest for beats.

Beating a Scene

I was introduced to the concept of beats by colleague Christina Porter, who had been introduced to it as an undergraduate at St. Anselm's College. In a drama course taught by Dr. Landis Magnuson, Porter and her classmates were frequently engaged in a performance-based form of chunking used specifically for dramatic literature, and defined here by Robert Barton, author of *Acting: Onstage and Off*:

> [Beats are] Changes within the scene, signaling that some kind of transaction has been completed and a new one is starting—for example, a topic of conversation is changing; another attack is being tried; a new person is changing the direction of the conversation; or a new objective is being pursued. (14)

Porter was convinced that beating a scene in Shakespeare could be scaffolded for high school students, and she introduced it to her first-year students as they read *Romeo and Juliet*. The next year, I introduced beating to my Shakespeare class and continue to use it at least once in the reading of almost every play we study. Though we continue to share with students Barton's definition of beats, we quickly realized that some decoding was order, so we constructed this list:

According to Barton, a change or beat occurs within a scene when:

- A topic of conversation changes
- A character changes the direction of a conversation
- A character is not getting what he or she wants and attempts a new approach

In addition to these reasons, a new beat may begin when:

- A character enters or exits
- A character's emotional state changes
- A shift in power occurs between two or more characters
- A character finally gets what he or she wants

Since beating is best suited for long, busy scenes, and since students are looking for shifts that occur in less obvious ways than with chunking (a character enters or exits; a new action begins), it is helpful to begin the process by distributing copies of scenes with the first few beats boxed off and marked with a title or short summary. Porter distributes the Folger edition of act 1.5 of *Romeo and Juliet* with the first beats clearly marked and titled:

Beat 1: Preparing for the Guests

Servingmen come forth with napkins

First Servingman: Where's Potpan that he helps not to take away? He shift a trencher? He scrape a trencher?
Second Servingman: When good manners shall lie all in one or two men's hands, and they unwashed too, 'tis a foul thing.
First Servingman: Away with the joint-stools, remove the court-cupboard, look to the plate.—Good thou, save me a piece of marchpane, and, as thou loves me, let the porter let in Susan Grindstone and Nell.—Antony and Potpan!
Third Servingman: Ay, boy, ready.
First Servingman: You are looked for and called for, asked for and sought for, in the great chamber.
Third Servingman: We cannot be here and there too. Cheerly, boys! Be brisk awhile, and the longer liver take all. *They move aside. Enter Capulet and his household, all the guests and gentlewomen to Romeo, Mercutio, Benvolio, and the other Maskers.*

Beat 2: Let's Party!

CAPULET:
Welcome, gentlemen. Ladies that have their toes
Unplagued with corns will walk a bout with you.—
Ah, my mistresses, which of you all
Will now deny to dance? . . .

The first step, then, is to read the scene looking for both the obvious and subtle changes that occur within it. The second step is to write titles that summarize each beat. I encourage students to segment the scene first, then go back and write titles, since this encourages rereading and rethinking. Sometimes, I challenge students to emulate Shakespeare's wordplay by using song titles for each beat in a comic scene, or headlines for a history. In 2006, when students beat act 2.4 of *Henry IV Part I*, each reading company tried to out-Falstaff the other by writing tabloid headlines. What follows is a list of the best (or should I say worst?) headlines for *Henry*:

Beat 1: The Prince Rejoins Poins, Pickled

Beat 2: The Prince Torments the Pauper

Beat 3: Falstaff Hates All Cowards

Beat 4: The Facts Grow Fat!

Beat 5: Prince Presses Perjury—Falstaff Folds!

Beat 6: Falstaff Saves Face

Beat 7: Falstaff Plays the Bouncer

Beat 8: Details of Their Disgraceful Disguise

Beat 9: Duty Calls—Hal Must Answer

Beat 10: Prodigal Prince Practices with Posing Papa Falstaff

Beat 11: Falstaff Sells Himself

Beat 12: Roles Reversed!

Beat 13: Prince Predicts Falstaff's Fall from Power!

Beat 14: Sheriff Pursues Thieves—Prince Promises Results

Beat 15: Prince Sobers Up

The final challenge is to explore the characters caught up in these dynamic exchanges. Though beating a scene may seem like a strategy for exploring a scene's structure, look closely at each bulleted item listed earlier: the word *character* appears in six of the seven lines and is the subject in five. At its performance roots, beating is a tool actors employ to take the pulse of a scene, to understand the ebb and flow of "structural energy" at work in each scene and to be nurtured by it (Rodenburg 120). As an extension, for each beat that they identify and title, students can focus on one character in the beat and articulate that character's objectives using this sentence template:

Character	Objective/Verb	Receiver	Desired response
Capulet	wants to showcase	Juliet	to seal the deal with Paris.
Juliet	wants to like	Paris	to please her parents.

Porter's complete lesson, "Beating Shakespeare," is published at the Reading Shakespeare website. Figure 8.4 brings the essentials of beating a scene together into one handout for students.

There is simply so much to see on a Shakespearean page that even the most experienced readers are often overwhelmed. Imagery, rhetoric, pronouns, punctuation, verse, prose, implied stage directions, characterization, tone, mood—on any given page almost any one of these and more can be at work. In an essay in *Adolescent Literacy* that reads like a meditation on what it means to understand, Ellin Oliver Keene enjoins teachers to "Focus, focus, focus—make decisions about which concepts matter most for students" (38). Early in my teaching of Shakespeare's plays, I found myself reading and rereading the next scene in an attempt to answer these questions: *What matters here? What moves me to care? What captures my attention?* Rather than relying on a list of broad essential questions or a framework of ELA standards as the basis of tomorrow's lesson plan, I learned to look inward and to trust Shakespeare's text. Look behind the scenes, and they will tell you what to focus on tomorrow.

Identify Beats

"[Beats are] Changes within the scene, signaling that some kind of transaction has been completed and a new one is starting—for example, a topic of conversation is changing; another attack is being tried; a new person is changing the direction of the conversation; or a new objective is being pursued." (14)

Robert Barton, *Acting: Onstage and Off*

According to Barton, a change or beat occurs within a scene when:

- A topic of conversation changes
- A character changes the direction of a conversation
- A character is not getting what he or she wants and attempts a new approach

In addition to these reasons, a new beat may begin when:

- A character enters or exits
- A character's emotional state changes
- A shift in power occurs between two or more characters
- A character finally gets what he or she wants

Entitle Beats
Write a title for each beat that summarizes the changes or transactions in the scene.

Identify Character Objectives
Within a "beat" each character should have an objective. Simply stated, an objective is a character's purpose within that beat. Objectives should be stated using strong verbs in their infinitive form. Objectives should have a receiver and often, a desired response. In some beats, a character, a verb, and a receiver are sufficient.

Character	Objective/Verb	Receiver	Desired Response
We	want to inspire	students	to become lifelong readers of Shakespeare
Ophelia	wants to win	Hamlet's	undying devotion
Macbeth	wants to deceive	King Duncan	

Figure 8.4. Beat handout.

9 Reading in Companies

*Good Nurse, God save you and good night. I would stay asleep my whole life
if I could dream myself into a company of players. (21)*

Marc Norman and Tom Stoppard, *Shakespeare in Love: A Screenplay*

There are so many ways to name them, the configurations in which
we group students when they read together in class—reading
workshops, reciprocal teaching groups, literature circles, Socratic
seminars. But it was Norman and Stoppard's screenplay that gave me the
name I needed—reading companies—for the team reading we do with
Shakespeare. Sometimes students name their companies after theaters in
Shakespeare's London: The Rose, The Swan, The Globe. Sometimes they
remake the names of Elizabethan troupes into The Admiral's Angels or
Dakin's Demons. And sometimes it's Mad Chick Productions.

Whether they name their companies or not, students need to know
that reading Shakespeare is not the part they skip. Nor is it the kind of
reading that should be limited to a single approach. As Bonnie Ericson
points out in *Teaching Reading in High School English Classes*, "guided
reading, independent reading, group reading, and reading aloud"[3] all
have their day in the English classroom (4), and that must include the
days we read Shakespeare. Teachers are good at reading the room, at
knowing what is right (to borrow from the mantra of the National Board)
for these students at this time in this place, but sometimes we fall into
patterns so comfortable that we rob our students of the risk-taking necessary for growth and independence. Though the varieties of reading
Ericson catalogs—guided, independent, group, and oral—overlap, this
chapter will focus on group reading.

Reading Shakespeare is like reading life itself—sensuous, immediate, baffling—and we do students a great disservice when we shield
them from the intense, exploratory, cooperative reading they must learn
to conduct with less dependence on teachers and translators and greater
dependence on themselves.

The Process at a Glance

In the beginning, especially in the first act, our reading is almost exclusively whole-group guided read-alouds conducted by the teacher and
student volunteers, with frequent pauses for questions, clarifications,

discussion, and the kind of modeled annotation described in Chapter 7. In the middle acts, or as soon as the class seems ready, more of the reading will be done by the students themselves in small, supportive groups I call reading companies, often prefaced with prereading mini-lessons and post-reading summarizers that continue the process of guiding students, even as they work within their reading companies. Independent reading most often takes the form of *re*reading a scene or speech in order to perform an active reader's task, such as summarizing or analyzing, or to craft each student's contribution to a group project. Slowly, the Shakespeare teacher hands off a seventeenth century text to twenty-first century readers and *Retires*, more or less depending on the group, to the wings.

Let the company of players in Al Pacino's film *Looking for Richard*, with their expert guides in the form of directors and scholars, their dynamic group sessions, and their individual preparations for the roles each plays, be the working model of collaboration, exploration, risk-taking, and support that reading Shakespeare requires.

A Company of Teachers

In the era of No Child Left Behind, we all teach to somebody's test. All of our students must be equipped to read excerpts from texts of varying complexity, answer multiple-choice questions about those texts, and write open responses and essays that demonstrate their comprehension of text. And they must do these things on their own.

One day after school, I scribbled my standardized test anxiety into a series of questions. But the questions I wrote that day were not so much about how to help my students pass an eight-hour test as they were about how best to spend our forty weeks together, including those dozen or more weeks in which we flickered like moths around William Shakespeare's flame. The answers mattered beyond test scores, beyond adequate yearly progress, beyond Shakespeare's plays themselves, because the answers could empower twenty-first-century American students from myriad ethnic cultures to take up the bonfire of words as light and fuel necessary for their futures. After much crossing out, two of the essential questions on my list read:

> What do accomplished readers do to understand Shakespeare's text?
>
> How can we teach these things to students?

The long search for answers brought me closer to students and colleagues, as well as to educators and researchers from around the country whose work is documented in books, journals, conference sessions, and on websites.

In the summer of 2007, while reading a book about literacy in the secondary English class, I was introduced to Harvey Daniels's work with literature circles by way of Sandra Okura DaLie. Her chapter, "Students Becoming Real Readers: Literature Circles in High School English Classes," describes an approach to reading literature that is student-centered and authentic. Citing Daniels, she lists the basics of literature circles:

- Students choose their own reading materials and form groups based on book choice, with different groups reading different books.
- Groups meet regularly to discuss their reading.
- Students create notes, questions, or drawings to guide their discussion. . . .
- Initially, while learning to interact in literature circles, students assume designated roles with specified tasks.
- The teacher serves as a facilitator only, not as a participant (85).

I reread DaLie's chapter several times, made copies for colleagues, purchased Daniels's book, *Literature Circles: Voice and Choice in Book Clubs and Reading Groups*, and began to experiment with literature circle applications in the grade 10 English classroom and in the Shakespeare elective that I teach to juniors and seniors. A team of colleagues coalesced around the project—Christina Porter, Kim Talbot, Kelly Andreoni, Nancy Barile, Althea Terenzi, Ben Murphy, Allison Giordano, and Logan Takahashi—and what follows is the results of our collaboration.

Reciprocal Teachers

In the fall of 2007, Christina Porter, the literacy coach at our high school, launched a content literacy initiative by introducing the members of her interdepartmental team to a carefully chosen list of seven reading strategies to test-run in our classes. Her long-term goal was and remains the schoolwide adoption of a set of common strategies for improving the reading comprehension of our students in all subject areas. One of the seven strategies on her list is reciprocal teaching.

As summarized by Deschler et al. in *Informed Choices for Struggling Readers*, reciprocal teaching "involves explicit instruction in and modeling of a particular set of strategies coupled with increasing opportunities for practice in a collaborative environment" (197). Though reciprocal teaching was originally designed by researchers in the early 1980s as a reading comprehension intervention program for elementary students scoring below the 35th percentile on standardized reading tests, it has been documented as an effective approach to reading for elementary, middle, and secondary students of all ability levels (Deshler 123, 197–98). Through practice and repetition, students process and comprehend what they read by taking turns questioning, clarifying, summarizing, and predicting. Over time, students internalize these reading strategies to become more independent readers.

One of the first teachers at our school to successfully incorporate reciprocal teaching into her practice is Kim Talbot, an accomplished veteran in the Foreign Language Department and a member of the literacy team. Talbot quickly learned that if reciprocal teaching was going to work with her students in Spanish 1, she would need to introduce the roles one at a time, and each of the roles would need a series of "stem starters" to focus students on the kind of thinking each strategy requires.

In jigsaw fashion, Talbot's students were assigned a common reading passage and a role, and at first they worked independently, then joined others who were working on the same role. In these homogeneous groups, they conducted a "give one, get one" activity. "Even students who didn't have too much," Talbot observed, "were now able to join their group with something." Finally, in heterogeneous groups, each student modeled his or her assigned strategy. Using a four-square worksheet constructed by Porter, her students recorded what they learned from one another about the assigned reading passage. Keeping notes on what they learned is an important part of the process because it requires active listening and documents what students learn from each other.

Talbot adapted the model to her content area by eliminating the role of Clarifier ("My students associate 'clarify' with language and not with content") and adding the role of Connector to encourage her students to connect each reading passage to the essential question or the theme of the unit, or with their personal experience. She renamed the role of Questioner to Excavator because "Questioner evoked literal questions instead of deep-thinking, 'I wonder' questions. The simple name change really got the kids thinking, and their questions were much better."

Porter and Talbot collaborated on classroom sets of index cards to distribute to student groups. Each card names one of the roles on the front and a series of four or five commands and stem starters appropriate to each role on the back.

As her work with Talbot progressed, Porter became convinced that the methods of reciprocal teaching could be a valuable first step in team-reading Shakespeare, especially with younger and/or less skilled readers. Together, we wrote Shakespeare-based starter statements for each of the five roles and enlisted the artistic talent of student Richard Bonilla to illustrate each role. Bonilla was acquainted with reciprocal teaching because his history and English teachers had both incorporated it into their instruction. Still, Porter and I were struck by the inventive ways in which he connected the roles to Shakespeare's plays. See Figures 9.1 through 9.5.

For students who might still have trouble saying something in their role, Porter used a handy list of "stem starters for 'Say Something' comments" in Figure 7.2 of *When Kids Can't Read* by Kylene Beers. Porter

1. Read the assigned scene carefully.

2. Think about the action and dialogue in the scene.

3. Jot down 3–4 "I wonder why" statements. For example, in *Romeo and Juliet*, you might write, "I wonder why Lady Capulet is so angry with her daughter."

4. Turn your statements into questions, "Why do you think…" and ask your partner/group for possible answers. Share your thoughts, too. Sometimes there will not be one "correct" answer because your questions will require the reader's opinion or interpretation.

5. Discuss the rest of your questions.

Figure 9.1. Questioner role.

1. Read the assigned scene carefully.
2. Note the things that confuse you—a long sentence or speech that seems important, or something a character does, for example.
3. Try to clear up the most confusing things and turn your confusion into statements. For example, "At first I thought this speech was about ____, but now I think . . ."
4. Share the most confusing things with your partner/group. Together try to clear up the confusion.
5. Ask your partner/group what confused them. Try to clear up the confusion.

Figure 9.2. Clarifier role.

eliminated "Make a Comment" starters from Beers's chart and added Summarizer stem starters so that each of the five reciprocal teaching roles—Questioner, Clarifier, Summarizer, Predictor, and Connector—is represented. Figure 9.6 shows Porter's stem starters for the role of Summarizer.

Meanwhile, Kelly Andreoni was looking for a way to bring the success of the book club she had founded at our school into her grade 11 English classes, and I was looking for ways to nurture interdependence in the Shakespeare class. Just beyond the realm of reciprocal teaching

1. Read the assigned scene carefully.

2. Think about the most important events in the scene. Look for 3–4.

3. Jot down the main events in chronological order, in the form of a timeline.

4. Tell your partner/group what the scene is mainly about by creating a good title for the scene. Or prepare a summary sentence: "This scene is mainly about . . . "

5. Avoid retelling all the minor details.

Figure 9.3. Summarizer role.

lay the unexplored terrain of literature circles. Developed a decade later, in the early to mid-1990s, by different educators for different purposes, literature circles struck me as the big sister to reciprocal teaching. I gave Kelly a copy of DaLie's chapter, "Students Becoming Real Readers: Literature Circles in High School English Classes," and she set off before me.

Modeling and adapting her work from DaLie, Andreoni wrote job descriptions for seven literature circle roles: Discussion Director, Illustrator, Literary Luminary, Vocabulary Enricher, Connector, Summarizer, and Investigator. She distributed the job descriptions, along with job qualifications and responsibilities, to her students in two sections of grade 11 English. Here is an example, cited from DaLie:

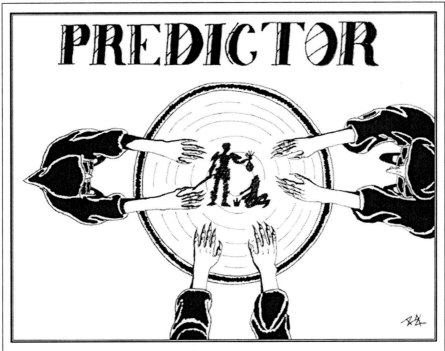

1. Read the assigned scene carefully.
2. Think about what happens in the scene.
3. Based on what you have just read, predict what you think will happen next.
4. Turn your predictions into statements that begin with, "I think that . . ." or "I predict that . . ." or "Because of . . . I predict that . . ."
5. Tell your partner/group about your predictions. What do they think will happen next?

Figure 9.4. Predictor role.

Literary Luminary
Job Description: Brings attention to key lines, quotes, and details from the text. The selections can focus on that which is interesting, powerful, funny, important, puzzling, or worth hearing.
Qualifications: Must be able to read closely and recognize humor, irony, and important ideas. (89–90)

Andreoni added text for the Literary Luminary's responsibilities:

Responsibilities: For each reading assignment, you must provide at least five passages and your reasoning for choosing those passages. Your reasoning should include all explanations of humor, irony, and/or importance, etc.

1. Read the assigned scene carefully.

2. Think about the connections between your world and the characters, events, and setting in the scene.

3. Jot down 2 connections between the scene and yourself or people you know. For example, in *Romeo and Juliet,* you might write, "Juliet reminds me of my sister because . . . "

4. Jot down 2 connections between the scene and people or characters you know in popular culture (celebrities, movie or TV characters), history, or literature. In *Macbeth,* you might write, "The invasion of Scotland reminds me of . . . because . . . "

5. Share your connections with your group. What connections can they make?

Figure 9.5. Connector role.

Summarizer Stem Starters
   • This part was mainly about . . .
   • First this happened _____(*fill in event*) and then_____ and then_____ . . .
   • The most important things that happened were . . .

Figure 9.6. Summarizer stem starters.

Her students filled out job applications in which they named their top two role choices and explained why they would be good at each. Andreoni interviewed students in case more than one student applied for a particular job in a particular group.

Throughout the time that her students read books independently, prepared for their roles in literature circles, and met with their peers, Andreoni kept meticulous notes on the process unfolding before her:

> I think their excitement grows every day because they feel as though they are part of these "secret societies" that no one else in the class understands. They are forging relationships with classmates in their literature circles, and in most cases, those classmates are not the same students they are friends with outside of class. When I went around to check in on the groups today, they were involved in some of the most intense and intelligent conversations about the literature. In fact, in most cases their discussions were far more advanced, and they used higher level thinking skills than I could have gotten from them in a "regular" class. There were boys sharing emotional revelations regarding *Tuesdays with Morrie* . . . students shared personal experiences with depression and attempted suicide in *The Bell Jar* group . . . I heard wonderful conversations about gender roles in the *Thousand Splendid Suns* group . . . When I was circling the room and tried to chime in or ask a question to the group, they were trying to keep from shushing me; they didn't want any interruptions because they knew they were doing a fine job on their own. They didn't even need me there.

Andreoni's is a tale of two cities in that for the group she describes, the experiment literally soared, whereas for a second group there was enthusiasm but insufficient follow-through in doing the independent reading and preparation necessary for the success of literature circle meetings. Still, Andreoni describes her first experience with literature circles as "the best thing I ever did with my junior class." Coming from such a groundbreaking teacher, her words were all I needed to hear.

As happy prologues to the swelling act, Porter and Talbot's work with reciprocal teaching and Andreoni's decision to adopt the literature circle model for independent reading in her English classroom paved the way for the next act, Shakespearean literature circles.

Reading in Circles

At first, I wasn't at all sure that literature circles would work with Shakespeare's plays. Literature circles were developed by Harvey Daniels and his colleagues to nurture independent readers by giving them choice—students select their own reading materials—and voice—students meet in a "peer-led reading discussion group" (Daniels 1). In both the Shakespeare elective and in most English classes where Shakespeare is required reading, students have no choice and, as Daniels defines it, not enough voice, and I wasn't sure that the literature circle model could work given such major modifications. Finally, if I were the only teacher in the building to attempt Shakespearean literature circles and succeed or fail, the results would be equally inconclusive. I needed a company of players.

As a mentor to novice teachers, I knew that teaching *Macbeth* and *Hamlet*, required reading for all sophomores at our school, can quickly petrify into a rigid and demanding pattern of teacher-directed lessons that leaves new teachers drained and their students surly and indifferent. So I brought a packet of my ideas for Shakespearean literature circles to several first-year teachers and hoped that if we tried this student-centered approach to reading *Hamlet* together, we could establish (in my case, reestablish) a balance in the Shakespeare class somewhere between whole-group and independent learning. Little did I know how much I would learn from them. And I knew another mentor teacher in my department, Nancy Barile, who gravitates perpetually toward risk and innovation. I made my pitch, and Nancy was game.

The packet of ideas I refer to in the previous paragraph was, at best, a work in progress that contained four handouts I had begged, borrowed, and stolen from almost everyone named in this chapter:

Shakespeare Literature Circles

1. Introduction to Shakespeare Literature Circles
2. Job Application
3. Role Sheets
4. Assessments

The first handout, a detailed introduction to ten active reading roles I thought most pertinent to understanding Shakespeare, was five pages of text in 10-point font, written to inform and (somehow) inspire students. Okay, so it's wordy, I thought to myself, but a necessary first step. On the day I distributed it to the juniors and seniors in the Shakespeare elective, just before we would read *Twelfth Night*, I prefaced "step 1" with an apology for its length and a plea for patience as we read through the entire document. Miraculously, they seemed intrigued and enthusiastic, but I knew I had taken a walk on thin ice. What if I had fallen in right then?

Two weeks later, I distributed the packet to colleagues, mentioned the verbosity of the first handout, and cheerfully wished them Godspeed. The next morning, I got an email from first-year teacher Althea Terenzi. "I knew my sophomores would never sit through that first handout, so I came up with this idea. What do you think?" she wrote. Attached to the email was the first draft of a one-page document she named "Shakespeare Classifieds." From my pedantic and tedious introduction she had fashioned an elegant and witty help wanted sheet that informed students of the nature of the jobs they could choose and inspired them to apply. As the weeks passed, we continued to add to, subtract from, revise and refine the handout to its current composition (Figure 9.7).[4]

In spite of this vastly improved introduction, Terenzi experienced problems with her sophomores similar to the problems Talbot first encountered when she introduced reciprocal teaching to her students in Spanish 1. They needed to start small, with one or two roles at a time and lots of classroom modeling. Because the students in Shakespeare class were prepared throughout the first semester to explore Shakespeare with increasing independence, we had been able to launch into Shakespeare literature circles with minimal instruction on my part. Terenzi's teaching context is more typical.

After introducing her students to my preliminary drafts of the role sheets reproduced at the end of this chapter, Terenzi led her students in a guided, whole-group read-aloud of *Hamlet* 3.1, with a focus on the Third Soliloquy ("To be, or not to be . . . "). Modeling one of the tasks for Summarizer, she turned Hamlet's soliloquy into a fill-in-the-blank word game by leaving out most of the nouns, verbs, adjectives, and adverbs, indicating beneath each blank which part of speech was needed. As her students worked in pairs on their "silly soliloquies," she wrote the original on the board.

About twenty minutes later, after students had finished their word games, she asked for four students who had volunteered the day before to take up the roles of Vocabularian, Summarizer, Prophet, and Questioner. Vocabularian went to the board to underline all the confusing or unfamiliar words; with the help of the whole group, these words were defined and their meanings written on the board. Next, Summarizer went to the board and made notes in the margins about the main ideas in the soliloquy; students copied these notes into their books. Questioner came up and threw out to the class some questions she had about the soliloquy; some students in class gave possible answers. Finally, Prophet got up and predicted what he thought would happen next. "Based on this soliloquy," he asked, "do you think that Hamlet will eventually commit

Shakespeare Classifieds
Help Wanted

Literature Circles Corporation *Looking for tomorrow's experts today*	**Questioner** Are you naturally curious and stubborn about getting the facts straight? Do you question everything? Can you translate wonder and confusion into insightful, thought-provoking questions? Must have the ability to spark group discussion and lively conversation. Apply now!	**Connector** Can you connect the dots between past and present? Position available in connecting the world of the play to our world. If you are up on pop culture and current events, if you can see connections between literature and life, we want to hear from you. Apply today!
Literary Luminary Do you live for alliteration and die for dramatic irony? Do you crave imagery? Do you know a symbol when you see it? Do you make metaphors when you speak? Expert close-reader wanted to analyze aesthetic language. Starving poets accepted! Apply now!	**Illustrator** Do Shakespeare's words paint pictures in your imagination? Put your artistic skills to work in this exciting position! Make visible Shakespeare's richly imaginative speeches and scenes using your knowledge of color, perspective, and line. Show how a picture is worth a thousand of the Bard's words! Apply now!	**Character Captain** Are you a people-person? Do you love watching strangers in a crowd and wondering who they are and what makes them tick? Psychoanalyze some of the most complex characters in literature! Cast celebrities and classmates in their parts! If the study of the human heart is your beat, then this job is for you. Apply!
Director Take Shakespeare's words from page to stage! Director wanted to select dramatic scenes and explain how you would coach actors for those scenes. If you are good at getting scenes on their feet, if you are both practical and creative, if you have a little Hollywood in you, apply today!	**Wordsmith** Get thee to work on words and word patterns in Shakespeare! Employ thy sensitivity to rhythm and rhyme, to *thee*, *thou*, and *thine*! Get thee to a punnery, and quickly too! Applicants should love words —their denotations and connotations, their meaning and sound. Apply!	**Prophet** Are you good at predicting? Do you have an eye for patterns and foreshadowing? Put your skills to work by making connections between past, present, and future. Write missing scenes! Show cause and effect relationships! Help your team see the future! Apply immediately!
Vocabularian Find a rewarding career in words! Your job will be to look up unfamiliar and confusing words. Applicants should be interested in words and competent in using dictionaries and other reference sources. Having a rich personal vocabulary a plus! Apply today!	**Summarizer** Your logical mind, your creativity, and your strong leadership skills will pay off in this position. Duties include identifying major events and important details. Ability to communicate ideas with clarity a must. Find exciting ways to get main points across to your team. Apply now!	

Figure 9.7. Shakespeare classifieds.

suicide?" In the final minutes of class, Terenzi asked all her students to respond in their journals to this question: *If thought causes inaction, what do you think will happen, or fail to happen, in the rest of the play?*

The next day, Terenzi's students filled out the job applications for literature circles, read Terenzi's summary of act 3.2, and took part in a whole-group, guided read-aloud of 3.3, a short but critical scene in which Claudius prays and Hamlet delays. Terenzi's lesson plan for the first official day of *Hamlet* act 3.3 literature circles reads:

- Hand out job assignments with complete job descriptions/role sheets.
- Review grading policy for lit circles. Share rubric.
- Students prepare for their roles: fifteen minutes.
- Groups convene and discuss.
- Students prepare self-evaluation and one peer evaluation for homework.
- Teacher will keep his or her fingers crossed.

Terenzi's experience underscores one major advantage that conducting literature circles in the Shakespeare class provides. An underlying assumption of book clubs and the literature circle model devised by Daniels is that the first reading is done independently. Even when students are free to select their reading materials from classroom sets, and even when those reading materials are written at a level appropriate to independent reading, too many classrooms are populated with adolescents who, through lack of motivation, skill, and/or time, won't read on their own. Andreoni experienced this problem firsthand with one of her groups to the extent that it became almost impossible for traditional literature circles to function. On the other hand, reading Shakespeare is team reading. If we structure the days and weeks in such a way that Shakespearean literature circles meet after whole- and small-group readings of a major scene or an entire act, students (with the exception of those who are chronically absent) will have something to contribute and much to learn from each other.

At about the same time that first-year teacher Terenzi was incorporating literature circles into the teaching and reading of *Hamlet*, veteran Nancy Barile was sending me emails that read, "You've GOT to come see these kids! They're working in lit circles right now—they are SO engaged!" Though Terenzi and I usually structured our classes so that students spent one full, 54-minute period both preparing for and taking part in their literature circles, Barile found it more beneficial to give her sophomores two class periods to prepare and one full class period to

Figure 9.8. Photograph of Nancy Barile's students in class.

meet, share, and assess their work. After I visited her classroom the first time, I could see why. Her students (Figure 9.8) could barely contain their enthusiasm. Moving as unobtrusively as possible from group to group, I was struck by the rich conversations about *Hamlet* that I overheard.

One student with the job of Summarizer was sharing a summary poem for act 1, "Young Fortinbras's dad was murdered by the king, / Even had his land stolen, ouch that's gotta sting . . . ," while a Literary Luminary showed her collection of allusions in Hamlet's first soliloquy—Hyperion, satyr, Niobe, Hercules. When I asked what sense any of these made in the speech, she said she learned that "satyrs are creatures associated with sexual innuendoes and Hyperion is a titan, so Hamlet is implying that his father was a god and his uncle is an animal."

During my second visit, a student in the role of Questioner showed me a long list of questions she had composed about act 2. Impressive as the list was, I was forcefully struck by this student's casual observation that many of her questions had both a *yes* and a *no* answer. "Does Hamlet really love Ophelia?" she asked us all. Then she offered an answer. "No, it's just an act, part of his plan to act crazy. Or yes, he's really hurt when she obeys her father and stops seeing him, and he really wants to hurt her back."

"Which answer do you think is correct?" I asked her.

"Both?" she replied. I hope my smile reassured her to remain unsure. Adolescents and ambiguity generally don't mix—it's either yes or no, black or white. For many students, reading Shakespeare is their first literary sojourn in the grown-up's gray zone.

In another group, a student in the role of Connector was sharing a disturbing link between Ophelia's relationship with her father and brother and the first "honor killing" of the year 2007. I didn't understand, so she showed me a printout of a news story about a Jordanian father who had killed his seventeen-year-old daughter on January 25, 2007, because he suspected her virginity. (Though I didn't know this student, Barile later told me that she is from the Middle East.) Until that moment, I never truly understood the weight that culture and gender roles impose upon Ophelia, and I marveled at this young woman's obvious determination to shed these burdens.

Before leaving Barile's classroom that day, I visited a group of students who were eager to share the artwork their Illustrator had done. Bridging two cultures, a young man named Huy Nguyen had produced a series of illustrations for *Hamlet* in the anime style. A collage of his work is reproduced in Figure 9.9.

As if echoing Hamlet's *To be or not to be* conundrum, Barile later told me that the experience of literature circles might be very difficult for certain teachers. "It was so hard for me to step back and let the kids *be*," she admitted. In fact, the three veteran teachers who experimented with literature circles—Kelly Andreoni, Nancy Barile, and me—all felt how unneeded we were as teachers when, as Barile put it, "the students facilitate their own learning." With a combined total of forty-four teaching years between the three of us, incorporating literature circles into our classrooms constituted a necessary but not necessarily easy shift away from teacher-directed learning and toward student-centered learning.

While Althea Terenzi made significant contributions to the introduction of Shakespearean literature circles and Nancy Barile explored the full potential of the process by giving her students the space and time they needed to plan, prepare, and share, it was first-year teacher Ben Murphy who harp'd my fear aright by continually addressing what he came to see as the biggest challenge of literature circles—finding ways for students "to somehow make their group presentations interactive."

Even with the students in the Shakespeare elective, I had witnessed instances of students creating highly detailed handouts for their

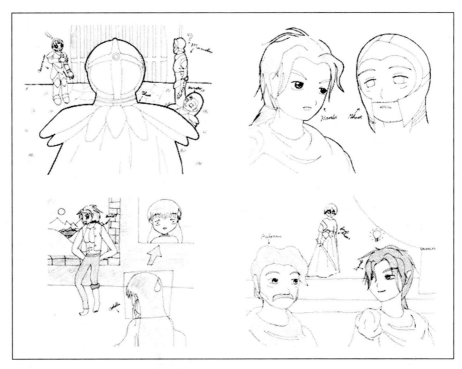

Figure 9.9. Student illustrations of *Hamlet*.

group but simply distributing them and reading them verbatim in the worst manner of teacher-directed instruction. In a series of conversations and emails between us, Murphy identified the strengths and weaknesses of the role sheets I had developed, and he invited me to visit his classroom during one of the Shakespearean literature circle meetings to observe some of the ways in which he and his students had figured how to more actively share what they were learning. "Just as we teachers do," Murphy insisted, "students have to find a way to engage their group members in some active learning."

The ten role sheets that comprise the last ten pages of this chapter bear the mark of many hands. Wherever possible I incorporated Ben Murphy's suggestions, along with suggestions from my students, for a more interactive framework by specifically assigning tasks that invite group interaction and cooperation. Althea Terenzi's fill-in-the-blank word game activity for the Third Soliloquy inspired a new task for Summarizer. Student Francisco Ospina pointed out the need for a role sheet that focuses on Shakespeare's complex characters, and he even coined the name, "Character Captain." And though I tried to compose tasks for each role sheet that range from less to more challenging, teachers and students still noted differences between the roles. Murphy's students voted Wordsmith "the most difficult" and Director "the most fun." Student Lena Staples suggested that Vocabularians could tackle the more challenging task of paraphrasing a difficult speech. Barile suggested that the Connector role sheet could be made more challenging with the inclusion of a news media task.

Daniels stresses that role sheets are temporary support structures ("book club training wheels") that should be removed after the first full reading of a whole work with its accompanying cycle of literature circle meetings (99–100). He even recommends telling students to start literature circle meetings with the role sheets face down, to be referred to only if and when needed. Finally, Daniels and his team of Chicago teachers emphasize that the "roles are meant to rotate with each time the groups meet" (104).

DaLie, however, finds that "assigned literature circle roles provide students with boundaries and clear expectations" (87) and that her students' group meetings are more productive with them than without them. She allows her students to stay with a role "through the completion of a book" (88). Having her students take up different roles over the course of time "supported all of my students in acquiring the behaviors, skills, and vocabulary of readers" (87). Since most teachers who adopt Shakespearean literature circles will teach a play by Shakespeare only once in a term or an academic year, the question of whether to phase out the role sheets and whether to reassign roles (with or without the sheets) before completing the play is left to our own judgment.

Assessing the Circles

No one gets a grade for book club, but assessment and evaluation come with the territory of school. While students meet in literature circles, teachers are free to listen, observe, and record their holistic impressions, and at the end of a literature circle meeting (or for homework) students should assess themselves and one of their peers. For this purpose, DaLie developed a streamlined peer evaluation rubric for students to use that requires them to assess the degree (*often, sometimes, never*) to which a student in their circle was cooperative, respectful, on task, and prepared (91–93). I adapted DaLie's peer evaluation form to align it more closely with the skills I would be evaluating at the end of the process (Figure 9.10).

Literature Circles Peer Evaluation

Student's Name: _____ Role: _____

Performance during Literature Circles	✓+	✓	✓–
Provoked new insights and lively discussion			
Fulfilled responsibilities in a meaningful and creative way			
Prepared thoroughly for the meeting			
Shared information in an understandable and logical way			
Treated group members with respect			

Overall, this student has earned a (circle one):   ✓+   ✓   ✓–   for today.

Student's Name: _____ Role: _____

Performance during Literature Circles	✓+	✓	✓–
Provoked new insights and lively discussion			
Fulfilled responsibilities in a meaningful and creative way			
Prepared thoroughly for the meeting			
Shared information in an understandable and logical way			
Treated group members with respect			

Overall, this student has earned a (circle one):   ✓+   ✓   ✓–   for today.

Student's Name: _____ Role: _____

Performance during Literature Circles	✓+	✓	✓–
Provoked new insights and lively discussion			
Fulfilled responsibilities in a meaningful and creative way			
Prepared thoroughly for the meeting			
Shared information in an understandable and logical way			
Treated group members with respect			

Overall, this student has earned a (circle one):   ✓+   ✓   ✓–   for today.

Commentary: Respond to one of these prompts for the person in your group (other than yourself) who earned your highest praise today:

Student's Name: _____ Role: _____
    Explain one specific thing you learned today from this student; *OR*
    Describe one specific thing you liked today that this student did:

Figure 9.10. Literature circles peer evaluation.

Students earn two cumulative grades in my class for the work they do in Shakespearean literature circles—one grade for their performance in the circles (this is based on the collection of peer and teacher evaluations that accumulate over time) and a second grade for their contributions to the collection of notes, questions, connections, annotations, illustrations, graphic organizers, lists, storyboards, scripts, predictions, definitions, rebuses, paraphrases, fill-in-the-blank word games, outlines, and lyrics that make up the pages of their reading company portfolios.

Though I originally intended to assign one final grade for each reading company portfolio, I found it more equitable to grade each student's individual contributions to the portfolio. In fact, Barile, Murphy, and I all felt that certain roles are inherently more challenging than others, and this can complicate grading. DaLie views the inequities of traditional literature circle roles as an advantage in classrooms with students of mixed abilities (88), but as Barile points out, "In a class of honors students or AP students, every job needs to be challenging." In the end, teachers can choose whether to assess students' contributions to the group portfolio individually or by group. The rubric I developed (Figure 9.11) can be adapted from an individual to a group grade report.

Read, Reading, Reads

Soft you. A word or two before you go.

Throughout this chapter, and indeed throughout this book, iterations of the verb *read* appear countless times. *The American Heritage Dictionary* provides this definition:

> To examine and grasp the meaning of (written or printed characters, words, or sentences). To utter or render aloud (written or printed material): *read poems to the students.* (1455)

Whether reading Shakespeare aloud in the company of our students is guided, independent, or group, and whether we adopt the methods of reciprocal teaching or literature circles, the temptation, according to Ralph Alan Cohen, "is to get carried away and keep reading." In his list, "Ten DON'Ts of Teaching Shakespeare," Number Ten is "Don't read in class (or have your students read) more than two sentences at a time (except sometimes)" (67). Reading on and on because we love the sounds of Shakespeare, or listening to the near incoherent droning of a reader who ignores the traffic signals of commas and question marks, puts a stop to the social construction of meaning that Shakespeare's text demands. "You must always be building a theatre in their minds," Cohen reminds teachers, "and to do that you must frequently interrupt yourself and comment on the text" (67).

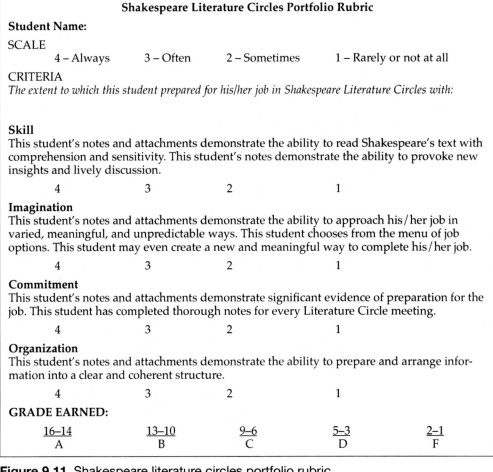

Figure 9.11. Shakespeare literature circles portfolio rubric.

More than any work of literature in the secondary classroom, reading Shakespeare is what Louise Rosenblatt calls "a doing, a making, a combustion fed by the coming together" of particular readers with a particular text at a particular time (xvi). I agree with Cohen that we must always be building a theatre in our minds, and to do that we must frequently interrupt ourselves to comment, question, clarify, connect, summarize, and predict. But as a college professor, his teaching context differs from my own and his students can be expected to have a higher tolerance for close first readings.

So hoist a playhouse flag on the days when you and your students read Shakespeare in whole groups or small, and let the motto read: *Pause Every Page or Two (Except Sometimes).*

Shakespearean Literature Circles Role Sheets

QUESTIONER

Name:

Play:

Act:

Your job is to write questions for the things you wondered about or didn't understand in an act, scene, or speech. Your job is not to answer your questions, but to spark group discussion and to promote deep understanding and lively conversation.

Who? What? When? Where? Why? How? Most questions begin with one of these words. Do any of your questions begin with these words? For example, as you read a scene or a speech, were you wondering who one of the characters is, or what he or she is feeling, or when and where a turning point in the conflict might be reached or how you might have reacted to a situation in the play? Were you wondering why Shakespeare wrote a particular speech or scene? Share your questions with the members of your company.

Your questions might address the big ideas, or themes, in the play you are reading. According to scholars, these four themes can be found in every play written by Shakespeare: "conflict, appearance and reality, order and disorder, change" (Gibson, Field-Pickering 105). What questions does this play raise about any or all of these themes?

Each of Shakespeare's plays raises more specific questions about themes particular to a play. For example, *Romeo and Juliet* raises questions about love and hate; *Macbeth* raises questions about loyalty and ambition; *Julius Caesar* raises questions about honor. What particular questions does this play raise?

Questions about this act:

CONNECTOR

Name:

Play:

Act:

Your job is to connect the world of the play to you and your world.

How do the problems in the play connect to your personal experiences, or to the experiences of people you know at school or in your family? What personal connections can members of your reading company share?

What connections can you make between this act or scene and songs you have heard, or movies you have seen, or famous people and events in our world? Make a list of these connections and ask members of your company to add some connections of their own.

Take the twenty-first century into the Elizabethan era by rewriting the events of the play into a newspaper or a television newscast. In the manner of the modern news media, your news production should include both facts in the form of news stories and opinion/commentary. You might want to include news about Elizabethan celebrities, fashion, food, or entertainment of the time period. Encourage the members of your company to contribute to your newspaper or newscast in the form of Letters to the Editor (that's you!).

Record your work here or attach it to this sheet.

LITERARY LUMINARY

Name:

Play:

Act:

Your job is to select vivid lines and powerful speeches in a scene for your company to reread, analyze, and discuss.

Locate the most vivid and powerful lines and/or speeches in this act. What's going on with the language? Is it written in verse or prose? Is the meter regular or irregular? Do you see similes and metaphors, personification, antithesis, irony? Do you hear repetition, alliteration, onomatopoeia, rhythm, and/or rhyme? Box off and mark up with commentary, lines, symbols, and color the most important speech or set of lines and label everything you find. Read the passage you have selected aloud in your group, then explain why you like it and why you think the language is powerful. Finally, ask each member of your group to select his or her own vivid passage to read aloud and comment on.

Shakespeare knew Greek and Roman mythology; he knew the Bible. You can locate allusions to mythology and/or the Bible in this act. Research what you don't know about the allusions; try to find visuals that show the person, place, event, or poem/written work to which the allusion refers. Discuss with your company why a character in this act alludes to these figures and stories from mythology or the Bible.

People in Shakespeare's world placed a great deal of symbolic importance on things like flowers, plants and herbs, and animals. If there are repeated references to these things in the act, research their symbolism and their significance in this act. Talk with your group about the significance of these symbols and the ways that we might use symbols to represent things today.

Record your work here or attach it to this sheet.

Reading Shakespeare with Young Adults by Mary Ellen Dakin © 2009 NCTE.

ILLUSTRATOR

Name:

Play:

Act:

Your job is to make visible Shakespeare's richly imaginative speeches or scenes.

Draw illustrations for key lines in the act or scene. See if the members of your company can identify the lines you have illustrated.

Design costumes for characters in the act. Consider the historical period and geographical location of the scene; consider the characters' status and wealth; think about the symbolism of colors. Sketch your designs and write a brief explanation for your choices. Without explaining your designs, show them to the members of your company and see if they can link the costumes with the characters.

Design before-and-after costumes and makeup for the characters in the play that undergo a radical change. Sketch your designs and write a brief explanation for your choices.

Show the conflict, or a relationship between characters, or a connection between events in this act and in earlier acts *visually* in a graphic organizer.

Record your work here or attach it to this sheet.

CHARACTER CAPTAIN

Name:

Play:

Act:

Your job is to adopt one or more characters in the act or scene to study closely.

Write a series of interview questions for one of the characters in the act. Write the questions as if you were that character's friend, enemy, physician, psychiatrist, lawyer, conscience, or something else. Members of your reading company can answer your questions as that character would answer them, citing things that the character says and does in the scene that support the answers they give.

Make a character vocabulary list for the characters in the act or scene and the character traits they demonstrate in the act. For example, if we were reading *Macbeth* and the first character on your list is the Weird Sisters, your character vocabulary might begin with *equivocating, manipulative,* and *mysterious.* Your character vocabulary list should have two columns, one for the names of the characters, and a second column for the character traits each character demonstrates. In your companies, look for literary evidence (what a character says or does; what others say about a character) that demonstrates the character traits you have listed.

If you were to cast the parts for this act or scene today, what artists, celebrities, and/or public figures would you choose to play each part, and why? Or, which of your classmates would you cast for each part, and why? What modern settings would work well? Construct a modern cast list and a modern set and justify your choices to the members of your company.

Record your work here or attach it to this sheet.

Reading Shakespeare with Young Adults by Mary Ellen Dakin © 2009 NCTE.

DIRECTOR

Name:

Play:

Act:

Your job is to take Shakespeare's words from the page to the stage.

Select the most dramatic scene in the act and plan a performance. What concrete details do you need and want to know in order to fully imagine this act for stage or film? (You can research the culture, music, architecture, fashion, religion, art, food, etc. that would shed light on the world of this play and this act.) Explain to the members of your reading company how you would coach the actor(s) about line delivery, movement, gesture, and props. Copy the scene and write your ideas in the form of directorial commentary for stage or film. OR storyboard the scene. If time permits, cast the scene and rehearse it in your company.

Plan one or more tableaux vivants (living pictures) in which students in your group, frozen together in a carefully planned preliminary pose, come to life one by one, speak a line from a scene that conveys special meaning, and refreeze into a final group pose. Select the lines carefully; decide the order in which the lines will be spoken; plan the most appropriate opening and closing poses; decide what actions best accompany each line as it is spoken; cast the parts. Finally, rehearse the tableaux.

Storyboard a speech or scene from the play. Visualize the action—what is happening at the moment the words are spoken—*and* the actions and images suggested by the words. Freeze the action at key lines and sketch them as individual frames of film. Write the words from the speech or scene being spoken for each frame. Include ideas for camera work and a sound track.

Record your work here or attach it to this sheet.

Reading Shakespeare with Young Adults by Mary Ellen Dakin © 2009 NCTE.

WORDSMITH

Name:

Play:

Act:

Your job is to look closely at word patterns in the play.

Note pronoun shifts in a scene. For example, do speakers shift from "you/your/yours" to "thee/thy/thou/thine," and if so, what does this reveal about their relationship or about conflict? Does a royal speaker shift from the royal "we" to the personal "I," and if so, what does this signify in the scene? Identify the places in the act where these shifts occur and discuss the significance of these shifts in your company.

Each of Shakespeare's plays is unique in part because of the word families that run through it. For example, the play you are reading might be interlaced with the language of law, religion, commerce, theater, warfare, disease, the natural world, animals, plants, love, sex, and/or death. These word families intensify the emotions and ideas in the play; they intensify its meaning and mood. Identify the word families in this play and collect specific words from the act that belong to each family. Organize your collection and share it with your company. Think about the significance of these word families and be prepared to discuss what they suggest about the play's characters, conflicts, and themes.

Punning is a word game that plays with the different senses or meanings of the same word. Puns can be lighthearted and playful, but they also can be used to disguise a speaker's intentions. Note the use of puns in the act and the possible reasons why the speaker(s) uses puns. What modern puns do the members of your company know?

Record your work here or attach it to this sheet.

PROPHET

Name:

Play:

Act:

Your job is to recognize the connections between past, present, and future in this play.

What events may have led up to act 1 of this play? Make a graphic organizer that illustrates the connection between events in act 1 and the pre-act 1 events that may have caused them. Show the members of your company the act 1 events on your graphic organizer and ask them to supply their own ideas about what might have happened before act 1. Share your ideas.

What events will probably happen after the act you have just read, or after the play ends? Make a graphic organizer that illustrates the events that have already happened and the events that will probably happen as a result. Ask members of your company to make their own predictions about what will happen next.

Write a missing scene for the play. This scene might take place between acts, or at the beginning or end of the play. Be sure that your missing scene dramatizes some action that is implied but not included in the play. Lead the members of your company in a dramatic reading of your missing scene.

Record your work here or attach it to this sheet.

Reading Shakespeare with Young Adults by Mary Ellen Dakin © 2009 NCTE.

VOCABULARIAN

Name:

Play:

Act:

Your job is to learn about unfamiliar and confusing words in a difficult speech or a short but important section of dialogue.

In a speech or short scene, locate words that are confusing, unusual, or frequently repeated, words that seem important to the speech or scene but are not clearly defined in the footnotes. Write a good definition for each word, one that considers multiple meanings of each word. Help the members of your company to locate and discuss these words. Create a vocabulary activity that requires your company members to learn the definitions and use the words.

A rebus is a representation of words in the form of pictures or symbols (for example, "I ♥ you.") Show the meanings of difficult words in a speech by creating a Shakespearean rebus. Select the most difficult words in each line or sentence to represent with a picture or symbol. Share your work with the group. See if they can read your rebus without peeking back at their books for the missing words.

Apply your understanding of Shakespeare's unfamiliar words and context clues by paraphrasing (putting into your own words) a particularly difficult speech. Divide the speech into sentences, and then write a paraphrase for each sentence. Members of your company read each of Shakespeare's sentences aloud then pause as you read your paraphrase. Encourage feedback.

Record your work here or attach it to this sheet.

Reading Shakespeare with Young Adults by Mary Ellen Dakin © 2009 NCTE.

SUMMARIZER

Name:

Play:

Act:

Your job is to accurately identify the major events and most important details in the act.

Write a fully developed summary of the act or scene as a fill-in-the-blank composition in which you leave out key words; the readers in your company accurately fill them in.

Chunk the longest scene into a B-M-E (beginning-middle-end) and write a title or a short caption for each chunk. Before you share your titles and captions with your company, have them write their own. Compare the results.

Write the lyrics to a Rap Review that tell the story of the act, weaving keywords and phrases from the act into the lyrics and incorporating rhythm and rhyme.

Retell the story of an act or scene in one of these ways:

A fairy tale
A breaking news report
The latest gossip
A political cartoon
A nursery rhyme
A comic strip

Record your work here or attach it to this sheet.

10 Reading Single Characters as Plural

The greater plays leave us knowing we should be perplexed.
Norman Rabkin, "Rabbits, Ducks, and *Henry V*"

We're supposed to struggle when we read Shakespeare. What we need to teach our students is that "the struggle isn't the issue; the issue is what the reader does when the text gets tough" (Beers 15). Independent readers know *how* to struggle with challenging text. Dependent readers give up. Or worse, they let us tell them what to think.

"Polonius is an old fool."

"Brutus is a naïve idealist."

"Romeo is in love with love."

We've all done it.

Too often the most interesting characters in Shakespeare's plays are limited by the dominant, or most common, readings of their character. We bring these instant, prepackaged readings into our classrooms from our high school and college days, from film and stage performances we have seen, and from the materials we read as we prepare to teach a play. Reading Bottom as an ass or Ophelia as innocent victim are two examples of a dominant reading: Shakespeare's text supports these readings, but does it require them and them only? With the gusto of a wrecking crew, Irish theater critic Fintan O'Toole dismantles one of the most pervasive dominant readings in Shakespeare, that of Hamlet as "isolated neurotic," and reconstructs Hamlet as "a man with a keen political sense and a sharp social knowledge" (64). One fundamental way to get Shakespeare's youngest readers to join the fray is by challenging them to engage in multiple readings of a single character.

Reading Plurally

In *The Genius of Shakespeare*, Jonathan Bate asserts that there "are two laws which all the plays obey. The first law is that truth is not singular" (327). He illustrates this law with an image of a gestalt beast, drawn here by student Jennifer Pollard (Figure 10.1), which I project at the overhead early in our reading of a play. The rabbit-duck provides the perfect visual frame for this approach to character study.

Figure 10.1. Jennifer Pollard's illustration of a gestalt beast.

In spite of what Bate calls "the first law" of Shakespeare, every major character and many of the minor ones in the plays we read with adolescents come to us narrowed through cultural, social, moral, or political forces into something like a singular (*i.e., common, predictable, dominant*) reading. Therefore, it isn't difficult to select characters whose dominant readings limit their complexity. This is a list of plays likely to be taught in secondary schools and of characters that invite multiple readings:

> *Romeo and Juliet*: Romeo, Juliet, Capulet, Lady Capulet, Friar, Nurse
>
> *A Midsummer Night's Dream*: Theseus, Hippolyta, Oberon, Titania, Bottom
>
> *The Taming of the Shrew*: Katherina, Petruchio
>
> *The Merchant of Venice*: Shylock, Jessica, Prince of Morocco, Portia, Antonio
>
> The *Henriad*: Henry IV, Prince Hal/Henry V, Falstaff, Katherine
>
> *Julius Caesar*: Brutus, Portia, Cassius, Caesar, Mark Antony
>
> *Twelfth Night*: Orsino, Viola, Antonio, Sir Toby Belch, Malvolio, Feste

Hamlet: Hamlet, Ghost, Claudius, Gertrude, Polonius, Ophelia, Rosencrantz and Guildenstern

Othello: Othello, Desdemona, Iago, Emilia

Macbeth: Macbeth, Lady Macbeth, Banquo, Ross, the Weird Sisters

King Lear: Lear, Cordelia, Goneril and Regan, Kent, Edmund

The Tempest: Prospero, Miranda, Ariel, Caliban

One way to introduce students to dominant and alternative readings of a character is to provide them with excerpts from the essays of Shakespearean scholars that express the polar ends of a critical continuum. In *Reading Hamlet*, Bronwyn Mellor cites two diametrically opposed interpretations of Ophelia; at one end of the spectrum, Ophelia is described by Rebecca West as passive, unchaste, and "disreputable," whereas Fran Richmond insists that she is "innocent and pure in motive" and capable of both wit and independence (52–53). Which Ophelia do you read? Why?

Nick Bottom in *A Midsummer Night's Dream* is one of those Shakespearean characters that inspires radically different critical interpretations. The chart in Figure 10.2 provides a graphic and textual representation of the extremes to which scholars go in their assessment of Nick the Weaver. These extreme readings of Bottom can mark the spaces between which students position themselves as they read the character and the play.

However, critical citations are not necessary. Simply share with students what you know about the range of interpretations of the character(s) you are studying. Better yet, ask them what they think, but wait until they have read a significant portion of the play. When my students completed the first three acts of *A Midsummer Night's Dream* in the fall of 2008, just before I shared with them the Greenblatt-Goddard dichotomy in Figure 10.2, we listed the cast members on the board, and then I drew a horizontal line the width of the front board, with the words LEAST APPEALING and MOST APPEALING at either end. Calling this a character continuum, I distributed strips of legal size paper (to dramatize the notion of a continuum) and asked them to arrange each character's name along their own continuum (Figure 10.3).

"We're all reading the same play, right?" I asked them the next day as I displayed an overhead transparency of the results. The students were visibly surprised.

Reading Bottom		
Reading the Critic	*Reading the Reader*	*Reading the Critic*
Dominant Reading Stephen Greenblatt: *Will in the World*	Which Bottom do you read and why? Review your responses to the reader's survey. What predispositions do you have that would cause you to see this character as you do?	**Alternative Reading** Harold C. Goddard: *The Meaning of Shakespeare* Volume 1
"Bottom, to be sure, is asinine, but it takes no magical transformation to reveal that fact. Indeed, what is revealed is not so much his folly—he does not have one moment of embarrassment or shame, and his friends do not laugh at him—as his intrepidity. 'This is to make an ass of me,' the ass-headed Bottom stoutly declares, when his friends have all run away in terror at his appearance (3.1). . . . He is surprised at the Fairy Queen's passionate declaration of love, but he takes it in his stride: 'Methinks, mistress, you should have little reason for that. And yet . . . reason and love keep little company together nowadays' (3.1). And he is entirely at his ease in his new body: 'Methinks I have a great desire to a bottle of hay . . . ' (4.1). **When the ass's head is finally taken from him, he does not experience a moral awakening; rather, as Puck puts it, he merely peeps at the world once again with his own fool's eyes"** (35)		"To Puck, Bottom is an ass. Yet Titania falls in love with him, ass's head and all. 'And I will purge thy mortal grossness so That thou shalt like an airy spirit go,' she promises (3.2). And she keeps her promise by sending him Bottom's dream. **The moment when Bottom awakens from this dream is the supreme moment of the play.** There is nothing more wonderful in the poet's early works and few things more wonderful in any of them. For what Shakespeare has caught here in perfection is the original miracle of the Imagination, the awakening of spiritual life in the animal man. **Bottom is an ass. If Bottom can be redeemed, matter itself and man in all his materiality can be redeemed also. Democracy becomes possible. Nothing less than this is what this incident implies. Yet when it is acted** . . . this divine insight is reduced to nothing but an occasion for roars of laughter. Laughter of course there should be, but laughter shot through with a beauty and pathos close to tears" (1:79–80).

Figure 10.2. Reading Bottom.

LEAST APPEALING	MOST APPEALING
Egeus: 9 votes	Puck: 5 votes
Puck: 2	Hermia: 4
Bottom: 1	Helena: 2
Hippolyta: 1	Bottom: 1
Quince: 1	Demetrius: 1
Titania: 1	Hippolyta: 1
	Quince: 1

Figure 10.3. *A Midsummer Night's Dream* character continuum.

Note that four of the characters identified as "Least Appealing" by some students are also identified as "Most Appealing" by other students. We had not been reading this play in solitary confinement but in lively small- and whole-group companies, and still each student was surprised to see his or her favorite character listed as someone else's least favorite.

In reading *The Tempest*, I encourage students to monitor their reading of the enigmatic Prospero by periodically marking a notch on the line between "patriarch" and "tyrant" with the act and scene numbers of their reading (Figure 10.4). In discussions, students need to explain their thinking by noting the narrative fragments (*what a character says, what a character does, what others say about the character*) that support their readings. In the give-and-take that ensues, students are forced to consider a broad range of interpretations of the same narrative fragments:

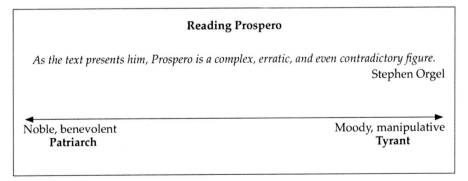

Figure 10.4. Prospero continuum.

The modifiers at either end of the spectrum are my own, based on a general knowledge of the interpretations of Prospero.

The key to character study in Shakespeare is to keep it plural. Remember that "truth is not singular" in Shakespeare.

Reading the Reader

I suspect that Bate's first law of Shakespeare resonates with me in part because of Nick Bottom. He is one of my favorite characters, yet I have found myself defending him with the same passionate intensity as an adolescent whose friends reject the boy she loves as not good enough for her. I paid a price for my loyalty to Bottom when Janet Field-Pickering, director of education at the Folger, invited me to present with her at the annual NCTE convention in San Francisco in 2003. Her presentation was entitled "Imagination bodies forth . . . ," and my role was to present a series of summative projects for engaging students in thoughtful and constructive rereadings of *Midsummer*. Back at Revere High School, the Shakespeare students had just completed these projects, and I was eager to share their work and the lessons I had developed to help them walk the fine lines in this play between high and low status, comedy and pathos, fantasy and reality. Just as I had done weeks earlier in my classroom, I displayed at the overhead Bottom's prose speech from the Folger edition of act 4.1, reproduced in Figure 10.5.

With the sixty-plus teachers in the audience standing in for adolescents, we worked our way into the speech, and into (so I hoped) Bottom's tragicomic complexity.

"What might the punctuation reveal about Bottom's state of mind?" I asked them. *Lots of question marks in the beginning*, someone said, *but then they stop. The rest are periods. Maybe he's becoming less confused.*

Lots of pauses within sentences—the punctuation shows him thinking things out, slowly and logically, someone else observed.

"What words and phrases are repeated? What seems important to Bottom in this speech?" I asked.

Me. My. I. E-y-e, a teacher in the front row said. *He's full of himself.*

Man. Dream. Thought, a teacher in the crowd countered. *It's not just about him.*

"Divide this speech into a beginning, a middle, and an end. What patterns do you see?"

Past to future. Fantasy to reality. Player to poet, some said. I should have read the body language, the rolling eyes, and the frown of the teacher in the front row. But instead I said, "Bottom is a character with

---

Bottom wakes

BOTTOM: When my cue comes, call me, and I will answer. My next is 'Most fair Pyramus.' Heigh-ho. Peter Quince? Flute the bellows-mender? Snout the tinker? Starveling? God's my life! Stolen hence, and left me asleep?—I have had a most rare vision. I have had a dream past the wit of man to say what dream it was. Man is but an ass if he go about t'expound this dream. Methought I was, and methought I had—but man is but a patched fool if he will offer to say what methought I had. The eye of man hath not heard, the ear of man hath not seen, man's hand is not able to taste, his tongue to conceive, nor his heart to report what my dream was. I will get Peter Quince to write a ballad of this dream. It shall be called 'Bottom's Dream,' because it hath no bottom, and I will sing it in the latter end of a play, before the Duke. Peradventure, to make it the more gracious, I shall sing it at her death. *Exit*

Figure 10.5. Bottom's dream speech.

little education, no wealth, no status, and no hope of advancing in his world beyond the role of weaver. He is also the butt of this play's cruelest joke. Why do you think Shakespeare wrote this speech for him? What does it add to your understanding of Bottom?"

He's an ass. He was an ass before his dream, he's an ass in his dream, he's an ass after his dream. His name is Bottom. This is a comedy. End of story, the teacher in the front row said.

It felt like a slap. I mumbled something about the Goddard essay I had recently read, and stumbled to paraphrase the soaring claim that Bottom makes democracy possible, a claim that felt silly now. I wanted to explain in my own words why I believe in Nick Bottom, but I wasn't sure why I did.

Since that awkward moment in 2003, I have come to understand why Bottom matters so much to me, largely through the work of Louise Rosenblatt. In her 1938 treatise on literature and teaching, Rosenblatt enjoins English teachers to help their students explore themselves as readers. "What the student brings to literature," she asserts, "is as important as the literary text itself" (78). Adolescent preoccupations with their social, psychological, and ethical selves can limit and distort their reading of a literary text. Yet these preoccupations can also spark an adolescent's empathy for literary characters and enrich his or her understanding of the text. Rosenblatt outlines the complex network of attitudes, values, and emotions that the adolescent reader brings to literature in Chapter 4 of her book, *Literature as Exploration*. Issues of authority, group dynamics, relationships, individuality, and culture "possess whole constellations

of fixed attitudes and automatic emotional reflexes" (92). Since reading her book, I have struggled to make visible the ways in which my
students and I transact with Shakespeare's literary text. As for Bottom,
I ask students at the end of act 3 to respond to this prompt:

> Bottom appears to be vain and foolish, yet the other workmen
> genuinely admire him. Describe the Bottom in your life. Draw par-
> allels between the person you know and the character of Bottom.

At the end of act 4, after Bottom has spoken his dream speech,
I write the word "dreamers" on the board and students cluster their
personal associations with the word in a word web. Though most of the
students we teach will have positive associations with the word—in 2008,
one student wrote on his web that dreamers "reshape reality"—some
will not. On the same day in the same class, another student wrote on
her web that dreamers are "lazy" and "not conscious of reality." Then I
ask students to respond in writing to this prompt:

> Who are the dreamers in this play? Who aren't? Among which
> group would you feel more at home, and why?

Year after year, the vast majority of my students rank themselves among
the dreamers, most often identified as the lovers Hermia, Lysander,
and Helena, and the mechanicals Bottom, Peter Quince, and company.
Michael, whose favorite character is Bottom, wrote, "Dreamers are
more human, they have hopes and work toward them; whereas the
non-dreamers—Oberon, Egeus—take shortcuts to get what they want."
Less often, students also include Duke Theseus and Titania among the
dreamers, with the reasoning that Theseus hopes to change history by
marrying an Amazon queen and actually making her happy, while Titania seeks to raise as her own the son of a mortal who died giving birth.
Hanan, who wears a hijab at school and struggles as so many Middle
Eastern students do with negative stereotypes, wrote, "I would feel more
at home with the dreamers in this play because like them I do not like
the conventional world and want to make a change."

Still, some of the most compelling observations are reserved for
the non-dreamers in this play and in this world. Mariany wrote, "Dreamers work for their dreams to come true, while non-dreamers just work,"
and Carlos, who expressed disappointment in the Amazon queen's
acquiescence to marriage, wrote of non-dreamers, "They have all either

accepted their fate and the fate of others, or they are too down-to-earth to have any dreams left."

In the process of writing and thinking about dreamers, our students cannot help but write and think about themselves—their attitudes, values, and emotions.

This is for the teacher in the front row in San Francisco: Nick Bottom matters to me because he is all the students I have ever known who wouldn't or couldn't conform to the stereotypes imposed upon them; he is every student who didn't think he or she was smart enough but kept learning anyway. He is every waking dream I have ever had that someone labeled foolish. Thank you, Ms. Rosenblatt.

Rereading the Text

The character readings chart (Figure 10.6) lists contradictory readings of five characters from five different plays, key scenes in which each character appears, and a framework for rereading these scenes. In the play they are reading, after they have reread key scenes and discussed the ways in which the text supports multiple, even contradictory readings, students (and most readers) will tend to gravitate toward the reading they prefer. Challenge students to explain how the three most fundamental building blocks of information in a dramatic text—what the character says, what the character does, and what others say about the character—can yield so many different constructions of a single character.

According to Mellor, this focused rereading and analysis of key scenes should help our students to see that single readings, or single constructions, of a character result from:

- emphasizing particular narrative fragments
- ignoring or suppressing particular narrative fragments
- reading particular narrative fragments to make them "fit" an interpretation
- gap-filling from particular positions [cultural, social, moral, or political] (53).

This approach to reading characters can open our eyes not only to the complexity of Shakespeare's characters but also to the complexity of our own. How often, in our dealings with ourselves, with others, and with characters in literature, do we willfully or unintentionally see what we want to see and hear what we want to hear? The habit of questioning not only the text but ourselves is more than a reading skill, it is a life skill.

Character Readings		
Character	**Range of Readings**	**Key Scenes, Narrative Fragments** *Reread these scenes for:* • What the character says • What the character does • What others say about the character How do these pieces of information, called narrative fragments, support multiple and even contradictory readings of the character?
Bottom *MND*	Static; a fool; an unredeemable ass Dynamic; capable of insight, growth, and spiritual awakening	Reread acts 1.2, 3.1, and 4.1
Ophelia *Ham.*	Passive, unchaste, and disreputable Innocent and pure but capable of wit and independence	Reread acts 1.3, 3.1, and 4.5
Henry V *H5*	Machiavellian hypocrite Epic hero; ideal monarch	Reread acts 1.2, 2.2, 3.1, and 4.3
Brutus *JC*	Vain egotist Naïve idealist	Reread acts 1.2, 2.1, 3.1, and 4
Caliban *Tmp.*	Monster and slave Poet Rightful master of his island	Reread acts 1.2, 2.2, 3.2, 4.1, 5.1

Figure 10.6. Character readings chart.

Directing Plurally

In his critical introduction to the Oxford edition of *The Tempest*, Stephen Orgel states, "Shakespearean texts are by nature open. . . . It is performances and [critical] interpretations that are closed" (12). Explore with students the ways in which a performance is also a reading of the text. Assign one key scene to different groups of student-performers, each with an alternative reading of the character in question. This activity will spark discovery of the ways in which even small choices about line delivery, movement, gesture, and props can have radically different consequences. A helpful resource for multiple readings of Shakespeare's text is Ralph Alan Cohen's *ShakesFear and How to Cure It*. In Part Two of this book, Cohen identifies "scenes for alternative readings" in twenty-two of Shakespeare's plays. Another way to approach plural readings in performance is by having students write film scripts for a key scene, a process more fully addressed in Chapter 11.

Reading Film Comparatively

I remember hurrying to my parents' house in 1990 with a newly purchased videocassette of Kenneth Branagh's *Henry V*. I knew how much they loved Sir Laurence, as they called him, and I knew that for their generation, Olivier's 1944 production of *Henry V* transcended the screen to become a part of the mis-en-scene of life during World War II. But Branagh's *Henry V* was better, hands down, and they were going to love it.

"What's he doing?" my mother impatiently asked when, seconds into the film, Derek Jacobi flicks a match as he speaks, "O for a muse of fire . . . " (*brilliant!*) and walks across an empty sound stage in modern dress.

"Remember those stage-y, *Book of Days* sets in the Olivier film? I think Branagh's paying homage to Olivier here," I gushed.

They looked at me as if I had just dropped in from the moon, or the vasty fields of France, but decided to give Branagh ("the new kid") a chance. That is, until King Hal is book-ended by two suspicious-looking clerics, one of whom entreats, "Unfurl your bloody flag."

"This isn't *Henry V*! Downright unpatriotic."

They never made it to the tennis balls.

One of the best ways to help students begin to see that every performance is a reading is to key up two or more film productions of a scene students have reread and analyzed for the ways in which the

Shakespearean text supports multiple and even contradictory readings of a character. What reading have the director and the actors chosen? How will we know? John Golden, teacher and author of books and articles on using film in the English classroom, maintains that one of the most common aspects of textual analysis—characterization—is also one of the most fundamental aspects of film analysis (61). Putting aside for now the cinematic effects, which are addressed much more fully in Golden's books, students can immediately grasp the potential significance of the set (light or dark? interior or exterior? old or modern?), props, the actor's costume (its colors, style, and condition), and the actor's behavior and tones of voice. If some students can also "read" the camera work or the sound track, the discussion will be even richer.

Two film productions of *A Midsummer Night's Dream* 4.1 that provide a fascinating contrast are the 1935 production directed by Max Reinhardt and starring James Cagney as Bottom, and the 1999 production directed by Michael Hoffman and starring Kevin Kline as Bottom. Cagney's Bottom is dark and manic; he pulls himself from the brink of understanding, suggested in the repetitions of "Methought I was . . . methought I had . . . ," to walk out of frame singing, whistling, and laughing as his former, foolish self. Kline's Bottom awakens to sunlight and speaks his speech with gentle knowing; before it ends, he has found a golden fairy's ring and with it, evidence that his dream was substantial.

Writing Plurally

Though analytical essays may feel like the English teacher's albatross, there are times when our students need to engage in the formal analysis of literature. Still, writing and reading essays need not be all gnashing of teeth. If students have engaged in lively classroom conversations about themselves as readers, if they are learning to read single characters as plural personalities, and if we expand our notions of reading and writing to include digital compositions, then the shift from analytical reading to analytical writing can be meaningful, constructive, and authentic. In his book, *The Director in the Classroom*, Nikos Theodosakis writes, "In theatre, they say, 'If it's not on the page, it's not on the stage.' The same applies to filmmaking. The details of a good production originate from the fingertips of the writer, and they are communicated through words . . . and images" (127).

In the spring of 2007, the stars were finally aligned to tackle a multimodal project inspired by something rich and strange I had once seen in an office at the Massachusetts Institute of Technology. Seven years earlier, while working with a team of educators on a website cosponsored by the Folger Shakespeare Library and MIT, Professor Peter Donaldson showed me some "essays" that students in his Shakespeare on Film class were composing. I place quotation marks around the word "essays" because these were digital compositions with links embedded in the text to film clips that illustrated the points the student writers were making about some literary, theatrical, or cinematic aspect of the film. In one of the digital essays, the student authors examined the religious imagery in Baz Luhrmann's *Romeo + Juliet*, and links activated multiple film clips of madonnas, crucifixes, and the bleeding heart of Jesus. In another, students analyzed Kenneth Branagh's interpretation of the character of Henry V, and one link in the text activated a close-up shot of Branagh speaking his ultimatum to the governor of Harfleur. Not content with the close-up shot of Branagh's face, the students narrowed the field of vision to Branagh's eyes in order to show that throughout the speech he never blinks. *O brave new world*, I kept thinking to myself.

What I saw at MIT in 2000 was not part of the project we were working on, but I never forgot it, and in 2007 when I was describing these digital compositions to colleague Christina Porter, who had recently earned a master's degree from Tufts University, she said something that stopped my breath: "What a minute, I've seen something like that at Tufts, and I know who to contact." Two weeks later, Dan Cogan-Drew, director of the Department of Education Curriculum Resource Center at Tufts University and codesigner of the software program for what is called VideoPaper, came to Revere High School to meet with me, Porter, technology teacher David Kaufman, and Director of Humanities Jon Mitchell. The crown jewel in this collaboration was a student-written, student-performed, and student-produced multimodal essay on the character of Ariel in *The Tempest*. Never before had I worked on a more dynamic inquiry-based project with students and colleagues.

I introduced the project with a single-page handout, reproduced in Figure 10.7. Looking back now on the neatly numbered steps (only three!), the imperative verbs (*form, collaborate, write, perform, produce*), and the exclamation at the end, I marvel at my optimism.

From the open-mouthed expression on their faces, I quickly realized that my single-page handout was only a starry-eyed start. We would spend that day and the next hammering out a list of possible topics at the board.

Introduction to the VideoPaper Project

Shakespearean texts are by nature open . . . It is performances and interpretations that are closed, in the sense that they select from and limit the possibilities the text offers in the interests of producing a coherent reading.
                    Stephen Orgel, Introduction to *The Tempest*

In this project, you will explore the open nature of Shakespeare's play, *The Tempest*, by constructing multiple and even contradictory readings of one or more characters, relationships, or themes in the play. Each reading, no matter how contradictory, must be supported by Shakespeare's text.

The Process
(1) Form three teams:

      Writers

      Performers

      Producers

(2) Collaborate within your own team and between teams to construct a multidimensional reading of a character, relationship, or theme in *The Tempest*, and choose one reading over the others.

The Product
(3) Write, perform, and produce an interactive essay called a VideoPaper, described by Dan Cogan-Drew, director of the Department of Education Curriculum Resource Center at Tufts University and codesigner of the software program, as an "interactive document which links and synchronizes video, text, and images in a single, cohesive document that can be viewed in a web browser."

O brave new world!

Figure 10.7. Introduction to the VideoPaper project.

Caliban
Monster, slave, victim, villain, poet, dreamer, master (in the end) of his own island.

Miranda
The only woman in the play (if we don't count the goddesses in the masque). Docile, passive, innocent? Rebellious, sexual, independent? Aware of her father's shortcomings?

Prospero
Wise, all-knowing patriarch? Tyrant? Bully? Racist?

Ariel
Male? (only one or two places in the text where his sex is identified). Female? ("delicate," "dainty, "chick"). Androgynous?!

Gonzalo
Good? Foolish?

Relationships
Prospero's relationship with his brother? With Miranda, with Ariel, or with Caliban?

Themes
How is power defined in this play? Does power change? Does Prospero really renounce power in the end? Who has power in this play? (Don't forget the Boatswain!)

Though the class agreed that they were best prepared to focus on Prospero, in the end they were drawn to the question of Ariel's gender. Meanwhile, I got to work providing additional structure for this ambitious project, and composed the next handout (Figure 10.8).

Suffice it to say that on this first go at the VideoPaper, we got by with a little help from our friends. At the time, there were no digital cameras or computer software for such multimedia projects, so we borrowed some equipment from another school in our district. Since my director Jon Mitchell's knowledge of the cinematic aspects of film greatly surpassed my own, he spent a class period teaching students the basics of camera work, lighting, and sound. The technology teacher, David Kaufman, reserved one of the computers in his lab for the Shakespeare students' use and taught a small group of my students alongside his own. Since the VideoPaper program is written for Macs but at the time we only had PCs, Kaufman worked with the tech support staff to

Planning to Write and Produce the VideoPaper
An Open Letter to the Class

The Whole Group
Agree on the topic of your work.

Select places in the plays that are open to multiple readings of the character, relationship, or theme you have chosen. You may need to do a bit of narrowing here so that your analysis is sufficiently complex but also manageable.

Become specialists. Some will be the writers, some will plan and perform key lines/speeches/scenes, and some will film those performances, edit them, and construct the VideoPaper.

Writers
This structure is adapted from pp. 88–89 of *Reading Hamlet* by Bronwyn Mellor:

Introduction
This section acknowledges the topic—the character, relationship, or theme you have chosen— and indicates the direction and scope of the essay.

Range of Readings
In this section, give specific examples of the different, possible readings of the character, relationship, or theme that are supported in the text. You may choose to research critics' and performers' readings and incorporate them into your analysis, but you do not have to do this.

Construction of Readings
Begin with what seems to be the dominant reading of the character, relationship, or theme. Give examples of the ways in which this reading is supported in the text. You may want to comment on the values this reading affirms. For example, if the dominant reading of Ophelia in *Hamlet* limits her to the role of innocent victim, this may reinforce traditional notions of women as passive and weak.

Alternate, contradictory readings should then be explored. Examples of the ways in which these readings are also supported in the text should be made clear.

Choosing a Reading
This is where you give reasons for choosing or not choosing one reading over another, making as clear as possible the basis of your choice. If you do not feel able to choose one reading as more correct or accurate than the others, it is important to make as clear as possible on what basis a choice *might* be made.

Conclusion
Summarize your conclusions and comment on their significance. You may choose to speculate about the author, William Shakespeare's, intentions or values.

For all sources, verbal and/or visual, incorporated into the essay, include a Works Cited at the end. Use MLA format.

Figure 10.8. VideoPaper plans.

Figure 10.8. continued

Performers

Collaborate with the writers on the lines/speeches/scenes that support the dominant reading and the places in the text that support alternate, even contradictory readings.

Brainstorm for the ways in which a performance would convey each reading.

Collaborate with writers and producers on storyboards and/or film scripts for each scene.

Rehearse the scenes. Line delivery is the most important performance tool—"You can't act Shakespeare until you can speak him" (Rodenburg xi). Memorization of lines is not required; we can prepare small promptbooks for you to hold as you perform. Consider the full range of performance tools—line delivery, facial expression and gesture, action and interaction, props and setting.

Select the lines/speeches/scenes (we'll refer to your choices as mini-scenes) most critical to each reading, cast the parts, storyboard each mini-scene, and rehearse. Make choices about the set(s) and props. Make adjustments and changes as your work progresses.

Producers

Collaborate with the writers and performers on the ways in which camera shots, angles, lighting, and sound will contribute to the dominant and alternate readings.

Learn how to use the cameras.

Survey the campus for the best scene locations.

Film the performances and then view the footage, making decisions about editing.

Construct the VideoPaper.

patch together a platform that would support the construction of the VideoPaper. No sooner did the school year and this project end than I sat down to write a grant for multimedia technology at our school. Today we have a portable cart of twenty Macintosh laptops loaded with the iLife suite for multimodal compositions, a digital video camera and two digital cameras, a keyboard, and a printer. Things went much more smoothly in the production of the second VideoPaper in 2008. O brave new world? Amen.

Figure 10.9 shows the VideoPaper screen with its three frames for video, slides or still images, and text. The final product for *The Tempest* VideoPaper project can be viewed at http://www.revereps.mec.edu/caliban/Videopaper/index.htm.

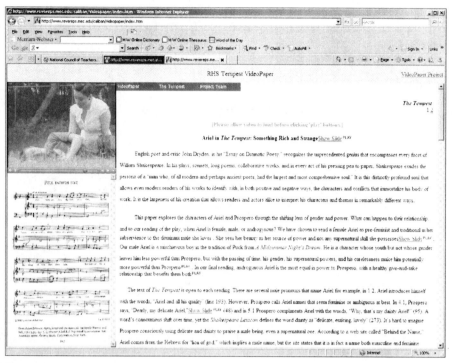

Figure 10.9. VideoPaper screen.

During the last days of school in 2007, I asked the students to write down what they had learned about reading Shakespeare. Throughout the year I had worked with them on all of the skills and strategies codified in this book, but again and again they commented on the discovery that there is more than one way to read Shakespeare's words.

"I learned to see all the different sides that each character has," Chanta wrote, "and the possibility of more than one personality in one character."

"His language is rich and complicated; very little of what is said in the lines can be interpreted as meaning one thing. His characters . . . are open-ended," wrote Justin.

Alejandro wrote, "There is more in the text than is actually written."

But Sodavy's six words say it all: "Shakespeare leaves room for the reader."

11 Reading with Eyes and Ears

The eye of man hath not heard, the ear of man hath not seen, man's hand is not able to taste, his tongue to conceive, nor his heart to report what my dream was.

A Midsummer Night's Dream 4.1.208–211

In the theater, Shakespeare is first and foremost aural. Because the action is in the word, a Shakespearean actor must speak with clarity and conviction, and the audience must listen (Rodenburg 53). In the movie house, Shakespeare is primarily visual. In fact, the first Shakespearean film, *King John*, was produced in Britain in 1899, almost three decades before the first commercial talking picture would be released in 1927, and as Judith Buchanan points out in *Shakespeare on Film*, modern film productions of Shakespeare's plays owe much to the groundbreaking cinematic pantomime of the silent Shakespeares (22, 51–52).

In the classroom, whether we approach Shakespeare's plays as working scripts or as literary texts, there is no getting around the words or past the act of reading them. Reading Shakespeare is both visual and aural. "The physical nature of the word," writes Patsy Rodenburg in *Speaking Shakespeare*, "is the fabric of the play" (72).

Seeing Shakespeare's words means seeing double and triple. Meanings collide. When Hamlet enjoins Ophelia to get herself to a nunnery, he means a convent, or a whorehouse, or both. When Mercutio calls his wound "a scratch, a scratch," he means that he is dying (3.1.93). When Othello calls himself "merciful," he finishes the job he started of smothering Desdemona because she is "not yet quite dead" and he would not have her "linger in . . . pain" (5.2.95–97). "Words are very rascals," the clown Feste observes in *Twelfth Night*, and "A sentence is but a cheveril glove to a good wit. How quickly the wrong side may be turned outward!" (3.1.11–13). Seeing Shakespeare means seeing what isn't there—Juliet's waking nightmare of the tomb, Macbeth's dagger of the mind, Chorus's kingdom for a stage.

Hearing what we read begins with the eyes—in *Macbeth* we read *Thunder and lightning*, but soon we listen for the striking of a bell and hear the sudden knocking at the gate. Caliban tells us not to be afraid, "the isle is full of noises" (*The Tempest* 3.2.138). Hamlet enjoins us to "speak the speech . . . trippingly on the tongue" (3.2.1–2), while Gertrude cries out, "O, speak to me no more! These words like daggers enter in mine ears. No more, sweet Hamlet" (3.4.84–86).

"Writing," observes Randy Bomer, "leaves almost everything out, and one of the jobs readers can take on is to put some of the world back in" (528). The strategies in this chapter help students to see, hear, and produce Shakespeare's richly imaginative speeches and scenes by attending closely to the words, imagining the poetry, playing with the possibilities, and putting "some of the world back in."

Seeing Shakespeare: The Rebus

When we read g-h-o-s-t, which is in itself a symbol formed from letters with a shape and a sound of its own, we construct "mental images and personal associations" with the word, making even the most abstract word concrete (Costanzo 18). To borrow from the Bible, the word is made flesh. A simple strategy for helping students to see the words in a speech or soliloquy, especially the abstract words, is the Shakespearean rebus. This activity is local in that it is line- and word-specific; the first step should be universal and address the question, *What is this monologue about?* One way to unlock the big ideas of a speech or soliloquy is to chunk it: see Chapter 8 for a fuller discussion of this strategy. Another way is to provide students with a short list of potential main ideas, arm them with colored highlighters, and let them have a go at rereading to determine the ideas developed in the lines. For example, after students have read aloud Hamlet's first soliloquy, "O, that this too too sullied flesh would melt," I distribute colored highlighters and ask them to color-code every reference to:

> FATHER
>
> MOTHER
>
> TIME
>
> MARRIAGE

After they work on this in small groups, I ask, *What's this soliloquy about? What is Hamlet debating?* Of course, it's about all these things, but students will generally piece together a one-sentence summary that concludes, "Hamlet is mad at his mother for remarrying so quickly."

As a follow-up to this sort of big-picture approach, the rebus requires students to look closely at keywords in the lines, to explore their emotional connotations, and to draw them symbolically. After distributing sheets of unlined paper (legal size paper is preferable), I display these directions on the overhead projector:

Seeing Words: The Shakespearean Rebus

A rebus is a word-picture puzzle in which certain words are represented by images:

I ♥ you.

Directions: In pencil, copy out each line of the soliloquy on un-lined paper. Select keywords in each line, preferably words that name ideas and emotions, and erase them. In their place, draw symbols for these words. A symbol is something that stands for something else. Think of creative ways to symbolize the words.

Figure 11.1 is the first page of student Linda Veasna's rebus, completed in her sophomore year. Though some of the words Veasna chose to illustrate are concrete words (the word *flesh* in line one is drawn as a bleeding piece of steak!), her illustrations make them more vivid. And she plays with the multiple meanings of a word when, in line three, she symbolizes the word *fixed*—"Or that the Everlasting had not fixed his canon"—not as it is used in this line, to mean *fastened*, but as a broken vase, mended. Each time students do this work, they better appreciate Feste's observation that words are very rascals.

Another way to approach this is to extract five or six key lines from a scene or act, type them with white space in between, and challenge students to paraphrase Shakespeare's words not with more words but with images. Figure 11.2 is one such handout I prepared for a scene from *Macbeth*. For the second quote, " . . . he died As one that had been studied in his death, To throw away the dearest thing he owed . . . ," one student drew the traitor as a reader with an open book in his hand; the front cover read "Life" and the back cover read "Death;" Cawdor was in the process of tearing out a page of "Life" and throwing it away.

Seeing Shakespeare: Living Pictures

Photography opens another window onto Shakespeare's words. Halfway between the still image and live or filmed performance lies the photo-essay, and in the Shakespeare classroom this child of journalism takes on a new persona. I stumbled onto this approach when a group of shy English language learners in my grade 10 classroom begged me to excuse them from a performance project. After making every compromise that I could justify and still call their work a performance, the three girls began to cry. Then one of them asked, "Could we take pictures instead?" Assisted by a cast of neighborhood extras, they posed and photographed the sequence of events in the mad scene in *Hamlet*, using dialogue as captions. The full lesson, adaptable to any of the plays, is published on the PBS website, "In Search of Shakespeare."

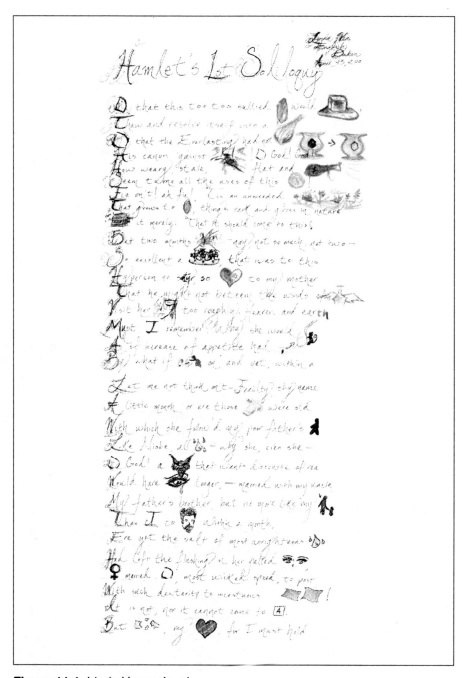

Figure 11.1. Linda Veasna's rebus.

Paraphrasing 1.4 with Images

Most often, teachers ask you to paraphrase someone else's words with more words! Today, I want you to use images (pictures, drawings) to translate the meaning of these key lines.

Directions: Find a way to *show* what is being said in these quotations by sketching or diagramming the speaker's main idea(s) on a separate piece of paper. Use this sheet to record your ideas.

"The Prince of Cumberland! that is a step On which I must fall down, or else o'erleap, For in my way it lies." (Macbeth to himself after Duncan announces that Malcolm will be named Prince of Cumberland, and second in line to the throne of Scotland)

"Nothing in his life Became him like the leaving it; he died As one that had been studied in his death, To throw away the dearest thing he owed As 'twere a careless trifle." (Spoken by Malcolm to King Duncan about the traitor Cawdor)

"There's no art To find the mind's construction in the face: He was a gentleman on whom I built An absolute trust." (Spoken by Duncan about the traitor Cawdor)

"I have begun to plant thee, and will labour To make thee full of growing." (Duncan to Macbeth)

"Stars, hide your fires; Let not light see my black and deep desires. . ." (Macbeth in an aside)

" . . . The eye wink at the hand; yet let that be Which the eye fears, when it is done, to see." (Macbeth, continued from #4, in an aside)

Figure 11.2. Paraphrasing with images.

The photo-performance project is cousin to another kind of performance, the tableau vivant, or living picture. Long before it was a performance-based reading strategy, the tableau was a form of entertainment that combined elements of the theater with elements of art and photography. People posed themselves into striking compositions and held the pose without moving or speaking. It was Peggy O'Brien and her team at the Folger's Teaching Shakespeare Institute that adopted the tableau as a strategy for getting students to explore the dramatic core of a Shakespearean scene and the physicality of the words. I modified the directions for teachers written in Lesson 14 of *Shakespeare Set Free: Teaching Romeo and Juliet* into a handout for students (Figure 11.3) to help them organize and rehearse their tableaux. Before students perform, they fill out the "Shakespearean Snapshots" chart on page 167 of *Set Free*, which provides a written record of student work. The tableau is an excellent way to get students involved in reading for key lines in a scene and for speaking and moving the words.

This strategy, however, can serve another purpose. I sometimes have different groups of students work the same scene into different and even contradictory "messages," guiding them in the process toward an understanding of the ways in which selective editing not only expedites a scene but can distort it. Act 3.1 of *Julius Caesar*, for example, provides students with the opportunity to shape, or in the current political vernacular, to spin the events of Caesar's assassination. In the process, students become more aware of the ways in which a deliberately selective combination of words and images can misrepresent the events in a scene. This approach to living pictures is outlined in Figure 11.4, and can be used effectively with any of the problem plays—*The Merchant of Venice, Othello, The Taming of the Shrew*—as well as with the political plays. Challenge students to spin the invasion of France or the siege of Harfleur in *Henry V*; challenge them to spin the gender wars in *Shrew*.

Seeing Shakespeare in Art

Beyond asking students to produce their own still or moving images of a word, a sentence, or a scene, having students examine the art related to Shakespeare's plays holds the potential to enrich their comprehension of Shakespeare's text while introducing them to the grammar of images. The *Hamlet on the Ramparts* website produced by MIT in fellowship with the Folger Shakespeare Library houses an art database of 165 images of act 1.4–5, the scenes in which Hamlet confronts the Ghost of his father. Soon after this site was published in 2000, I composed a handout to guide

Rehearsing the Living Picture
Adapted from *Shakespeare Set Free: Teaching Romeo and Juliet*, Lesson 14

- How many characters are in this scene? How many students are in your group? If the numbers don't agree, make adjustments.

- Assign each student in your group to speak the lines of one character.

- Reread/skim the scene together, extracting key lines that serve your group's purpose. Carefully copy your lines onto index cards.

- Decide the order in which each player will speak: Who will be First Player, Second Player, etc.? Practice speaking your lines with clarity and conviction.

- Agree on the order in which each player in your group will speak. Practice speaking your lines in order.

- Decide what actions best accompany your lines. Practice speaking your lines as you perform this action.

- Block the scene. First arrange yourselves in an appropriate opening tableau and then freeze like a photograph.

- One at a time each player comes to life, speaking his or her line while performing an action, and then freezes in a final image or closing tableau.

- Rehearse the tableau.

- Prepare a brief opening and closing to accompany your presentation. The opening should identify the scene and your group's interpretation of the scene. The closing should briefly explain how the lines and actions your group chose conveyed your interpretation of the scene.

- The entire presentation should use words, action, and images to convey the group's purpose.

Figure 11.3. Rehearsing the living picture.

students in their exploration of the images inspired by this father-and-son reunion (Figure 11.5).

Though students enjoyed exploring the images, after reading their summary compositions I realized how little experience students have in observing and analyzing nonverbal texts. They used the most basic art language carelessly, rarely distinguishing between paintings, sketches, and prints. Though students were somewhat successful in interpreting the different relationships between Hamlet and the Ghost ("Hamlet looks scared," "The Ghost looks mean," "You can tell that this Ghost loves Hamlet"), they barely got beyond the facial expressions and they

---

Living Pictures: Spinning the News of Caesar's Assassination

But men may construe things, after their fashion,
Clean from the purpose of the things themselves.
Comes Caesar to the Capitol tomorrow?
(Cicero, 3.1.34–36)

The **Tableau Vivant** (living picture) is an activity in which characters, frozen together in a carefully planned preliminary pose, come to life one by one, speak a line from the scene that conveys special meaning, and refreeze into a final group image.

Our own culture, so drawn to the frozen images of photography and the moving pictures of film, stores part of its identity in the "living pictures"/images of our national life recorded in pictures.

Think of photographs and/or documentary news clips of events that have seared themselves into modern memory. Try reading these images for both their objective and subjective qualities, guided by these definitions:

ob·jec·tive
- Uninfluenced by emotions or personal prejudices; fair.
- Presented factually.

sub·jec·tive
- Influenced by emotions or personal values and experiences; biased.
- Expressing the individuality of the artist or author.

Then return to Rome on the Ides of March to form living pictures of the assassination of Julius Caesar. To build on your growing awareness of the shifting relationship between objective and subjective truth, you will work in three groups to create three versions of the same event.

Julius Caesar Act 3.1: Enter the No-Spin Zone?!

Group A: Your group, the <u>objective news reporters,</u> will form a living picture of the events in 3.1 that seeks neither to blame nor praise the participants.

Group B: Your group, the <u>Brutus spin-doctors,</u>[1] will form a living picture of the events in 3.1 that emphasizes Brutus's patriotism and Caesar's ambition.

Group C: Your group, the <u>Caesar spin-doctors,</u> will form a living picture of the events in 3.1 that emphasizes Caesar's greatness and Brutus's treason.

---

[1] " . . . Individual experts who interpret events for viewers by framing, directing, and focusing remarks to favor one side or the other." Encyclopedia of Television. Newcomb, Horace, ed. 3 vols. Chicago: Fitzroy Dearborn, 1997.

Figure 11.4. Living pictures: Spinning the news of Caesar's assassination.

Hamlet on the Ramparts Website

Today, we will continue to explore the complex and ambiguous relationship between Hamlet and the Ghost by visiting a site that includes a variety of textual and nontextual resources for act I, scenes 4 and 5.

Follow this path:

shea.mit.edu/ramparts

- Enter the site and then select READING ROOM on their menu bar.
- Click on **1.4. 42–62,** which will bring up the text of Hamlet's speech, "Angels and ministers of grace, defend us!"
- In the right hand column, click on ART.

You now have access to thirty-three images of this scene produced by a wide variety of artists over a period of 150 years.

(1) **Task:** View the images and then collect five or six that strike you as interesting in some way. Create a file labeled "Ramparts" and save these images in your student file. Then use the following questions to guide your analysis of each image.

Analyzing the Art: How to Begin
What was the purpose of the image—to model an actual stage set, to advertise, to illustrate—and how do you know?

How would you describe the style of the image—realistic? idealized? cartoonish? abstract?

What means did the artist use to convey the personality of the Ghost? of Hamlet?

What relationship between the Ghost and Hamlet is reflected in the image?

What means did the artist use to convey the mood of the scene?

(2) **Summarizer:** Select any two images and compare and/or contrast a significant component—for example, their style, their interpretation of the relationship between Hamlet and his dead father, or their mood.

Figure 11.5. *Hamlet on the Ramparts* website instructions.

all struggled to describe the style of an image. The words I gave them— *realistic, idealized, cartoonish, abstract*—didn't help them at all.

The following year, before sending students online to examine Henry Fuseli's eighteenth-century paintings of scenes from *Macbeth, Hamlet, A Midsummer Night's Dream,* and *The Tempest,* I took nothing for granted and composed the "Seeing and Reading a Painting" handout in Figure 11.6. After closely "reading" Fuseli's paintings, students were better prepared to discuss the ways in which an artist paraphrases a poet.

Seeing and Reading a Painting
Adapted from a student guide published by the Museum of Fine Arts, Boston, Massachusetts

Title of the Painting:

Artist:

A. FORM: In a painting, the basic structure is composed of color, light, line, and texture.

Color: Cool colors suggest rest and calm (blues, greens, purples).
            Warm colors suggest agitation and emotion (reds, yellows, oranges).
1. Describe the ways in which the artist uses color:

Light: The presence of light tends to suggest openness, honesty, and/or
            tranquility. Light tends to create the feeling that all is well.
            The absence of light, in the form of darkness and shadows, tends to
            suggest mystery, fear, and sometimes danger.
2. Describe the ways in which the artist uses light and shadow:

Lines: Vertical lines suggest strength.
            Horizontal lines suggest rest.
            Diagonal lines suggest motion and energy.
3. Describe the ways in which the artist uses lines in this painting:

B. COMPOSITION: Paintings can tell a story without words. In a painting, the subject, the setting, the characters, the pose, the mood, and the use of symbols create the "composition."

Subject or Theme: Most realistic paintings have a recognizable subject, such as a landscape, a person or groups of people, and/or an event like a battle.
4. What appears to be the subject of this painting?

Setting:
5. Describe the place in the painting (the indoor or outdoor space):

Figure 11.6. Seeing and reading a painting.

Figure 11.6. continued

6. What is the weather like?

7. What time of day is it?

8. What year or historical period is it?

Characters:
9. Who are the people in the painting? What are they doing?

10. If there are many people in the painting, describe the most dramatic facial expressions:

11. Describe the "body language": the position of the bodies, the gestures, etc.

12. How are the people dressed? Describe details of clothing and/or jewelry that stand out:

Pose: People in a painting can be close together or separated. They can look relaxed and natural or stiff and formal, or caught in the middle of some great action.
13. How are the people in the painting arranged?

Symbols: A symbol is any object that stands for something greater than itself. For example, a serpent may be a symbol for evil, a lily may be a symbol for purity, an eagle may symbolize freedom. In painting as in writing, objects often function as symbols.
14. Are there objects in the painting that may be symbols of the painting's theme?

Mood and Tone: The emotional impact of the work of art is of central importance. How the artist feels about the subject, and how he or she wants us to feel, is expressed in a variety of ways, through the elements of form and composition.
15. What is the mood of this painting? What is the artist's attitude toward his or her subject? Why do you think this?

Paraphrase may be unfair. Shakespeare's text "is inherently a document of possibilities" (Buchanan 3), and to some extent the relationship between poet, literary painter, and performer will be symbiotic. Predating the modern era of lavishly illustrated promotional posters for plays and films are the thousands of "literary paintings" produced by hundreds of artists. In his introduction to the online *Shakespeare Illustrated*, which houses the paintings of almost one hundred fifty artists who painted Shakespeare's scenes, Emory University professor Harry Rusche notes that of the total number of literary paintings composed between 1760 and 1900, approximately one-fifth are pictures from Shakespeare. "The boards of the theatre and the canvass," writes critic John Eagles, "are the same thing—the eye is to behold, and the mind to be moved" (qtd. in Rusche).

When students arrive at some of the most vivid speeches in Shakespeare's plays, I often ask them to look closely through several lenses. Though I will use the example of Gertrude's speech on the death of Ophelia in *Hamlet* 4.7, this approach to reading Shakespeare with eyes and ears can be adapted to almost any speech or scene that has been paraphrased into film and art. In this particular activity, students peer through the lens of the poet-playwright himself, a modern performer, and a nineteenth century painter. We begin by reading aloud Gertrude's speech, they from a handout (Figure 11.7) and me from a transparency of the handout projected at the overhead.

Then working in small groups, students focus first on the poetry. I distribute a set of questions, and after about ten minutes, we share observations and conclusions:

> **Language: How does Gertrude's language describe, or "see,"
> Ophelia?**
>
> 1. Highlight/color-code words and phrases that appeal to any of the five senses—sight, sound, smell, taste, or touch. Explain in detail what kind of a place this is.
>
> 2. Underline and label examples of personification. Explain what things are being humanized. Why do you think there are so many examples of personification in this speech?
>
> 3. How does this passage sound when you say it out loud? Do you hear a rhythm? Are the words soft and musical or harsh and discordant? Why is the last line so short?
>
> 4. What is the mood of this speech? How do the imagery and the personification contribute to the mood?

After a brief discussion of these questions, I key up Kenneth Branagh's

---

Reading with Eyes and Ears: *Hamlet* **Act 4.7.138–155**

QUEEN: There is a willow grows <u>aslant</u> the brook	*beside*
That shows his <u>hoar</u> leaves in the glassy stream.	*old*
Therewith fantastic garlands did she make	
Of crow-flowers, nettles, daisies, and long purples,	
That <u>liberal</u> shepherds give a grosser name,	*crude*
But our cold maids do dead men's fingers call them.	
There on the <u>pendent boughs</u> her crownet weeds	*hanging branches*
<u>Clamb'ring</u> to hang, an <u>envious sliver</u> broke,	*climbing: spiteful branch*
When down her weedy trophies and herself	
Fell in the weeping brook. Her clothes spread wide,	
And mermaid-like a while they bore her up;	
Which time she chanted snatches of old tunes,	
As one <u>incapable</u> of her own distress,	*unaware*
Or like a creature native and <u>endued</u>	
<u>Unto</u> that element. But long it could not be	*suited to live on*
Till that her garments, heavy with their drink,	
Pulled the poor wretch from her melodious <u>lay</u>	*song*
To muddy death.	

Figure 11.7. Reading *Hamlet* with eyes and ears.

1996 production of the scene. Before watching the film clip, students receive the second set of questions:

> **Performance: How does Julie Christie's performance "read" the words?**
>
> 5. Listen closely. Explain how the actor uses her voice as a performance tool.
> 6. Watch closely. What else does the actor do to add meaning and emotion to these words? For example, how does she use gestures, facial expressions, and movement to enrich the words?
> 7. How do the camera shots and angles contribute to the drama of this scene?

Figure 11.8. Millais's painting of Ophelia. ©Tate, London 2009. Used with permission.

After small-group discussions run their course, we share as a whole group. Finally, I display Millais's iconic painting at the overhead (Figure 11.8) and distribute these questions for small- and whole-group discussion:

> **Painting: "Ophelia" by John Everett Millais. How does the painter "read" the words?**

8. Reread Gertrude's words and study the artist's portrait of Ophelia. Find the lines in Gertrude's speech that are illustrated here. Is this a painting of Ophelia in life or death? How do you know?

9. What words would you use to describe the mood of this painting? How does color contribute to the mood? How do Ophelia's facial expression and the gesture of her hands contribute to the mood?

10. Each text, the written and the painted one, describes Ophelia's death. What are the strengths of the written text? What are the strengths of the painted text? Which do you prefer, and why?

As a summarizer to this lesson, I ask students if Ophelia's death is a suicide. Arguments ensue, and students cite sources beyond the text to support their reasoning. Millais's painting emphasizes, indeed almost romanticizes, Ophelia's passive passage into death, and students who focus on this medium tend to reject suicide. "She's out of it," they say. "She has no idea what she's doing. It's an accident." One year, a student expressed the stunning conclusion that Ophelia's death wasn't a suicide or an accident but a murder. Though I suspect that the camera work, with its dissolve from Julie Christie to Kate Winslet, had something to do with his interpretation, this student employed logic. "How would Gertrude know all those details about the flowers and the brook if she didn't witness Ophelia's death?" he asked us all. I was momentarily speechless, but another student spoke up. "I think Gertrude saw it happen," she said, "but from a distance and she couldn't get to Ophelia in time to save her." Her evidence? "In the movie, Julie Christie's hair is messed up a little. That shows that she was there, probably running through branches, but it was too late." Through exposure to multiple perspectives, students can learn to see the possibilities of the text.

Seeing and Hearing Shakespeare: The Storyboard

In the age of film and the graphic novel, Shakespeare's plays are infinitely at home. Critics often proclaim the cinematic quality of Shakespeare's writing, and there are directors and scholars who postulate that if the Bard had been born four hundred years later, he would be making movies today. Constructing storyboards and writing scenes into film scripts are two modes of expression in which young readers bring their mind's eye and ear to Shakespeare's page.

Today, almost every book and article that addresses the use of film in the classroom includes information on storyboards and templates for their construction, but I was first introduced to this format in 1993 when I took a television production course at a community cable television outlet. We were assigned to write and storyboard a thirty-second public service announcement (PSA) in this way: draw ten to twelve blocks onto a large piece of paper, imagine an equal number of film frames, sketch an image in each block, and write a script for narration and sound in the white space beneath each frame. The classroom applications were immediately apparent, but when I searched local bookstores for teacher support materials, the only book I found was Irwin R. Blacker's *The Elements of Screenwriting: A Guide for Film and Television Writing*. To this day, I include Blacker's explanation in my storyboard assignments:

> Storyboards are made by sketch artists in the preproduction months before shooting begins. They help the director, cameraman, set designers, and others to visualize key scenes and to save valuable production time. If the script is in the proper form and

carries all of the relevant description, the director and sketch artists together can easily visualize what is going to be shown on the screen. (92)

For most of the years that my students constructed storyboards, they did as I once did, dividing large pieces of unlined paper into ten to twelve blocks, sketching key frames, and writing explanatory notes for narration and sound at the bottom of each block. Recently, I found templates in two different sources for storyboards, both of which improve upon my homegrown model. The first is in Nikos Theodosakis' 2001 book, *The Director in the Classroom*, and the second is in another 2001 publication, John Golden's *Reading in the Dark*. Golden provides a two-step storyboard template that scaffolds student reading from literary to cinematic. Using Golden's Storyboarding Activity #1, students Carlos Monroy and Jaime Vasquez began to translate King Lear's speech in 3.2.1–11 into a voice-over narration for the storm (Figure 11.9).

After students complete five or six shot sketches with comments on what they want to demonstrate and the lines of text that help them to see the words, Golden introduces (or reviews) cinematic techniques and students return to the scene with an arsenal of strategies for transforming literary text into film. Their new knowledge often empowers students to see the lines of text with a new set of eyes and ears. Though Shot #1 is still a long shot, Carlos and Jaime call for a Dutch, or tilted, angle that distorts the natural landscape. Compounding the natural sounds of wild weather, they add the nondiegetic sound of "dramatic music" (Figure 11.10).

Golden's commentary on storyboarding, with examples of student work, can be found on pages 53–57 of *Reading in the Dark*, and his storyboard charts are in Appendix B, pages 160–161. In Chapter 1 of his book, Golden explains and illustrates film terms and techniques students need to understand in order to read the "text" of film.

Storyboarding Shakespeare is particularly effective with passages that evoke images of the supernatural, but any scene or speech that begs imagination is fertile ground. Students in my classes have had particular success constructing storyboards for these passages in the plays:

- *Romeo and Juliet* 4.3.14–57: Juliet's waking nightmare before drinking the potion
- *A Midsummer Night's Dream* 5.1.2–22: Theseus's pronouncement on lunatics, lovers, and poets
- *The Tempest* 4.1.1148–158: Prospero's revels, ended

Storyboarding Activity #1
Template from *Reading in the Dark* by John Golden

SHOT #1

What did you want to demonstrate?

I wanted to show the strength and terror of the storm. The tempest is raging right out in the open, without much cover. The land is bare, without one creature moving to emphasize how alone Lear is.

What lines helped you see this?

"Blow, wind, and crack your cheeks! Rage!"

"all shaking thunder"

"Crack nature's moulds"

Figure 11.9. Storyboard activity #1.

Storyboarding Activity #2
Template adapted from *Reading in the Dark* by John Golden

SHOT #1

Intended Effect of Shot: The intensity of the storm should correlate with Lear's feelings toward his daughters.

Dialogue & Diegetic Sound: "Blow, winds and crack your cheeks! Rage! Blow!"
Wind howling. Tree branches shaking.
Thunder, lightning, and rain.

Nondiegetic Sound: Dramatic music, fast-paced to emphasize the chaos.

Shot Type: Long shot

Angle: Dutch angle

Lighting: Low-key with occasional flashes of light.

Movement: Pan

Edit: Crosscutting to Shot #2

Figure 11.10. Storyboard activity #2.

- *Henry V* Prologue: No ghosts, dreams, or hallucinations, but a panorama of imaginary armies clashing on imaginary battle-fields
- *Julius Caesar* 4.2.326–337: The brief appearance of Caesar's Ghost offers subtle possibilities, in part because, as Coppelia Kahn points out, "the 'monstrous apparition' that appears to Brutus in his tent on the eve of battle calls itself not Caesar but 'Thy evil spirit' and says only 'thou shalt see me at Philippi'" (224).
- *Hamlet* 1.4.19–38: Hamlet struggles to name what he sees as the Ghost enters and beckons him to follow.
- *Macbeth* 2.1.44–77: Macbeth's hallucinatory soliloquy before killing Duncan

Figure 11.11 shows student Jennifer Pollard's storyboard of Macbeth's second soliloquy in act 2.1, modified from its original size of 11 × 17 inches. Though Pollard is a talented student artist, I was struck by her innate sense of storytelling with a camera. When she did this work in 2005, I discussed cinematic techniques with students in the most superficial of ways, by asking them to think about their favorite suspense films and the ways in which the camera added to the suspense.

Only now, using the film terminology outlined in Golden's first chapter of *Reading in the Dark*, can I name some of the cinematic techniques Pollard used to storyboard Macbeth's hallucinatory soliloquy:

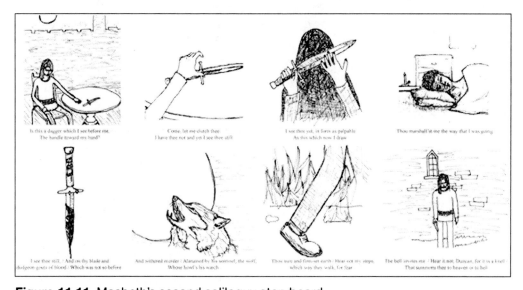

Figure 11.11. Macbeth's second soliloquy storyboard.

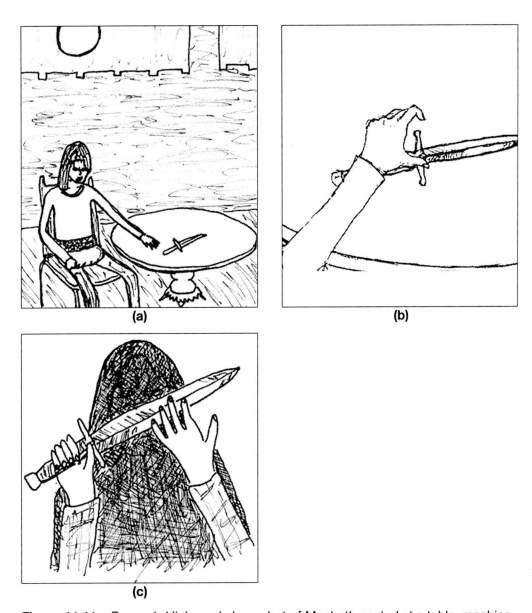

Figure 11.11a. <u>Frame 1</u>: High-angle long shot of Macbeth seated at a table, reaching toward a dagger, backlit by a full moon: "Is this a dagger which I see before me, / The handle toward my hand?"

Figure 11.11b. <u>Frame 2</u>: High-angle close-up shot of Macbeth's hand reaching for the dagger: "Come, let me clutch thee. / I have thee not, and yet I see thee still."

Figure 11.11c. <u>Frame 3</u>: Medium shot, eye-level, of Macbeth holding a different dagger: "I see thee yet, in form as palpable / As this which now I draw."

What strikes me most about Frame 3 is that it defies the logic of the eye-level medium shot, which Golden describes as the most "neutral" shot and the one preferred in television because it is common and doesn't call attention to itself (5). The low-key lighting on Macbeth's face, the high-key lighting on his dagger and hands, the rack focus that sharpens the weapon in the foreground and blurs the human face behind it—all of these cinematic choices combine with the "normal" eye-level medium shot to create contradiction, tension, and imbalance.

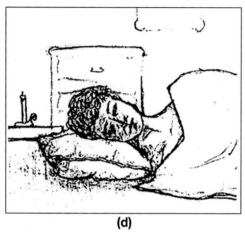

(d)

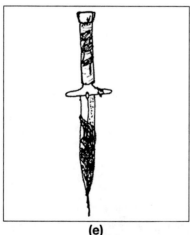

(e)

Figure 11.11d. <u>Frame 4</u>: Camera cuts to the sleeping King Duncan, with a voice-over: "Thou marshall'st me the way that I was going . . . "

Figure 11.11e. <u>Frame 5</u>: Close-up of the dagger Macbeth can't grasp; it is now vertical and bleeding: "I see thee still; / And on thy blade and dudgeon gouts of blood, / Which was not so before."

I wonder if Pollard would choose to soften the focus in Frame 5 to suggest that this image may be in Macbeth's imagination.

Figure 11.11f. <u>Frame 6</u>: Cut to a low-angle close-up of a howling wolf, backlit by the moon, suggested by Macbeth's voiceover, " . . . and wither'd murder / Alarum'd by his sentinel, the wolf, / Whose howl's his watch . . . "

I would call the sounds of a wolf howling diegetic, since it is a "sound that could be logically heard by a character within the movie environment" (17). Nondiegetic sound "is intended only for the audience and is not a part of the movie environment" (19).

Figure 11.11g. <u>Frame 7</u>: Close-up of Macbeth's foot: "Thou sure and firm-set earth, / Hear not my steps, which way they walk, for fear . . . "

Up until Frame 7, Pollard has been creatively translating Shakespeare's words into images and sound, but in this frame she takes the liberty of adding flames in the background that suggest that Macbeth's decision to follow the bloody dagger is leading him into hell.

Figure 11.11h. <u>Frame 8</u>: Long shot of Macbeth, oddly still. It is not clear if the dialogue is spoken or recorded as a voice-over: " . . . the bell invites me. / Hear it not, Duncan, for it is a knell / That summons thee to heaven, or to hell."

Now, when I introduce film terms and Golden's two-step storyboard activities, I also reproduce Pollard's storyboard of Macbeth's soliloquy, and shot-by-shot, we move from the questions in Golden's literary storyboard to the techniques listed in the more cinematic one, identifying and analyzing her choices. Pollard tells us what lines helped her to see each shot, and we infer what she wanted to demonstrate. "I think she wants to show Macbeth's temptation," one student remarked about her first shot, whose composition seats Macbeth at a table, his hand reaching toward a dagger. Then, with the same shot, we talk about the type of shot, the focus, the angle, the lighting, the suggestions for sound, and the ways in which these things contribute to the shot's overall effect. After closely reading someone else's storyboard, students are eager to construct their own.

Students need to be reminded that a storyboard is not a comic strip. Figure 11.12 is a collection of shots students have produced in

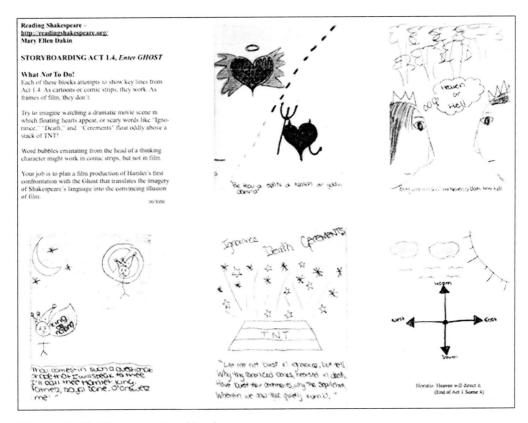

Figure 11.12. Storyboarding *Hamlet*.

the past that are clever illustrations of literary elements, but cinematic disasters. For example, when Hamlet asks the Ghost, "Be thou a spirit of health or goblin damn'd," one student drew the antithesis by splitting the screen into an angelic heart and a demonic one. In another shot, a student illustrates the verb *burst* as a box of TNT spraying stars of ignorance and death.

Seeing and Hearing Shakespeare: The Film Script

In 1993, as I searched for teacher support materials for storyboarding, I also became intensely interested in the genre of the film script and its applications in the literature classroom. Once again, Blacker's book, *The Elements of Screenwriting*, gave me a framework to build upon. With the set of directions that I adapted from Blacker, students began to see and hear Shakespeare as screenwriters and directors do (Figure 11.13).

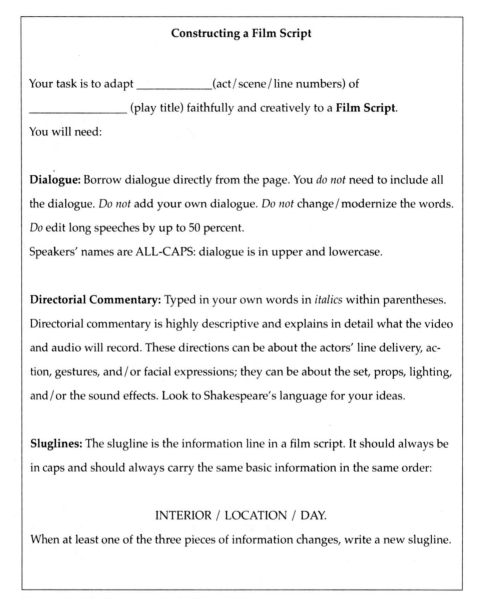

Constructing a Film Script

Your task is to adapt _____ (act/scene/line numbers) of

_____ (play title) faithfully and creatively to a **Film Script**.
You will need:

Dialogue: Borrow dialogue directly from the page. You *do not* need to include all the dialogue. *Do not* add your own dialogue. *Do not* change/modernize the words. *Do* edit long speeches by up to 50 percent.
Speakers' names are ALL-CAPS: dialogue is in upper and lowercase.

Directorial Commentary: Typed in your own words in *italics* within parentheses. Directorial commentary is highly descriptive and explains in detail what the video and audio will record. These directions can be about the actors' line delivery, action, gestures, and/or facial expressions; they can be about the set, props, lighting, and/or the sound effects. Look to Shakespeare's language for your ideas.

Sluglines: The slugline is the information line in a film script. It should always be in caps and should always carry the same basic information in the same order:

INTERIOR / LOCATION / DAY.

When at least one of the three pieces of information changes, write a new slugline.

Figure 11.13. Constructing a film script.

Students need to see samples of Shakespearean film scripts. I was fortunate to find Kenneth Branagh's film script for the 1996 production of *Hamlet* on the shelves of a bookstore. But thousands of film scripts (and a small collection of storyboards) are available at very reasonable prices from an online source called Script City. Furthermore, student

---

Adapting Shakespeare's Stage Script to Film
A Midsummer Night's Dream Act 3.1
By
Alandria Cimino and Jenna Forgione

EXTERIOR / CARNIVAL / NIGHT
(*Camera pans from fireworks to city lights, then to the entrance of a parking lot carnival. Set in the 1950s, the players, PETER QUINCE, NICK BOTTOM, FRANCIS FLUTE, TOM SNOUT, and ROBIN STARVELING, are seventeen years old. After having a run-in with the law, these juvenile delinquents have been instructed to put on a play for their community service hours. They will perform on the opening day at the carnival, so they break into the carnival at night to rehearse. The players are a little drunk, and a little too loud. They meet at the entrance to the carnival, looking in.*)

(*Camera zooms in on each boy, but pauses three seconds longer on* BOTTOM)

BOTTOM: Are we all met?

QUINCE: (*Standing before everyone. Quince is skinny and his clothes don't fit, but he is the best dressed in the group and is clearly the leader of the gang. He lifts the front of his shirt and pulls out a crowbar, which he uses to open the gate. He throws the crowbar on the ground. The noise should make them nervous but it doesn't. They run inside and stop in front of the carousel.*) Pat, pat; and here's a marvelous convenient place for our rehearsal.

BOTTOM: (*Runs onto the carousel, grabs one of the poles with his right hand, stretches out his left arm, and swings 180 degrees to face his friends*) There are things in this comedy that will never please. (*Jumps down from the carousel, holds up one finger and shouts the word "First!"*) First, Pyramus must draw a sword to kill himself; which the ladies cannot abide. How answer you that? (*Looks at each of his companions' questioning faces.*) Not a whit: I have a device to make all well. (*Rubs chin.*) Write me a prologue (*he addresses* QUINCE) and let the prologue seem to say, we will do no harm with our swords, and that Pyramus is not killed indeed; and, for the more better assurance, tell them that I, Pyramus, am not Pyramus, but Bottom: this will put them out of fear. (*Crosses arms and stands proudly smiling.*)

QUINCE: (*Takes a pack of cigarettes from his pocket and lights one.*) Well, we will have such a prologue; and it shall be written in eight and six.

BOTTOM: (*Snatches the cigarette from QUINCE's mouth and disapprovingly throws it on the ground. Stomps on it, then in a stern voice says . . .*) No, make it two more; let it be written in eight and eight . . .

Figure 11.14. Adapting Shakespeare's stage script to film.

models can be excellent sources of instruction and inspiration. Figure 11.14 is the first page of a student-produced film script that I treasure.

In *Great Films and How to Teach Them*, William Costanzo acknowledges that somewhere between one-third and one-half "of all films ever made" (3) are adaptations of literature, and he raises the question of fidelity—"What does it mean to be faithful to the book?" (10). In adapting act 3.1 of *A Midsummer Night's Dream* to film, students Alandria Cimino and Jenna Forgione took an approach that is both faithful and creative. They remained faithful to Shakespeare's dialogue and to the characterizations of Bottom and Quince, yet the Athenian woods becomes a traveling carnival, and the props include a crowbar, a carousel, and a pack of cigarettes.

Seeing, Hearing, and Producing Shakespeare

Almost every text written in the past decade that addresses adolescent literacy reminds the English teacher that words are "necessary, but not sufficient," and that the word *literacy* itself must be made plural—hence, *multiliteracies*—in order to name the integration of language with "art, movement, gesture, and music" that constitutes modern communication (Alvermann, "Multiliterate Youth" 22–23). While it is true that adolescents inhabit a world of text-messaging and digital broadcasts, many students lack the skills necessary to employ audio and visual media for anything other than entertainment. Part of our responsibility as educators is to build bridges between old and new technologies.

When it comes to technology, I inhabit the anthropological branch of the word—like much of the human race, I am adept at using tools (forks and spoons, needles and thread, scrapers and paintbrushes) to accomplish a task. But I am an immigrant in the high-tech Promised Land. Still, I have learned to get by with a great deal of help from my (younger, hipper, digitally native) children—Michael, Brian, and Beth—and colleagues. What follows is a series of strategies for getting students "to put some of the world back in" to Shakespeare's richly imaginative text using their eyes, ears, voices, and bodies, but also using microphones, digital cameras, and computers.

Podcasting "Others" in Shakespeare's Plays

In the weeks before my students began work on the first VideoPaper (see Chapter 10), we started small, with our first podcast. Several years before, while teaching *The Merchant of Venice*, I knew I needed a way to make students hear Shakespeare as they may never have heard it before. They needed to hear the way outsiders are named in Shakespeare's plays; they needed to understand that the words we use to name and describe others can limit them and us.

The human voice is a powerful instrument, and podcasting is one of the newest formats for exploring that power. According to the *New Oxford American Dictionary* and my daughter Beth Dakin, "A podcast is 'a digital recording of a radio broadcast or similar program, made available on the Internet,' but the definition has expanded to include video as well as audio." Though the audio for this work could be done using an old-fashioned tape recorder, a friend in the tech department offered to let my students record their work in his computer lab. And so our foray into high-tech Shakespeare began.

"What's in a name?" I asked students one November day in 2007. "List all the names, titles, and labels people use to identify you." Figure 11.15 lists the accumulation of names they wrote on index cards, reformatted into alphabetical order. One student added a note to his card, "I left some out simply because the derogatory words people use when speaking about me are not school-friendly." Before collecting the index cards, I asked students to identify the name or label that they would keep and the one they would eliminate, and to explain their reasoning.

That day, students told me that the names they prefer to be called are specific to them and name some inner quality that few others see. Their favorite names have been given to them by someone who cares deeply for them. The names they hate are generic names that deny their individuality, or mock their individuality. They are names that isolate

---

What's in a name? List all the names, titles, and labels people use to identify and "name" you.

	Failure	New Age Hippie
Almond Eyes	Fat-ass	Nobody
Babu	Flirt	Over-achiever
Baby	Follower	Paco Man
Beautiful	Fool	Princess
Best friend	Freak	Rah-rah
Bitch	Geek	Smarty Pants
Bookworm	Hazel	Spick
Brat	Hopeless Romantic	Sasha Jade
Columbian (*i.e.* Coke Dealer)	Jelly Bean	Slut
Doctor	Kid	Stupid
Drama Girl	Liar	Suck-up
Dreamer	Liberal	Tree-hugger
Disappointment	Loner	Weirdo
Dork	Mirror Doll	Whore
Eccentric	Muslim	

Figure 11.15. Labels people use to identify you.

them from their peers. We were reading *The Tempest*, and Caliban was on my mind. Like Shylock in *The Merchant of Venice*, Katherine in *The Taming of the Shrew*, and Othello, Caliban is a misfit in the world of his play. Bastard child of an Algerian "witch" (1.2.264–266), he is named "monster" more than thirty times by the Europeans who have usurped his island, located somewhere between the Old World and the New.

No matter which of the problem plays you teach, it is worthwhile to have students scan the play for the list of words and phrases used to name the outcast. Figure 11.16 is a list I constructed of lines from four plays that name outsiders: Shylock the Jew, Katherine the Shrew, Othello the Moor, and Caliban the slave.

From this list or a play-specific list constructed by students, a derivative script entitled "Naming Shakespeare's Others," or more specifically, "Naming Caliban," for example, can be composed. After the whole class has made a list and students have formed groups of four or five, I share these directions with them:

> **Constructing a Derivative Script/Naming Caliban in *The Tempest***
> From the list of names, titles, and lines in Shakespeare's text that name the outsider in the play, construct a script. Determine your objective. How does your group "read" Caliban? Will you construct a script that dehumanizes him or one that humanizes him? Will your script attempt to do both? How? Will Caliban speak? When and how often will he speak?
>
> Once your group agrees on its objective, write a derivative script by arranging Shakespeare's words and lines into the order you think is most effective in achieving your objective.
>
> Once you have completed the script, cast the speaking parts and practice speaking your lines with clarity and conviction.
>
> In preparation for the audio recording, consider the human and technological tools available to you:
>
> Line delivery: Pitch, pace, pause, volume, stress, tone; choral voices.
> Line distinction: How will we know, beyond the script itself, when we are hearing Caliban's voice?
> Sound effects: What are the sounds natural to the setting of this play? What other sounds would be appropriate for your script? Will you include music?
> Images: If you plan to include them, what images would enhance the message of your script?

Naming "Others" in Shakespeare's Plays

"What, ho! slave! Caliban!"
"Shylock the Jew"
" . . . curst Katherine"
" . . . his Moorship"
"From all such devils, good Lord deliver us!"
"Caliban my slave."
"Thou tortoise!"
"Thou poisonous slave, got by the devil himself, come forth!"
"Misbeliever, cutthroat dog . . . "
" . . . an old black ram is tupping your white ewe!"
"Thou most lying slave, Whom stripes may move, not kindness!"
"Freckled whelp hag-born—not honour'd with A human shape."
"I know she is an irksome, brawling scold."
"The devil can cite Scripture for his purpose."
"I have used thee, Filth as thou art . . . "
"You'll have your daughter cover'd with a Barbary horse . . . "
"Come, come, you wasp!"
"Abhorred slave, Which any print of goodness will not take/ . . . "
"Thing most brutish . . . "
" . . . rich Jew"
"Thy vile race . . . had that in't which good natures could not abide . . . "
" . . . faithless Jew"
" . . . lascivious Moor"
"I hate the Moor . . . "
"Hag-seed, hence!"
"So, slave; hence!"
" . . . intolerable curst, And shrewd and forward . . . "
"What have we here? A man or a fish?"
"O be thou damned, inexecrable dog . . . "
"Strange beast . . . "
" . . . dead Indian."
" . . . Thick-lips"
"Harsh Jew, thou mak'st thy knife keen."
" . . . the lusty Moor"
"Legged like a man! And his fins like arms!"
"Then must the Jew be merciful."
" . . . the circumcised dog"
"A most delicate monster!"
" . . . a very shallow monster!"
" . . . a most perfidious and drunken monster!"
" . . . puppy-headed monster. A most scurvy monster!"
"Poor monster . . . abominable monster!"
"A most ridiculous monster . . . "
"A howling monster; a drunken monster!"
"O brave monster!"
"Monsieur Monster."
"Monster, I do smell all horse-piss, at which my nose is in great indignation."
"This Jew, my master."
"This is the way to kill a wife with kindness . . . "
"This thing of darkness I Acknowledge mine."

Figure 11.16. Naming "Others" in Shakespeare's plays.

The next step will depend on the resources available to you, but at a minimum, students will need a computer, a microphone, and recording software. Audacity is free recording software and is relatively easy to use. For more information on podcasting, see Chapter 8 of Will Richardson's *Blogs, Wikis, Podcasts, and Other Powerful Web Tools for Classrooms.* For a fascinating look at derivative and transformative creative writing projects in the digital age, see Unit 2 of Christopher Shamburg's *English Language Arts: Units for Grades 9–12.*

This approach to seeing and hearing Shakespeare's most hurtful words begs some sort of decompression. Once the "Naming Caliban" podcasts were complete, I asked students to reflect on the ways in which these activities contributed to their understanding of the characters in *The Tempest,* of Caliban in particular, and of us as players in our own lives. The young woman who wrote on her index card that one of the names she is called is "Columbian," which she explained is short-speak for "cocaine dealer," said that she has learned to ignore racial epithets "because the people who say them are ignorant." Still, she added that being outnumbered would matter. "There are enough people in this school who look and sound like me to help me feel included," she said. "I don't know what I'd do if I were alone." What's in a name? Juliet's question requires exploration in our classrooms.

Reporting from the Scene

Because I teach in a city immediately north of Boston, taking students on field trips to see and hear performances of a Shakespearean play is usually an annual event. In the winter of 2007–08, the conjunction of two stars made it possible for my students to see a play, record the experience, and produce a digital field trip report. The first star came in the form of a grant from our local cultural council that funded the field trip; the second star (the result of a different grant) came in the form of twenty Macintosh laptops loaded with the iLife suite for multimodal compositions, a digital video camera and two digital cameras, a keyboard, and a printer. For the first time, my students would be able to record the experience of attending a Shakespeare play in a medium as dynamic as the performance itself. As members of the audience reporting from the scene, they too would be players, in their own production.

There were glitches, the biggest of which was the fact that we had not yet read the play we would see, *Henry V.* Winter break, snow days, and final exam week had conspired against us. So I had to amend my list of essential questions for this project by eliminating the first one:

> How does a performance extend and/or limit Shakespeare's text?

Instead, we spent several class periods getting acquainted with *The Henriad* and, in particular, with the enigmatic Henry V. Then I shared with students the questions their work would explore:

> How can we capture the experience of seeing and hearing a live performance of a play?
>
> Who is our intended audience? What is the purpose of our report? How do the answers to these questions influence the images, sounds, and words that we use in our report?

After attending the brilliant Actors' Shakespeare Project (ASP) production of *Henry V*, we returned to school with almost thirty minutes of video and dozens of photographs. In the following weeks, I read the iLife teachers' manual that came with the equipment and practiced on one of the Macs, visiting the tutorials over and over again in preparation for the project. In the end, the tutorials would do the technical teaching for me, and would free me to focus on my students and the content of our work.

As soon as we started, I saw the need for small groups and more structure. The tutorials on skimming and trimming footage, on creating movies and adding music, voice-over, and titles were only one part of the picture. Using the model in Chapter 8, "Designing Great Filmmaking Projects," of Nikos Theodosakis's book, *The Director in the Classroom*, I adapted a project guide (Figure 11.17) and a timeline to keep us on task for the two weeks it would take three groups of students to learn the equipment and to produce their digital reports. Employing the high-tech model of backwards engineering, I constructed a rubric for the project only after viewing and re-viewing the finished reports (Figure 11.18). When students completed their reports, they were eager for an audience of their own so they sent the links to the cultural council that paid for the field trip and to the Actors' Shakespeare Project.

Technology equips students with such an expansive toolbox of audiovisual communication tools that the greatest challenge for English teachers may lay, at least for now, in restraint. Though the urban school district in which I teach embraces technology, the poverty rate in our community still impacts the access students have to updated computers, software, or the required bandwidth to properly access the Internet in their apartments and homes. In addition, the transient nature of some of their living arrangements—living at times with a grandparent, a friend, or between two separated parents—impacts their ability to work

	Guide to Designing Our Project Adapted from *The Director in the Classroom: How Filmmaking Inspires Learning,* Chapter 8, "Designing Great Filmmaking Projects," by Nikos Theodosakis and Ian Jukes	
Purpose:	*What is the purpose of our project?*	
Vision:	*In your wildest dreams, what would you love to see this finished project achieve?*	
Subject:	Field trip to: When:	
Questions:	*What questions will this project answer?*	
Audience:	*Who is our intended audience?*	
Venue:	*How can audiences see our work?* Mini DV VHS CD DVD Web Email	
Project Length:	*How many minutes, including head (beginning) and end titles?* Five to ten minutes	
Deadline:	One week from today	
Special Instructions:	Use both photos and video Use both interior and exterior locations Use diegetic and non-diegetic sounds Narrate the experience *and* critique the performance Include every student Give credit, whenever possible, to the videographers, photographers, and writers	
Assessment:	<u>Technical</u>: Camera work, sound, editing <u>Creative</u>: Is the project's purpose achieved? Are the questions answered? Are words spelled correctly?	

Figure 11.17. Project guide.

Digital Field Trip Report Project Rubric		
This project will be assessed on the extent to which it demonstrates mastery of these components:		
Content and Organization	The project clearly, fully, and creatively completes the assignment: *Students will plan, record, script, and produce a digital field trip report that tells the story of the field trip and analyzes what they learned.* The report is organized; it is enriched with appropriate detail; transitions are effective. Questions raised by the project are clearly and insightfully answered.	Maximum pts: 20 Points earned:
Purpose	Students can clearly and thoughtfully explain the main purpose of their project (*for example, the purpose may be to inform, to entertain, to critique, to explain, etc.*) and demonstrate appropriate choices made by the students to achieve their purpose.	Maximum pts: 15 Points earned:
Audience	Students can clearly and thoughtfully identify their intended audience and explain how choices made by the students (*for example, their word choice, images, audio, graphics, and/or editing*) appeal to their audience. A strong awareness of audience is consistently evident in the design of the project.	Maximum pts: 15 Points earned:
Images	Students combine photographs and video to tell a story and to comment on the experience. The images chosen support the content of the story and enhance the main ideas and/or claims of the project. The images contribute to the mood and tone. Text is added where needed; words and names are spelled correctly.	Maximum pts: 10 Points earned:
Audio	The sound is consistently audible. The voiceover enhances the story; the speakers are articulate. Music and sound effects evoke a rich emotional response that intensifies the project.	Maximum pts: 10 Points earned:
Project Length	Length is appropriate. Editing is economical and insightful, including what is most important and relevant without dragging on or hurrying.	Maximum pts: 10 Points earned:
Special Instructions	The project addresses all of the special instructions: Use both photos and video Use both interior and exterior locations Use diegetic and non-diegetic sounds Narrate the experience *and* analyze what you learned Include every student Give credit, whenever possible, to the videographers, photographers, and writers	Maximum pts: 10 Points earned:
Deadline	Work is completed on time.	Maximum pts: 10 Points earned:
		Total points:

Figure 11.18. Digital field trip report project rubric.

on digital projects when not in school. In commentary written for the *Journal of Adolescent and Adult Literacy* in September 2008, Donna E. Alvermann lists other factors: "Hardware malfunctions . . . too expensive for families of low income to fix, connectivity problems . . . and limited leisure time in which to learn from tech-savvy friends" because of the "need to work part-time jobs" (15). All of which means that for many teachers and students, projects requiring multimodal tools and applications still need to be done largely during class time. Devoting weeks to the student production of a complex digital project with all the bells and whistles may not always be the best way to tell a story.

In a different era and with a different set of tools, William Shakespeare seems to have learned this lesson, too. As his writing matured, Shakespeare's verse gave way to more prose, and the blank verse itself became more fluid and naturalistic. "For anything so overdone," Hamlet instructs the Players, "is from the purpose of playing, whose end, both at the first and now, was and is, to hold, as 'twere, the mirror up to nature" (3.2.14–16). Author, educational technology specialist, and former high school English teacher Christopher Shamburg declares, "Language arts education is about developing the power of words—words that are spoken, linked, recorded, written, shouted, enacted—for different audiences and with different media—from digital video to the vibrations in the air" (5). The highway, in other words, runs both ways, and when students walk the distance between Shakespeare's times and their own, they will build bridges from past to future and future to past.

III Fluency: Hearing and Speaking Shakespeare

> HAMLET: We'll hear a play tomorrow. (2.2.538)
>
> US: Let's see a movie.

Think about what that little shift in verbs reveals about our culture and Shakespeare's. Still, though our students navigate a daily visual maze of films, websites, video games, and television, the rhythm and rhyme of music compose the soundtracks of their lives, and no adolescent I know has taken a vow of silence. Few of my students were read to when they were small, but that has never stopped them from listening open-mouthed when I lunge at the reader who has volunteered to speak for Macbeth and in a hysterical, accusing whisper, pronounce, "Why did you bring these daggers from the place? / They must lie there. Go, carry them and smear / The sleepy grooms with blood" (2.2.46–48).

Kylene Beers describes fluency as "the rhythm of reading" (204). This final section of the book fuses the strategies of reading and speaking specialists, Shakespearean actors, and those rare adolescents who arrive at our classroom doors every year like the children of Mnemosyne and Zeus, gifted it would seem from birth with the power to read and speak Shakespeare fluently. There is only one chapter in this section because it builds upon strategies outlined in the vocabulary and comprehension sections. You cannot read Shakespeare fluently if you continually trip over high-frequency archaic words and phrases: see Chapters 1 and 2 in the vocabulary section. You won't read Shakespeare with sensitivity to the nuances of expression if you are tone-deaf or unaware of the social status embedded in certain pronouns: see Chapters 4 and 5. You cannot read Shakespeare with clarity and appropriate expression if you don't understand the speaker, the conflict, the mood, or the language: see Chapters 7, 8, 10, and 11 in the comprehension section.

In the Shakespeare classroom, fluent readers give life to words.

12 Exploring Sound, Meaning, and Expression

Speak the speech, I pray you, as I pronounced it to you—trippingly on the tongue; but if you mouth it, as many of your players do, I had as lief the town-crier spoke my lines.

Hamlet 3.2.1–4

Before becoming a teacher of Shakespeare, my formal study of his plays was conducted largely in silence and isolation. I'm not sure when I began to rebel, but by the time I graduated from college I had reverted to what I had been taught to believe was the telltale marker of poor silent readers—subvocalization—because I needed to hear Shakespeare's words in my head and speak them in my mouth. Decades later, a sentence in a poetry text felt like validation. "We hear poems," David Mason and John Nims assert, "even when we seem to be taking them silently from the page" (146). *Seem?* Were Mason and Nims suggesting that no reading is completely silent? Several months later, a passage in a chapter on reading in a college study skills textbook emphatically answered, "Yes." Subvocalization, or "silent speech," is both normal and necessary to comprehension (Pauk 108–109).

When I finally got the chance to teach a play by Shakespeare, I gleaned from the teacher support materials that accompanied the literature anthology that a good deal of the reading of *Julius Caesar* was meant to be done as silent reading for homework, or by playing records of British actors intoning the text. Apparently, reading Shakespeare aloud was much too challenging for American adolescents. Working at the time in a school for boys in blue-collar East Boston, I found that if I played the recordings any longer than ten minutes, I lost them. The 1953 film production with James Mason as Brutus and Marlon Brando as Antony held their attention a little longer (after I told them to watch for The Godfather in his prime), but what was the point, I wondered. Was I teaching Shakespeare on film or Shakespeare?

Gradually, I started reading the longest speeches aloud to students and found that there were usually enough volunteers in each group to read aloud the rest. We stopped a lot to talk about the words. We climbed on desks to orate, we stole plastic knives from the cafeteria to assassinate, and we read the final scene with the B-52's hit song, "Roam" (our Roman pun), blasting out an impromptu soundtrack. I wasn't thinking of teaching them *how* to speak Shakespeare but just to speak it—as silent reading, *Caesar* was deadly.

There is no getting around it—Shakespeare's text is like music, written to be heard. But getting Shakespeare's words to issue forth like music is, for most adolescents and their teachers, a challenge. The fluent reader, according to the late Jeanne Chall, possesses the ability "to unglue from print," to read aloud with clarity, rapidity, and conviction (Curtis). Some of the strategies outlined in this chapter are best suited to post-reading projects in which students select a speech or short scene for explication and delivery. Still, during our reading of a play I try to find at least one speech or scene in which we focus specifically on the sounds of Shakespeare. And early in our reading, sometimes even as a prereading warm-up to a play, I ask students to begin with the sounds of their world.

Constructing a Sound Inventory

Macbeth rants that life is "full of sound and fury, Signifying nothing" (5.5.26–27), but students need to speak and listen to words for the ways in which sound *is* significant. Not only as readers but as human beings, we place primary emphasis on the sensory experience of sight; in hypothetical situations, sight is the sense people are least willing to sacrifice. Still, it was in the course of a hypothetical argument with colleague and biology teacher David Eatough that I first realized the primacy of hearing. Of all the senses, Eatough argued, hearing is the sense that most effectively sustains our capacity for a social life. Silence isolates. Even before we enter the world, our first sensory experience is auditory, taking place in the echo chamber of the womb. From the biology teacher to the tragic hero, I have come to understand the price of silence—the inability to speak what is true in the heart—and the degree to which it weakens Hamlet in act 1—"But break, my heart, for I must hold my tongue"—and finally consumes him in act 5—"He has my dying voice. . . . The rest is silence."

Shakespeare's plays are set in a world where sound supersedes sight. To reacclimate the modern ear to that world, ask students to take inventory of the sounds in their world. For tragedies such as *Macbeth,* and histories like *Henry V*—"Hear the shrill whistle which doth give order / To sounds confused . . ." (3.0.9–10)—you might ask students to catalog the sounds of conflict in their lives, of victories and defeat. For

comedies such as *Twelfth Night*—"If music be the food of love, play on
. . . " (1.1.1)—have students assemble an audio montage of love songs
and note the common musical and verbal sounds they make, the rhythm
and the rhyme. Or ask students to list the most beautiful sounds in
nature. I have always taught city kids who love to tell me there are no
natural sounds in their lives, but once they really start listening they
make some pleasant discoveries—"There are crickets in the vacant lot
at night!" Let the play you are teaching guide you with its own organic
sound effects, stated and implied.

The Tempest is a play rich in "Sounds, and sweet airs, that give
delight" (3.2.139). In preparation for our reading of this play, I share my
list of sweet sounds with students—a heartbeat, distant church bells, my
grandfather's brogue, the cadence of rain, the mourning dove's coo. I
tell them about the sound of my mother's voice calling me back from
some deep, dark place after I had fallen in the elementary schoolyard
at recess, only to awaken flat on my back on the concrete, staring up at
dozens of young faces staring down in fright at me, no mother in sight
(it was Keats, not Shakespeare, alas, who claimed that "Heard melodies
are sweet, but those unheard Are sweeter. . . . "). Then I ask students
to construct a personal sound inventory by listing their own sweet and
soothing sounds. I encourage them to make it personal.

Telling Sound Stories

Hamlet says, "We'll hear a play tomorrow" (2.2.538–9). Note his choice of
verbs. One of the most basic ways to reacclimate students to a world in
which sound preempts sight is to challenge them to tell a story without
words. Expect silence and quizzical gazes. Then say it again: Tell a story
without words; tell a story composed of nonverbal sounds.

In Chapter 5 of *Seeing and Believing*, Mary T. Christel describes the
soundscape project she developed to help students appreciate the impact
of sound in film. "We cannot fully appreciate sound," she writes, "until
it is separated and isolated from the visual image" (57). With some combination of sounds that are natural to an environment—music, digital,
or student-produced sound effects—and no more than five words (these
are optional), Christel's students record and edit a collection of sounds
into a one-minute audio recording that creates a mood.

Before getting started, Christel's students brainstorm for sound
scenarios and the sequence of sounds that will drive the scene from beginning to end. She has found that "sinister scenarios" work best, such
as the sounds of breaking-and-entering a place—the intruder's gravelly

footsteps, the smash of broken glass, the exertion of climbing through the window frame, the thud of landing on the floor, the desperate rummaging through cabinets and drawers until the wail of a police siren sends the intruder to fling open a back door, with "You're under arrest!" punctuated by the metallic clank of handcuffs.

After brainstorming, Christel instructs students to write "a paragraph scenario that describes the situation, and includes setting, characters, and action" (58). Then students construct a cue sheet that lists each action (remember that each "action" will be the sounds produced by the action) and the start/end time of each action-sound in the sixty-second sequence. Using Christel's model, I developed Figure 12.1 as a worksheet for students. As an extension of this activity, students can exchange their soundscapes and create storyboards that illustrate the visual component of these audio scenarios.

Christel's soundscape is an excellent pre-viewing activity for any of Shakespeare's plays; students should not be limited to scenarios like the ones they will encounter in the play they are about to read. Still, it is also an excellent activity for specific scenes in a Shakespearean play. Before students read act 4 of *Henry V*, which recounts the epic Battle of Agincourt, we brainstorm for the sounds of a modern battle; sometimes we listen to the opening sound track of *Saving Private Ryan*. I provide some historical information about the battle—the terrain, the conditions of the field, the positions of the English and French armies, the kinds of weapons employed by each. Then, emulating Christel's process, I ask students to write a dramatic paragraph scenario that describes in vivid detail the setting, characters, and action at Agincourt. I tell them to describe sounds that convey a mood such as horror or heroism. Students compose a cue sheet for a one-minute soundscape. They need to listen backward from the sounds of modern warfare to the more primitive sounds of medieval conflict. They need to decide if and when music is appropriate, and whether the music they choose will be native to the culture of the play, classical, pop/modern, or some combination of each. Though Christel limits her students to five words or less, I give students key lines from act 4 and limit them to five or less. After completing their soundscapes, we read the battle scenes or a prose summary, then view-hear Kenneth Branagh's *Henry V*, a film production where the sound track contributes immensely to the script.

Exploring Word Sound

Once upon a time, I assumed that the study of word sounds was something appropriate only to the lower grades. In recent years I have found

---

Sixty-Second SoundScapes
Adapted from *Seeing and Believing* by Ellen Krueger and Mary T. Christel, pp.57–59

We'll hear a play tomorrow.
Hamlet to First Player, Act 2.2

Assignment: Shakespeare's world is a place where sound supersedes sight. Ours is a world in which sight supersedes sound. To reacclimate the modern ear to the early modern ear, follow these directions:

1. Write an action story with highly descriptive words in a paragraph scenario.

2. After writing your paragraph scenario, combine sounds that are natural to the action and the setting with music and sound effects. Use the **Cue Sheet** to write a title for your scenario and list each action (remember that each "action" will be the sounds produced by the action). Approximate the start/end time of each action-sound in the sixty -second sequence.

3. You can add up to five Shakespearean interjections as dialogue:

Hark	O	What ho	Zounds
Alas	Fie	Prithee	Fo
Alack	Ah	Lo	Illo ho ho
'Swounds	Yea	Holla	Woe
'Sblood	Nay	Hail	Well-a-day

Title/Scenario:	
Cue Sheet	
Action	**Time in Sequence**

Figure 12.1. Sixty-second SoundScapes.

professional and personal reasons to ask students to hear and speak words as well as to see them. About 75 percent of the human brain is devoted to processing sensory information, and though the entire human body plays a part in absorbing that information—the sights, sounds, smells, tastes, and touch of experience—only the hands command more brain space than the mouth (Mason 3–4, 145). It has been my experience that the vast majority of adolescents have no sense of the physicality of words, of the ways in which words sound and play with meaning. I also have found that most adolescents have limited patience with linguistics, so I tread lightly. Though they enjoy thinking about the sounds in their world, their pleasure rarely lies in the accumulation of vivid sensory words.

What do you know about word sounds? I ask students. They blink and look quizzical—*Words? Sounds?* Sometimes the classroom conversation begins with onomatopoeia, minus its fantastical Greek name. Words like *bang, buzz,* and *hiss* fill the air. Sometimes someone mentions syllables, but few secondary students can say exactly what a syllable is. We start to speak in syllables—"*Syl – la – ble!*"—and again, the room is abuzz in word sounds. Then I display a chart that telegraphs the basics of words and their sounds (Figure 12.2) and we talk some more. I let the group of students I am with set the agenda—I do not want to lose sight of our main goal, which is to speak Shakespeare with greater clarity and conviction. Still, just by jumping from the first element on the chart (*vowels*) to the last (*repetition*), most students begin to think more consciously about words, sound, and meaning. For example, students are usually surprised to think of vowel sounds as having an up-ness and a down-ness as if on a musical scale, with the *oo, oh, aw* sounds at the base (say *boo, bone, boss*) and the high-pitched long vowels sounds *ay, ee,* and *i* (say *bay, bee, by*) at the top. And they are equally surprised to think that something as simple as the repetition of a word (*Tomorrow and tomorrow and tomorrow . . .*) can convey more than just the time of day.

There are many excellent resources to guide the teacher who chooses to bring students on a journey through linguistics; many are written in the context of teaching poetry. For an in-depth analysis of words and sound in poetry, see David Mason and John Frederick Nims's *Western Wind: An Introduction to Poetry.* But most adolescents will be spooked by the sudden complexity of what they already see as a complex task—reading and speaking Shakespeare. So I put the chart aside and we continue to play with words as blocks of sound.

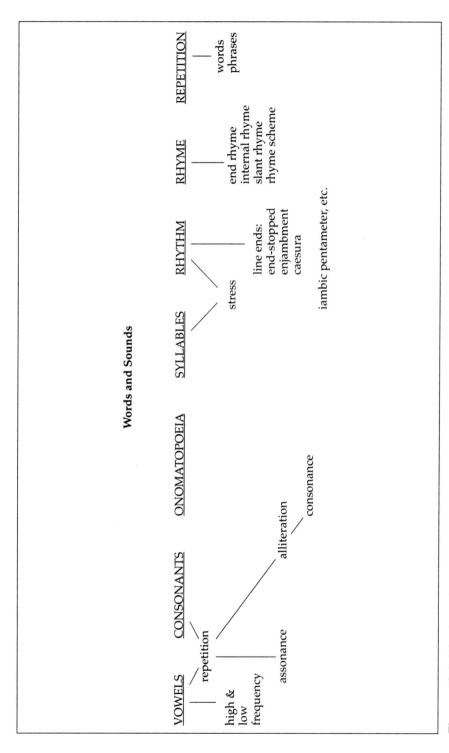

Figure 12.2. Words and sounds chart.

Metrical Soundings

Because meter is the heartbeat of a Shakespearean speech, we get to work listening for the systole and diastole of stressed and unstressed syllables. Give students a list of words, preferably from the play you are reading, and either break them into syllables together or syllabicate the words in advance. In their reading companies or as a whole group, have students practice sounding and marking the stressed and unstressed syllables. There are several symbols used in what is called scansion, some of which are highly technical. The authors of *Western Wind* remind us that stress all comes down to "more or less" and they recommend the simple, traditional way—"a firm straight line for the accented syllable (‾) and a sagging little curve for the slack one (˘)" (207). For Caliban's speech in 3.2, "Be not afeard . . . ," we begin to think about syllables and stress with this short list of words, which I syllabicate in advance:

> isle
>
> a-feard
>
> de-light
>
> twang-ling
>
> in-stru-ments
>
> me-thought

The vocabulary in this speech is straightforward, but if it weren't, I would choose words for this preliminary exercise whose meanings might not be clear to students. In that way, we address word sound and word meaning simultaneously. For an excellent exercise in pre-scansion, see Chapter 3 of *Accent on Meter* by Joseph Powell and Mark Halperin.

The next step is to distribute copies of one or more speeches from the play you are reading—enlarged, double-spaced, *and* pre-scanned. You may wonder why I scan the text for students instead of having them transfer what they have just practiced (marking words for stressed and unstressed syllables) to the speech themselves. My reasons are twofold: it saves valuable time, which keeps me from losing those students who will find scansion and meter boring and irrelevant. And secondly, it shows students that scanning Shakespeare's lines, or any poetry, is not a matter of mathematical precision. When caught up in marking the metrical sing-song of iambic pentameter, the tendency is to impose a strict *unstressed STRESSED unstressed STRESSED* pattern on the lines; that is what students generally do. But this violates the natural syllabication of words and does violence to both meaning and matter. However, if scanning lines from Shakespeare is something that will engage your students, by all means let them at it.

This is what I give my students from the Oxford edition:

> Be NOT aFEARD. The ISLE is FULL of NOISes,
> SOUNDS, and SWEET AIRS, that GIVE deLIGHT and HURT not.
> SomeTIMES a THOUsand TWANGling INstruMENTS
> Will HUM aBOUT mine EARS, and SOMEtimes VOICes
> That IF I THEN had WAKED AFter long SLEEP
> Will MAKE me SLEEP aGAIN; and THEN in DREAMing
> The CLOUDS meTHOUGHT would Open and SHOW RICHes
> READy to DROP upON me, that WHEN I WAKED
> I CRIED to DREAM aGAIN. (3.2.138–146)

But wait, you say! This pre-scanned text does not employ the straight line / slack line symbols that students used a few minutes earlier. Why? Because the capitalized syllables not only help students to immediately see stress, but to begin to see meaning. Old English words are primarily monosyllabic: students have told me that handouts like this one help them to understand what the speaker is saying because "the most important words" and word-parts "stand out." Once students have played with the text at the level of its stressed and unstressed syllables, they already know which monosyllabic words and word parts are being emphasized. This in itself can help them grasp meaning.

This format also helps students to see iambic pentameter and the places where irregularities occur. In fact, irregular meter (more or less than five stressed and unstressed syllables in one line), mid-line pauses or breaks, and half-lines are common in Shakespeare's verse. In Caliban's short speech alone, there are seven irregular lines, five mid-line pauses, one mid-line break, and one half-line at the end.

Read the speech metrically, devoid of tone, stressing and unstressing the sounds. Why, students may wonder, is it written like this?

Iambic pentameter is "the point of departure for all Shakespeare's verse" (Rodenburg 85) and the most common line in all poetry written in English (Mason 208). Ask students to think about the why of this—the possibilities are more than poetic. Students may be interested to hear that iambic pentameter mimics the rhythm of the human heart; furthermore, Powell and Halperin report that the length of a ten-syllable line is approximately the amount of text a speaker can comfortably speak aloud in one breath (11). "Among all people," Mason and Nims point out, "five is the natural unit of counting off" (208). Have students look to their hands.

Finally, the acoustics of a Shakespearean line can convey meaning, especially if we pay attention to the places where it becomes irregular. "If the iambic . . . is irregular," Rodenburg points out, "always take note of the content. Something is happening" (93). Iambic pentameter tends to convey order and harmony; irregular and broken lines disturb that order and often indicate "urgency . . . fragmentation . . . unease" (95).

From body language to body English, there are many reasons why Shakespeare wrote plays in iambic pentameter. But surely, he never intended his lines to be spoken metrically. Or did he?

In the fall of 2007, as part of an introduction to Shakespeare's language, I gave students a metrical rendering of the soliloquy Mark Antony speaks over the body of Caesar:

> O PARdon ME, thou BLEEDing PIECE of EARTH,
> That I am MEEK and GENtle WITH these BUTCHers.
> Thou ART the RUins OF the NOblest MAN
> That EVer LIVed IN the TIDE of TIMES.
> WOE to the HAND that SHED this COSTly BLOOD!
> Over thy WOUNDS now DO I PROpheSY—
> Which LIKE dumb MOUTHS do OPE their RUby LIPS
> To BEG the VOICE and UTterance OF my TONGUE—
> A CURSE shall LIGHT upON the LIMBS of MEN;
> DoMEStic FUry and FIERCE CIVil STRIFE
> Shall CUMBer ALL the PARTS of ITalY;
> BLOOD and desTRUCtion SHALL be SO in USE,
> And DREADful OBjects SO faMILiar,
> That MOTHers SHALL but SMILE when THEY beHOLD
> Their INfants QUARTered WITH the HANDS of WAR,
> All PIty CHOKED with CUSTom OF fell DEEDS;
> And CAESer's SPIRit, RANGing FOR reVENGE,
> With ATe BY his SIDE come HOT from HELL,
> Shall IN these CONfines WITH a MONarch's VOICE
> CRY HAVoc! AND let SLIP the DOGS of WAR,
> That THIS foul DEED shall SMELL aBOVE the EARTH
> With CARrion MEN, GROANing for BUrial. (3.1.257–278)

We read it aloud in an exaggerated, sing-song voice and agreed that this is not what Shakespeare wants from his speakers. Then, with the metrical rendering still displayed on the overhead, we listened to track 23 of the audio CD that accompanies the Sourcebooks Shakespeare edition of *Julius Caesar* and includes recordings of the speech by Orson Welles, Adrian Lester, and Herbert Beerbohm Tree. We heard variations in volume, pace, pitch, and tone in each audio performance, but we could still hear in each actor's recitation the iambic pentameter, not as sing-song but as natural speech.

Though each performer represented a different era and acting style, each one had in varying degrees found a way to express the emotional content of the speech—its remorse and rage—at least partially through observance of its metrical form.

The overall effect of speaking Shakespeare's lines metrically and devoid of tone may be, as Pritner and Colaianni write, "a mind-numbing sing-song" (30). Still, reading and speaking one of Shakespeare's speeches metrically can preview its meaning and mood.

Grammatical Soundings

It is not the line but the sentence that carries meaning in Shakespeare's plays. In the close reading of a speech, follow a metrical reading with a grammatical one. Box off every complete thought and examine the architecture of the speech. How many complete thoughts are there? Do you notice internal punctuation—commas, semicolons, dashes? Is every sentence declarative? Which sentence is longest? Mark the action verbs. Mark the nouns.

Most speeches will have three to five sentences. "If more," states Rodenburg, "the character might be unsure or emotionally hesitant. If less, they are very sure and emotionally charged" (113). Internal punctuation marks the twists and turns in a thought as it builds toward a conclusion. Declaratives state while questions and exclamations struggle. As sentences grow in length, the speaker's emotional momentum builds. Verbs are the muscle of the speaker's thoughts; nouns are the bones. Grappling with the grammar of a Shakespearean speech brings us closer to its power and meaning.

If you expect students to have trouble identifying the action verbs and nouns, then prepare a second handout that stresses these parts of speech. Make **action verbs** bold and underline <u>nouns</u>, for example, or make a color-coded transparency:

> Be not afeard. The <u>isle</u> is full of <u>noises,</u>
> <u>Sounds,</u> and sweet <u>airs,</u> that **give** <u>delight</u> and **hurt** not.
> Sometimes a thousand twangling <u>instruments</u>
> Will **hum** about mine <u>ears,</u> and sometimes <u>voices</u>
> That if I then had **waked** after long <u>sleep</u>
> Will **make** me **sleep** again; and then, in <u>dreaming</u>
> The <u>clouds</u> methought would **open,** and **show** <u>riches</u>
> Ready to **drop** upon me, that when I **waked**
> I **cried** to **dream** again.

Practice speaking Caliban's three sentences aloud, placing primary stress on the verbs and secondary stress on the nouns. Then practice speaking it again, picking up emotional momentum in the long third sentence. The abundance of internal punctuation in this sentence suggests a growing sense of wonder that culminates in pathos. The declaratives state without struggle—though he may not fully understand the magic, Caliban has experienced it.

Speaking Shakespeare grammatically, stressing the verbs and nouns, eliminates the "mind-numbing" effects of metrical stress and brings us closer to a meaningful, fluent speaking of the text. But what do we mean by *stressing* nouns and verbs? Most of us take this to mean saying them louder than the words around them. But how else can we stress a word? Next is a list of vocal tools discussed in Chapter 4 of this book:

> **Volume**: Speaking words in a range from soft to loud
>
> **Pitch**: Speaking words in a range from low to high-pitched
>
> **Pace**: Varying the rate of speech with which a word, phrase, or line is spoken
>
> **Pause**: Hesitating before or after a word or phrase is spoken
>
> **Tone**: Conveying attitude or emotion

When speaking Shakespeare, Rodenburg observes that "rhythm and stress are not as important as obedience to the musical use of tone" (90). Review the tone vocabulary charts in Chapter 4 or one your students have generated, and let them experiment with the vocal possibilities, guided by their advanced understanding of what the words, lines, and sentences mean, as well as their understanding of the context of the speech and the emotional subtext of the speaker.

Poetical Soundings

In a book about reading Shakespeare, devoting one full chapter to an examination of Shakespeare's poetic language might seem like a given. However, so much has been written about this aspect of Shakespeare's text that I decided to explore Shakespeare's figurative language in the context of speaking it. In the process of reading and speaking a speech or short scene from Shakespeare for its metrical and grammatical sense, most students will be satisfied with the discoveries they make about the connections between sound, meaning, and expression. But each year I teach a few students who plan to take Shakespeare with them when they go to college, either as English or theater majors. For these students, the process of owning Shakespeare can include one final step.

For Cal Pritner and Louis Colaianni, authors of *How to Speak Shakespeare* and professors in college theater departments, the final step in speaking Shakespeare is to "celebrate the poetry" (51). In what they call a "rhetorical reading," they provide a useful and streamlined guide to this advanced level of expression (51–66):

> Stress monosyllabic verbs, nouns, and modifiers.
> Be guided by the punctuation.
> Play with repeated sounds (alliteration, assonance, repeated words) but "let rhyme take care of itself" (60) lest it overpower everything else.
> Amplify *explaining* words/phrases and *contrasting* words/phrases.

In addition, Patsy Rodenburg, the director of voice at London's Royal National Theater and author of *Speaking Shakespeare*, has a great deal to teach about reading and speaking Shakespeare's poetical language. The following paragraphs on rhyme, poetic and rhetorical devices, and prose are based largely on her work.

Rhyme: Though it pleases the human ear, rhyme also unsettles, especially when it is used in a speech to express mischievous or sinister purposes. Think of the Weird Sisters in *Macbeth* or Puck in *A Midsummer Night's Dream*. Like modern-day rappers in a school hallway, rhymers in Shakespeare can be "showing off" their talent as they perform "bravura speech" (129). Rhyme also can be used to "disguise meaning" (think of the subversive political nature of many nursery rhymes) when truth is too dangerous to be expressed in blank verse or prose (146). Shakespeare's clowns and fools often speak in rhyme to powerful characters. When speakers shift from rhyme to blank verse, it can "often signal a change, a maturing" of thought or of character (131). Finally, rhyming couplets at the ends of speeches convey a sense of closure or resolution. When students select for close reading a speech or scene that rhymes or contains rhyme, they will need to consider why the speaker rhymes, and how the reasons for rhyming can influence the delivery.

Alliteration, Assonance, and Onomatopoeia: Students need to watch and listen for vowel and consonant sound patterns in a speech. Alliteration and assonance weave words together, "not necessarily through sense but sensually" (79). These verbal "pleasures" can be seductive and often sinister. *Othello*'s villainous Iago almost hisses in some speeches, so fond is he of words with *s* and *z* sounds. The up-ness of *ay*, *ee*, and *i* and the down-ness of *oo*, *oh*, and *aw* vowel sounds, mentioned earlier in this chapter, can convey in a deeply primal way the speaker's emotional state. Onomatopoeia expresses our most physical language—*mewling, puking, whining*—and tends to wed content with sound (81–82). When students select a speech in which these sound patterns stand out, they should find ways to stress the physical sounds of words. They should wonder why the speaker is drawn to such sensual devices.

Puns: Exploding like word bombs, puns pack a witty punch, and Shakespeare's play are filled with them. According to Joseph Papp and Elizabeth Kirkland, each of his plays averages "around eighty," and *Love's Labor's Lost* "has an estimated 200" (168). Whether single words with multiple meanings (like *arms* as in limbs but also as in weapons or heraldic insignia), multiple words with the same sound but different spellings (like *sun* and *son*), or clever word substitutions (as in Richard Lederer's "The *pun* is mightier than the sword"), puns are playful and in Shakespeare, often bawdy. Mercutio delights in sexual puns; so too does the team of Petruchio and Katherina in *Shrew*:

> *PETRUCHIO:* Who knows not where a wasp does wear his sting?
> In his tail.
>
> *KATHERINA:* In his tongue.
>
> *PETRUCHIO:* Whose tongue?
>
> *KATHERINA:* Yours, if you talk of tales, and so farewell.
>
> *PETRUCHIO:* What, with my tongue in your tail? (2.1.213–216)

Puns are best spoken knowingly, "to tease, mock, and confound—even yourself" (172).

Antithesis and Irony: When characters in Shakespeare employ these rhetorical devices, it is a mark of their education and intelligence. Antithesis is a form of reasoning that considers both sides and seeks to establish a balance; it explores the tension created by extremes (122). "To be, or not to be," Hamlet may *be* Shakespeare's most antithetical speaker. Characters in Shakespeare resort to irony when "straight talk hasn't worked or is inappropriate" (164). In this sense, irony can be a powerful tool; "By indirections," a character can "find directions out" (*Hamlet* 2.1.65) or, at the very least, conceal an insult with wit. Students have a difficult time recognizing irony, especially in a Shakespearean speech. Rodenburg's explanation is (ironically) direct: "If what your character is saying cannot be true but is not a direct lie, think irony" (167). How irony sounds is somewhere between straightforward and sarcastic.

Repetition: In logical appeals, the repetition of a keyword, phrase, or idea clarifies and emphasizes. But in Shakespeare, repetition often indicates a disturbance in the speaker's thought process. Words in Shakespeare's plays "act like stepping stones—each word a step forward," Rodenburg reasons. "Where there is repetition in a line . . . the character is momentarily overwhelmed" (177). She cites Hamlet's first soliloquy, "O, that this too too solid flesh would melt," as a speech jammed with repeating words and expressions and a prime example of a speech in which a character struggles, almost stutters, to speak fractured thoughts. Such is "the measure of his distress," Rodenburg concludes, that "his natural eloquence has been shattered" (177–179).

Prose: Though some characters in Shakespeare's plays speak prose because their lack of status and education means that prose is all they *can* speak, any character that can shift from prose to verse and vice versa is demonstrating that he or she is sophisticated enough to suit the word to the action. A linguistic shift in Shakespeare indicates a shift in motive, status, or state of mind. Hamlet's prose speech in act 2.2, "I have of late, but wherefore I know not, lost all my mirth," is one of my favorite speeches. Though some argue that Hamlet shifts here from verse to prose because he is addressing Rosencrantz and Guildenstern, inferiors whom he detests, I hear a different voice, a voice of bewildered, aching honesty. Imagine how two such deliveries of the same speech would differ in expression.

"Sometimes," Rodenburg writes, "form speaks almost louder than words" (162). When Brutus shifts from verse to prose to address the Roman mob after assassinating Caesar, he fatally misreads the mood of the crowd. They will respectfully hear him out, but by the time Antony has concluded his verse speech, Brutus is marked a traitor. Both speeches are rhetorically brilliant, but in these circumstances, the crowd hears Brutus's prose as informal and disrespectful. Antony's verse "heightens the debate . . . engages their allegiance—and thereby changes the course of history" (162). Since the ear of a modern audience would be far less sensitive to Brutus's verse, a speaker needs to convey such inappropriate form in the delivery itself.

Pritner and Colaianni's guide is compact and student friendly; Rodenburg's incisive analysis of Shakespeare's poetical devices is not something I can reduce to a checklist. Nonetheless, when I conference with students as they work on their speeches and scenes, my comments and questions to them are informed by her brilliant work.

Spoken Word Shakespeare

In a scene from the 1998 film *Shakespeare in Love*, Viola deLessups (Gwyneth Paltrow) dresses as a boy to audition for a part in Will's new play. After a string of poor players drives Will nearly to despair, his ear is caught by the sounds of an unknown actor reciting a speech from *Two Gentlemen of Verona*, "What light is light, if Sylvia be not seen?" (3.1.174). Like a dove among crows, Viola's recitation is so striking that Will comes suddenly alive and cries, "Where did you learn how to do that?"

After showing my students this film clip in 2008, I asked them what things Viola did well and scribbled their observations on an over-head:

"We can hear her," Samantha said.

"She speaks slowly," Mariany observed.

"Yes," I added, "she articulates every word."

"She pauses in the right places," said Shana.

"Can you be more specific?" I prodded Shana. "What are 'the right places'?"

"She probably let the punctuation guide her, but since we can't see that," Shana proceeded, slowly and thoughtfully as she unwound the string of her thought, "she pauses in order to emphasize the next word, or the next line. It's like she's thinking as she speaks, and not just speaking."

"She loves the speech," Meriam added. "She loves the words."

"Her body language," Jaime observed, "reinforces the words."

Using this conversation as a springboard, I broke the class into small groups and asked them to brainstorm for the essential elements of speaking Shakespeare with clarity and conviction. Synthesizing their ideas with my own observations, the work of professionals cited in this chapter, information about the hierarchy of Elizabethan acting companies in Papp and Kirkland's *Shakespeare Alive!*, and Hamlet's advice to the players in 3.2, I constructed a speaking Shakespeare rubric (Figure 12.3) to use as a guide when students prepare a dramatic reading of a Shakespearean monologue. If I were to use this rubric to arrive at a grade for final recitations, few or none of my students, apprentices all, would earn the A of poet. So we use it during rehearsal periods when students self- and peer-assess their recitations in supportive, small-group practice circles.

As your students read Shakespeare's play, encourage them to apply what they have learned about speaking Shakespeare by explicating a favorite speech or short scene from the assigned play. There is an

Speaking Shakespeare Rubric	Poet	Player	Apprentice	Mechanic
	Though by no means the most wealthy or powerful member of the Company, the poet-playwright is the artist who weaves straw into gold, dreams into reality, words into life.	*From the lowly travel-ing minstrel to the actor who owns a share in the Company, the player is the mature artist who embodies and interprets the words of the poet.*	*Inexperienced but determined to learn, the apprentice practices the parts of the whole – speaking, movement and gesture, singing and dancing, swordplay.*	*From ticket-taker to carpenter, the mechanic is essential to the daily workings of the Company but less concerned with the poetry and the play.*
Voice	Communicates mean-ing through an artful combination of volume, pitch, pace, pause, and tone. Each word is clearly articulated. Each sentence unfolds itself line by line in a natural yet heightened mode of expression. Conveys a keen understanding of the metrical, gram-matical, and rhetorical elements of the text.	Communicates mean-ing through a skillful combination of volume, pitch, pace, pause, and tone. Words are articulated; sentences are spoken with under-standing and appropri-ate emotion, though the effect may be more theatrical than natural. Conveys sensitivity to the metrical, gram-matical, and rhetorical elements of the text.	Communicates mean-ing inconsistently. The vocal tools of volume, pitch, pace, pause, and/or tone may be employed inappropri-ately or inconsistently to the words, lines, and sentences.	Communicates little or no understanding of the words. Fails to use the toolbox of volume, pitch, pace, pause, and/or tone with any sensi-tivity to the words.
Body	Suits the action to the word, the word to the action. Facial expres-sions, gestures, and movement are natural to the speaker and the words.	Facial expressions, ges-tures, and movements are appropriate to the words.	Facial expressions, ges-tures, and movements are limited, awkward, and/or inappropriate.	Saws the air in an in-explicable dumb show, and/or is too tame.
Effect	Holds a mirror up to nature. Speaks and moves with authority and passion tempered by thought. Owns the words.	Speaks and moves with an intuitive under-standing of the dra-matic power of the text. Performs the words.	Rehearses the words.	Mouths the words.

Figure 12.3. Speaking Shakespeare rubric.

excellent framework for speech explication in *Shakespeare Set Free: Teaching Henry IV Part 1*, Lesson 12.

At the end of the first semester in the Shakespeare class, I assign a summative project in which students choose a speech or short scene from one of the plays we have read, analyze in writing the language, the speaker, and the poetry, prepare a sound track and a storyboard, and perform a dramatic reading. By setting aside the last two weeks of the semester for focused review and guided practice, students take ownership of a passage from Shakespeare and apply what they are learning about reading, speaking, viewing, and hearing Shakespeare (Figure 12.4). This project, whose first draft I composed in the winter of 2003 and have continuously revised, reflects what I have learned from the experts cited in this chapter and throughout this book, and from the waves of students who have gathered with me over the pages of Shakespeare's text. It reflects in miniature the kind of daily work we do in the classroom, and informs my lesson plans and first semester course syllabus.

Speak, I Am Bound to Hear

As a teacher of Shakespeare's plays, I see a clear need to provide young adults with a series of steps they can take to become not only readers but also speakers of Shakespeare's text. His lines are written to engage the senses: reading Shakespeare only with the eyes constitutes a form of sensory deprivation.

As a teacher of the English language arts, I know from the Frameworks produced by each state that we are expected to teach not only reading and writing in our content area but also listening, speaking, and viewing in multiple modes. These are the five strands or building blocks of literacy. Since what's on the test (meaning state-mandated exit/competency tests) is reading and writing, it's all too tempting to focus on those skills and to disregard the fact that listening, speaking, and viewing are not only ELA skills but life skills.

These are my broad, professional reasons for asking students to listen more closely to Shakespeare's language and to practice speaking the words with clarity and conviction. But there are personal reasons, too.

One of my fondest memories of Rob Watson, head scholar at the Folger Teaching Shakespeare Institute from 1998 to 2004, would be repeated at the end of every brilliant lecture he delivered from the stage of the Elizabethan theater. "Cheated death again," he'd whisper with a wry little smile as he exited the theater. By speaking, I don't mean the

Reading, Writing, and Speaking Shakespeare

Choose an excerpt from a play by William Shakespeare that is personally meaningful to you. The excerpt should be from a play we have studied in this semester. The excerpt should be a monologue of about 20 lines in length. Tell me in advance which speech you have chosen.

Copy and paste the text from an online source into a Word document, or carefully type the text. Proofread for any errors in spelling or punctuation and for any omissions. Include the source (for example, *The Oxford Shakespeare, The Folger Library, The Arden Shakespeare*, etc.). If the lines of the text are not already numbered, number them yourself to use as reference markers in your writing. Do not mark every line with a number; number every fifth line (1, 5, 10, 15, and so on) in the far right margin.

Page 1: Vocabulary
List each word in the text that you do not understand and look it up in an unabridged dictionary such as the *Oxford English Dictionary* (OED). The beauty of the OED is that it gives a series of definitions in chronological order so that you can learn how we use the word today and how people in Shakespeare's time used the word. Pay close attention to the multiple meanings of a single word: Shakespeare often used a word because of its multiple meanings.

Instead of copying definitions, comment in writing on what you learned about each word.

Page 2: Primary Sources
Find the speech as it appeared in the **First Folio** of 1623 by going to an electronic archive or using our classroom edition of the Yale Facsimile. Print out or copy it and set it side-by-side with the text of the modern edition. Read both carefully for similarities and differences. Have any words, phrases, lines, or punctuation marks changed from the Folio text to the modern edition of the text?

Note any changes in writing. Comment if those changes strike you as interesting or unusual.

Page 3: Meter
Read the speech aloud several times, listening for its rhythm. For example, a line of iambic pentameter has five unstressed and five stressed syllables and would sound like "Ta DUM ta DUM ta DUM ta DUM ta DUM."

Based on your knowledge of meter and syllabication (you can check the way a word is syllabicated in a dictionary), type the text metrically, using lower case letters for unstressed syllables and capital letters for stressed syllables.

Comment in writing on how regular or irregular the meter is in the lines, and note lines that deviate from the norms of blank verse (unrhymed iambic pentameter). Remember that iambic pentameter tends to convey order and harmony while irregular and broken lines disturb the order and harmony. What is happening in the irregular lines? What is the connection between meter and meaning?

continued on next page

Figure 12.4. Reading, writing, and speaking Shakespeare.

Figure 12.4. continued

> **Page 4: Grammar**
> Annotate the grammatical elements of the text by formatting every **action verb** in bold. Format every <u>noun</u> in the text by underlining. Box off each sentence. Highlight in yellow every punctuation mark (commas, colons, periods, question and exclamation marks). Note the sentence lengths. Note the sentence types—declarative, interrogatory, exclamatory, and imperative. Read each sentence aloud for its full thought.
>
> Practice speaking the text aloud with primary stress on the verbs and secondary stress on the nouns. Practice speaking the text by "walking" it, speaking it aloud while moving, and changing direction at each punctuation mark. Practice speaking the text with greater emotional momentum in the longest sentence.
>
> Comment in writing on the extent to which the power and meaning of this speech is concentrated in its action verbs and nouns. Comment on the effects of the punctuation. Comment on the number and length of the sentences. Describe the emotional state of the speaker and comment on the ways in which the emotions can be seen and heard in the grammatical structures of the text.
>
> **Page 5: Tone**
> Tone is the speaker's emotional attitude. Tone often shifts during the course of a speech or scene as the speaker changes or clarifies his/her thinking. Annotate the text by marking it with tone words.
>
> Characterize in writing the tone(s) of the text. Does the tone shift? Where and why?
>
> **Page 6: Poetry**
> Annotate the literary elements of the text by marking figures of speech—imagery, similes and metaphors, personification, oxymorons, puns, irony, devices that enhance sound such as alliteration and rhyme; rhetorical devices such as repetition, parallelism, and antithesis. Label each example of figurative and rhetorical language that you find.
>
> Practice speaking the speech aloud, this time stressing the most playful and powerful literary devices.
>
> Comment in writing on the ways in which the figurative language (or the lack of it) conveys and enhances the meaning of the speech.
>
> **Page 7: Character Analysis**
> Answer these questions in writing:
> What (in the speaker) motivates the speech or dialogue?
> What does the text reveal about the speaker?
> Why did you choose this speech or scene?
>
> **Page 8: Sound Track**
> Practice speaking the text with clarity and conviction, paying attention to the approximate amount of time it takes to speak the speech or scene. What sounds
>
> *continued on next page*

Figure 12.4. continued

would be natural to the environment in which the text is spoken? (Remember that silence, or the absence of sound, can be part of the dramatic "sound" necessary to a scene.) What sounds are suggested by the words themselves? What added sounds (music, sound effects) would contribute to the dramatic impact of the text?

Construct a Cue Sheet with three columns and compose a sound track for a dramatic performance of the speech or scene:

Cue Sheet		
Sound	First 3–5 words of a line or sentence	Time in sequence

Page 9: Storyboard
Create a storyboard in six to eight frames that illustrate the dramatic sequence of the speech or scene for a film production:

Shot #

Line being spoken:

Intended Effect of Shot:

Diegetic Sound:

Nondiegetic Sound:

Shot Type:

Angle: Lighting:

Movement:

Edit:

Page 10: Speaking the Speech or Scene
Synthesize everything you now understand about the power and beauty of the speech or scene by preparing a dramatic reading of the text. Write directorial commentary in the margins of the text to guide your reading, with notes about volume, pitch, pace, pause, and tone. Perform your reading with clarity and conviction.

continued on next page

Figure 12.4. continued

You can memorize your lines for extra credit, and you can prepare a skeletal outline to guide you as you speak from memory.

Grading

You will earn a grade based upon these qualities of your work:

The written work
• is complete,
• is organized and easy to read,
• displays depth of thought.

The dramatic reading or memorization
• is complete and accurate,
• is articulate
• conveys understanding of and sensitivity to the words.

Component:	Maximum Points:	Points Earned:
Vocabulary	5 points	
Primary Sources	5 points	
Meter	10 points	
Grammar	10 points	
Tone	10 points	
Poetry	10 points	
Character Analysis	10 points	
Sound Track	10 points	
Storyboard	10 points	
Speech Delivery	20 points	
FINAL GRADE:		
Comments:		

sort of lively conversations with students, teachers, or parents that occur naturally in our profession; I mean those formal, official moments when we must step to the podium and deliver ourselves to others. And I mean something more: there is a direct connection between public speaking and speaking up, and it is speaking up and out—to power, to indifference, to injustice—that matters in a democracy.

What does this have to do with Shakespeare?

It was in a Shakespeare class taught by Caleen Jennings, author and theater professor at American University and colleague and friend at the Folger Teaching Shakespeare Institute, that I finally learned how to speak under pressure and to use my voice not only as a teacher but as a private person in some very public places. As I participated in her TSI theater classes in 2002, this teacher of teachers challenged us all to select a speech that appealed to us from the play we were reading, memorize it, and deliver it from the stage to an audience of our peers. She coached us every step of the way, and would brook no excuses from the shy. "It's you shy ones," she told me in private, "who have the most to say." And then she turned to the whole group and made us repeat her mantra, "Whose stage is it? *My* stage," to psyche us past our fears. In the years since 2002, I have spoken at the funeral of a dear friend and at the wedding of a young couple dear to me as my own children; I have spoken on behalf of a victim in federal court. In each of these situations, I heard Caleen's voice in my head reassuring me that I had already done this on a stage at the Folger, and that I could do it again, and better.

When we ask students to select a Shakespearean speech or passage that speaks to them in some fundamental way, and to read it again and again to gain some fuller understanding of its beauty and power, and then to speak it to us with clarity and conviction, we are asking them to expose some part of themselves—a need, a passion, a sorrow. I can't count the times a student has asked me if he or she can deliver the speech just to me, and if I could try not to look but just to listen. Beyond the nervousness that most of us feel about public speaking, these are moments when I sense that students have selected a speech that says what they wish they could say to someone who loves them or has hurt them. I always say yes, and even then there are tears and broken voices.

But that's okay. There will be times in the lives of these students when they will need both the courage and the skill to speak words that matter, out loud and in public. Then perhaps they too will remember the time they had to stand and deliver Shakespeare and see it as the dress rehearsal it was for what they now must do—raise their voices on behalf of themselves and others.

The most difficult words I have ever spoken in public were spoken because a Shakespeare teacher told me I could do it, and made me practice.

Epilogue: Independent Reading

Knowing I loved my books, he furnished me
From mine own library with volumes that
I prize above my dukedom.

The Tempest 1.2.167–169

In the fall of 2003, the library media specialist at Revere High School, Debra Molle, handed me a list of young adult literature titles related to Shakespeare's plays and lots of encouragement to consider adopting some for independent reading in my classes. Though Molle understood and supported my passion for teaching Shakespeare's *Macbeth* and *Hamlet* to sophomores, she was concerned about the amount of time teachers like me were devoting to this 400-year-old poet and playwright. Her timing was perfect: I was one of many English teachers at our school concerned about the classics-driven nature of our required reading lists and the lack of time relegated during the school day to independent reading.

With the support of my director, I started to set aside classroom time for independent reading. Students could borrow a book from our school library, bring in a book of their own, or borrow a book from the small but growing collection of Shakespearean spin-offs (and other YAL books) that I kept in plastic storage crates at the back of my room. Debra Molle continued to update the list with new titles and to order multiple copies of the best books for the school library. The list of YAL Shakespearean spin-offs can be found in the last section of this chapter.

Every English teacher knows what comes next, but I will nonetheless proceed: Providing a roomful of reluctant readers with a book and a chunk of time is the easy part; getting them to read (even high-interest, low-level books with enticing covers and colorful graphics) is the challenge. I decided to set aside most Fridays for independent reading, and there were a few Fridays with a few groups when independent reading was mistaken for recess. But for most of my students most of the time, the twenty- to thirty-minute independent reading sessions were just that, and the fifteen- to twenty-minute reading reports that they filed before the bell were thoughtful, interesting, and fresh. Since I didn't have multiple copies of most books, literature circles were not an option, but students would often recommend a book they had enjoyed to a friend, and even the students who never seemed to settle on one book that they liked enough to stick with usually enjoyed sampling a new book each Friday.

Through trial and error, I drafted a reading report assignment sheet (Figure 13.1) and a reading report form (Figure 13.2) for students to record their written work.

Once or twice in a ten-week quarter, at the end of class on the fifth Friday, I collated and stapled together five reading reports for one grade. At first, it was not my intention to have students write about their reading or to grade what they wrote, but I found it necessary to add this "incentive" to the project. Still, most of the students appreciated the balance that independent reading and YAL bring to the required reading of classical literature and teacher-centered instruction. And the students who chose to read the modern Shakespearean spin-offs consistently remarked that these books enhanced their comprehension and enjoyment of Shakespeare's early modern text.

Pop-Shakespeare

The interest level (IL) of most books on this list is characterized by Follett Library Resources as "young adult" (YA), but the reading levels (RL) range between grades 4 and 7. A few of the books on this list have been written for adult readers (AD), but I include them because some secondary readers can still enjoy them as independent reading. Though this list of books is by no means complete, it is a good place to start. The publication information for most of these books is supplied by Follett Library Resources.

Ariel by Grace Tiffany. The novel retells *The Tempest* from the point of view of Ariel, the airy spirit.
Publisher: Harper Collins
Year: 2005
IL: YA

Blue Avenger Cracks the Code by Norma Howe. A sixteen-year-old boy visits Venice, Italy, where he and his friends experience Shakespeare's *The Merchant of Venice* in their own contemporary lives.
Publisher: Holt
Year: 2000
IL: YA

Active Reading Reports

Good readers are active readers. An active reader is a reader who:
- questions the author and the text
- clarifies what is confusing in the text
- comments on the text
- summarizes the text
- predicts what will come next
- makes connections between the text and life.

Periodically, I will set aside twenty to thirty minutes of class time for independent reading. At the end of the reading period, you will file a reading report. Select any ONE of these activities for your report. As the weeks pass, be sure to attempt a variety of activities.

(A) Copy five to six short quotations from the text that interest, intrigue, and captivate you. They don't have to be connected—they can be from different parts of the text. After you copy each quote, comment in one to two sentences about what you like/learned/wonder about each quote.

(B) What confuses you as you read? Turn your confusion into three or more questions. Write down your questions, then attempt to answer them, using the text as your guide.

(C) Choose a part of the book that you do not like and turn your dislike into a question for the author. After you write your question, attempt to answer it as the author might, in five to seven sentences. You may choose to have the author admit that he or she could have written it differently, and better.

(D) If you finished the book and did not like the ending, write what you think should have happened, citing reasons and examples to support your opinion.

(E) If you are not near the end of the book yet, list several events in the book that you have read so far and based upon them, predict a possible ending to the book. Make sure you explain why you think this will or should happen based on the events you listed.

(F) Choose a character from the book who angers/frustrates/worries you. Write a letter of advice to that character in a minimum of five to seven sentences. Be sure that you letter helps me to understand why this character needs advice.

(G) Looking at the book in an historical context, what are some things that may have been different in the book if the book were set in a different time period (either a more modern or a more historical period)?

(H) Find five new words that you did not understand. Copy the sentence in which each word is found. Look up each word in a dictionary and copy the definition. Write a sentence using each new word—make sure your sentences have solid context clues.

(I) Create a quiz of five multiple-choice questions (with answers) for your reading today.

(J) Write about what you think a major theme/point of a selection is in five to seven setences.

(K) If you are near the end of the book, draw a timeline of the major events.

In order to receive full credit for these reports:
- Reports must be the minimum length stated in the activity.
- Reports must be legible—I must be able to read them.
- Reports must be completed during class—manage your time!
- Reports must show thought and effort.

Figure 13.1. Reading report assignment sheet.

Name:_____   Date:_____

Active Reading Report

Title of Book:_____

Author:_____

Chapter #:_____   Pages read today:_____

Label your entry with the correct letter (A–K). Then complete your entry on this page (*you may continue on the back if necessary*).

ENTRY LETTER:

Figure 13.2. Active reading report.

The Book of Sand and Shakespeare's Memory by Jorge Luis Borges. A collection of stories written by the Argentine writer.
Publisher: Penguin
Year: 2007
IL: AD

The Best of Shakespeare by Edith Nesbit. Simplified prose retellings of ten Shakespearean plays; includes photographs from modern stage productions.
Publisher: Oxford UP
Year: 1999
IL: YA

Dating Hamlet: Ophelia's Story by Lisa Fiedler. *Hamlet* retold as a romantic novel in the voice of Ophelia.
Publisher: Holt
Year: 2002
IL: YA

Enter Three Witches: A Story of Macbeth by Caroline B. Cooney. A fourteen-year-old ward of Lord and Lady Macbeth uncovers their secret plans. Includes lines from Shakespeare's play.
Publisher: Scholastic
Year: 2007
IL: YA

Hamlet's Trap by Janice Greene. Inspired by the play *Hamlet*, a young man investigates his father's death after his mother's hasty remarriage.
Publisher: Saddleback
Year: 2004
IL: YA

Loving Will Shakespeare by Carolyn Meyer. Written in the voice of Anne Hathaway, this novel tells the story of her marriage to Will Shakespeare.
Publisher: Harcourt
Year: 2008
IL: YA

Ophelia: A Novel by Lisa M. Klein. The story of *Hamlet*, retold (and reshaped) by Ophelia, who escapes.
Publisher: Bloomsbury

Year: 2006
IL: YA

The Playmaker by J. B. Cheaney. Set in 1597, a fourteen-year-old apprentice in a London theater company uncovers a mystery and a plot to overthrow the Queen.
Publisher: Dell
Year: 2002
IL: YA

Saving Juliet by Suzanne Selfors. A seventeen-year-old American actress is transported back in time to Verona, where she gives the real Juliet a happy ending.
Publisher: Walker
Year: 2008
IL: YA

Shakespeare's Criminals: Criminology, Fiction, and Drama by Victoria M. Time. A study of William Shakespeare's characterizations of criminal and deviant behavior, and the ways in which his works examine the effects of crime on society.
Publisher: Greenwood Press
Year: 1999
IL: AD

Shakespeare's Scribe by Gary L. Blackwood. A sequel to *The Shakespeare Stealer*; a fifteen-year-old orphan boy becomes an apprentice actor in Shakespeare's company.
Publisher: Penguin
Year: 2002
IL: YA

Shakespeare's Spy by Gary L. Blackwood. An orphan boy in William Shakespeare's acting company investigates several backstage thefts.
Publisher: Penguin
Year: 2005
IL: YA

The Shakespeare Stealer by Gary L. Blackwood. A young orphan boy is ordered by his master to infiltrate Shakespeare's acting troupe in order to steal the script of *Hamlet*.

Publisher: Penguin
Year: 1998
IL: YA

Something Rotten: A Horatio Wilkes Mystery by Alan Gratz. A contemporary retelling of *Hamlet*, reset in Denmark, Tennessee.
Publisher: Penguin
Year: 2007
IL: YA

Spanking Shakespeare by Jake Wizner. A high school student, teased because he is named after Shakespeare, gets his revenge through a school writing project.
Publisher: Random House
Year: 2007
IL: YA

The Third Witch by Rebecca Reisert. A rich prose retelling of *Macbeth* in the voice of Gilly, youngest of the three witches.
Publisher: Washington Square Press
Year: 2002
IL: AD, YA

This Must Be Love by Tui Sutherland. The worlds of *Romeo and Juliet* and *A Midsummer Night's Dream* collide in the lives of two high school friends.
Publisher: Harper Collins
Year: 2004
IL: YA

True Prince by J. B. Cheaney. A sequel to *The Playmaker*, this mystery focuses on London's finest boy actor, who is very much like Prince Hal of Shakespeare's *Henry IV*.
Publisher: Knopf
Year: 2002
IL: YA

Notes

1. This term is most often used to mean words that "a reader can 'see and say' instantly" (Ericson 16). Kylene Beers points out that "the terms *sight words* and *high-frequency words*" are sometimes used interchangeably (223).

2. The story of the textual authenticity of Shakespeare's plays is far too complex for an endnote, but suffice it to say here that quartos are small, printed, single-play publications that earned their name from the fact that their pages were about one-quarter the size of a "standard" sheet of 18-inch by 14-inch paper. Quartos were printed, most during Shakespeare's lifetime, from one or more handwritten texts, and preceded the printing of the First Folio in 1623, which was a large, bound collection of thirty-six of Shakespeare's plays published seven years after his death. About half of the plays in the Folio had already been printed as quartos, but there are many discrepancies between the quartos and the Folio texts (McDonald 194–199).

3. The term *reading aloud* invokes round-robin reading, "defined in *The Literacy Dictionary* as the outmoded practice of calling on students to read orally one after the other" (qtd. in Opitz & Rasinski 6). Kylene Beers describes round-robin reading as "taking turns up and down the rows with each student reading one paragraph aloud; the problem is, students count ahead to their one paragraph, rehearse it so they'll get it right, then tune out" (199). Neither Ericson nor Beers endorses this, but rather voluntary oral reading by fluent readers, as well as "readers' theater performances and choral reading" (Ericson 9–10).

4. I've settled on the final arrangement of jobs on the "Shakespeare Classifieds" sheet from Questioner first to Summarizer last by order of importance, not necessarily importance to the act of reading itself but to the act of reading Shakespeare. When you consider the relative unimportance of plot (either students already know what happens in the play or they are reading scene summaries supplied by us and/or others) and the fact that in most editions, there are ample footnotes to help them with the vocabulary, then the roles of Prophet, Vocabularian, and Summarizer are less pertinent than the roles listed before them.

Works Cited

Adler, Mortimer. "How to Mark a Book," from The Mercury Reader. *Building Academic Literacy: An Anthology for Reading Apprenticeship*. Ed. Audrey Fielding and Ruth Schoenbach. San Francisco: Jossey-Bass, 2003. 179–184.

Allen, Janet. "Mastering the Art of Effective Vocabulary Instruction." *Adolescent Literacy: Turning Promise into Practice*. Ed. G. Kylene Beers, Robert E. Probst, Linda Rief. Portsmouth, NH: Heinemann, 2007. 87–104.

Alvermann, Donna E. "Multiliterate Youth in the Time of Scientific Reading Instruction." *Adolescent Literacy: Turning Promise into Practice*. Ed. G. Kylene Beers, Robert E. Probst, and Linda Rief. Portsmouth, NH: Heinemann, 2007. 19–26.

————. "Why Bother Theorizing Adolescents' Online Literacies for Classroom Practice and Research?" *Journal of Adolescent and Adult Literacy* 52.1 (2008): 8–19.

Applebee, Arthur N. *Literature in the Secondary School: Studies of Curriculum and Instruction in the United States*. NCTE Research Report, No. 25. Urbana, IL: NCTE, 1993.

Barton, Robert. *Acting: Onstage and Off*. 2nd ed. Fort Worth: Harcourt Brace Jovanovich College, 1993.

Bate, Jonathan. *The Genius of Shakespeare*. London: Picador, 1997.

Beach, Richard, and David G. O'Brien. "Adopting Reader and Writer Stances in Understanding and Producing Texts." *Secondary School Literacy: What Research Reveals for Classroom Practice*. Ed. Leslie S. Rush, A. Jonathan Eakle, and Allen Berger. Urbana, IL: NCTE, 2007. 217–242.

Beck, Isabel L., Margaret G. McKeown, and Linda Kucan. *Bringing Words to Life: Robust Vocabulary Instruction*. New York: Guilford Press, 2002.

Beers, G. Kylene. *When Kids Can't Read, What Teachers Can Do: A Guide for Teachers, 6–12*. Portsmouth, NH: Heinemann, 2003.

Blacker, Irwin R. *The Elements of Screenwriting: A Guide for Film and Television Writers*. New York: Macmillan, 1986.

Bomer, Randy. "Reading with the Mind's Ear: Listening to Text as a Mental Action." *Journal of Adolescent and Adult Literacy* 49.6 (2006): 524–535.

Branagh, Kenneth, and William Shakespeare. *Hamlet*. New York: W. W. Norton, 1996.

Brown, Matthew D. "I'll Have Mine Annotated, Please: Helping Students Make Connections with Texts." *English Journal* 96.4 (2007): 73–78.

Buchanan, Judith. *Shakespeare on Film*. Harlow, England: Pearson Longman, 2005.

Burchers, Sam, Max Burchers, and Bryan Burchers. *Vocabulary Cartoons: Building an Educated Vocabulary with Visual Mnemonics*. Punta Gorda, FL: New Monic Books, 1997.

Cohen, Ralph Alan. *ShakesFear and How to Cure It: A Handbook for Teaching Shakespeare*. Clayton, DE.: Prestwick House, 2007.

Costanzo, William V. *Great Films and How to Teach Them*. Urbana, IL: NCTE, 2004.

Curtis, Mary E. "Adolescent Reading: A Synthesis of Research." National Institute of Child Health and Human Development. 20 May 2002 <http://216.26.160.105/conf/nichd/synthesis.asp>.

DaLie, Sandra Okura. "Students Becoming Real Readers: Literature Circles in High School English Classes." *Teaching Reading in High School English Classes*. Ed. Bonnie O. Ericson. Urbana, IL: NCTE, 2001. 84–100.

Daniels, Harvey. *Literature Circles: Voice and Choice in Book Clubs and Reading Groups*. 2nd ed. Portland, ME: Stenhouse, 2002.

Deshler, Donald D., Annmarie Sullivan Palincsar, Gina Biancarosa, and Marnie Nair. *Informed Choices for Struggling Adolescent Readers: A Research-Based Guide to Instructional Programs and Practices*. Newark, DE: IRA, 2007.

Encyclopedia of Television. Ed. Horace Newcomb. 3 vols. Chicago: Fitzroy Dearborn Publishers, 1997.

Ericson, Bonnie O. Ed. *Teaching Reading in High School English Classes*. Urbana, IL: NCTE, 2001.

Erne, Lukas. *Shakespeare as Literary Dramatist*. Cambridge: Cambridge University Press, 2003.

Flannery, Mary Ellen. "Born in the U.S.A.: And Other Things You Might Not Know about Today's English Language Learners." *NEA Today* 27.4 (2009): 24–29.

Garber, Marjorie B. *Shakespeare and Modern Culture*. New York: Pantheon Books, 2008.

Gibson, Rex, and Janet Field-Pickering. *Discovering Shakespeare's Language: 150 Stimulating Activity Sheets for Student Work*. Cambridge: Cambridge University Press, 1998.

Goddard, Harold Clarke. *The Meaning of Shakespeare*. 2 vols. Chicago: University of Chicago Press, 1951.

Golden, John. *Reading in the Dark: Using Film as a Tool in the English Classroom*. Urbana, IL: NCTE, 2001.

Greenblatt, Stephen. *Will in the World: How Shakespeare Became Shakespeare*. New York: W. W. Norton, 2004.

"Hamlet on the Ramparts." Dir. Peter S. Donaldson. Massachusetts Institute of Technology. Aug. 2008 <http://shea.mit.edu/ramparts>.

Heid, Jim, and Ted Lai. *The Macintosh iLife '06 in the Classroom*. Berkeley, CA: Peachpit Press, 2006.

Henry V. Dir. Kenneth Branagh. MGM, 1989.

Henry V. Dir. Laurence Olivier. MGM, 1944.

Hirsch, E. D., Jr. "Reading Comprehension Requires Knowledge—of Words and the World." *American Educator*. 27.1 (2003): 10–29.

Hunt, Douglas. *The Riverside Anthology of Literature*. 3rd ed. Boston: Houghton Mifflin, 1997.

"In Search of Shakespeare." Ed. Mark Love. 2003. PBS. Aug. 2008 <http://pbs.org/shakespeare>.

Kahn, Copellia. "Julius Caesar: A Modern Perspective." *The Tragedy of Julius Caesar*. The New Folger Library Shakespeare. Ed. Barbara A Mowat and Paul Werstine. New York: Washington Square Press, 1992.

Keats, John. "Ode on a Grecian Urn." *England in Literature*. 7th ed. Ed. Helen M. McDonnell, John Pfordresher, and Gladys V. Veidemanis. Glenview, IL: Scott, Foresman, 1985. 408–409.

Keene, Ellin Oliver. "The Essence of Understanding." *Adolescent Literacy: Turning Promise into Practice*. Ed. G. Kylene Beers, Robert E. Probst, Linda Rief. Portsmouth, NH: Heinemann, 2007. 27–38.

Krueger, Ellen, and Mary T. Christel. *Seeing and Believing: How to Teach Media Literacy in the English Classroom*. Portsmouth, NH: Boynton/Cook Publishers-Heinemann, 2001.

Lederer, Richard. *Get Thee to a Punnery: An Anthology of Intentional Assaults upon the English Language*. Layton, UT: Wyrick & Co., 1988 and 2006.

LoMonico, Michael. *The Shakespeare Book of Lists: The Ultimate Guide to the Bard, His Plays, and How They've Been Interpreted (and Misinterpreted) through the Ages*. Franklin Lakes, NJ: New Page Books, 2001.

Looking for Richard. Dir. Al Pacino. Twentieth Century Fox, 1996.

Mason, David, and John Frederick Nims. *Western Wind: An Introduction to Poetry*. 5th ed. Boston: McGraw Hill, 2006.

McDonald, Russ. *The Bedford Companion to Shakespeare: An Introduction with Documents*. Boston: Bedford/St. Martin's, 2001.

Mellor, Bronwyn. *Reading Hamlet*. The NCTE Chalkface Series. Urbana, IL: NCTE, 1999.

A Midsummer Night's Dream. Dir. Michael Hoffman. Twentieth Century Fox, 1999.

A Midsummer Night's Dream. Dir. Max Reinhardt. Warner Bros., 1935.

Mitchell, Jonathan. "Reading Shakespeare on Film: Thinking Like a Director to Improve Understanding." 29 Nov. 2005. *Reading Shakespeare*. 15 Aug. 2008 <http://readingshakespeare.org>.

Neergaard, Lauran. "Toddler talking takes off once enough easy words learned, researchers say." *The Boston Globe*. 3 Aug. 2007: A10.

Norman, Marc, and Tom Stoppard. *Shakespeare in Love: A Screenplay*. New York: Hyperion, Miramax Books, 1998.

O. Dir. Tim Blake Nelson. Miramax, 2001.

O'Brien, Peggy. *Shakespeare Set Free*. 3 vols. New York: Washington Square Press, 1993–95.

Opitz, Michael F., Timothy V. Rasinski, and Lois Bridges Bird. *Good-Bye Round Robin: Twenty-five Effective Oral Reading Strategies*. Portsmouth, NH: Heinemann, 1998.

Orgel, Stephen. *Imagining Shakespeare: A History of Texts and Visions*. New York: Palgrave Macmillan, 2003.

O'Toole, Fintan. *Shakespeare Is Hard, but so Is Life: A Radical Guide to Shakespearean Tragedy*. New York: Granta, 2002.

Papp, Joseph, and Elizabeth Kirkland. *Shakespeare Alive!* Toronto: Bantam, 1988.

Pauk, Walter, and Ross J. Q. Owens. *How to Study in College*. 9th ed. Boston: Houghton Mifflin Co., 2008.

Porter-O'Donnell, Carol. "Beyond the Yellow Highlighter: Teaching Annotation Skills to Improve Reading Comprehension." *English Journal* 93.5 (2004): 82–89.

Porter, Christina. "Beating Up Shakespeare." 16 Nov. 2005. *Reading Shakespeare*. 1 Sept. 2008 <http://readingshakespeare.org>.

Powell, Joseph, and Mark Halperin. *Accent on Meter: A Handbook for Readers of Poetry*. Urbana, IL: NCTE, 2004.

Pritner, Cal, and Louis Colaianni. *How to Speak Shakespeare*. Santa Monica, CA; Santa Monica Press LLC, 2001.

Rabkin, Norman. "Rabbits, Ducks, and *Henry V*." *Shakespeare: An Anthology of Criticism and Theory, 1945–2000*. Ed. Russ McDonald. Malden, MA: Blackwell Pub., 2004. 245–263.

Revere Public Schools Home Page. 15 Sept. 08 <http://www.revereps.mec.edu>.

Richardson, Will. *Blogs, Wikis, Podcasts, and Other Powerful Web Tools for Classrooms*. Thousand Oaks, CA: Corwin Press, 2006.

Rodenburg, Patsy. *Speaking Shakespeare*. New York: Palgrave Macmillan, 2002.

Rosenbaum, Ron. *The Shakespeare Wars: Clashing Scholars, Public Fiascoes, Palace Coups*. New York: Random House, 2006.

Rosenblatt, Louise M. *Literature as Exploration*. 5th ed. New York: Modern Language Association of America, 1995.

Saphier, Jon, and Robert R. Gower. *The Skillful Teacher: Building Your Teaching Skills*. Acton, MA: Research for Better Teaching, 1997.

Schmidt, Alexander, and Gregor Sarrazin. *Shakespeare Lexicon and Quotation Dictionary.* 2 vols. New York: Dover Publications, 1971.

Shakespeare Illustrated. Ed. Harry Rusche. Emory University. Aug. 08 <http://shakespeare.emory.edu>.

Shakespeare, William, Richard Andrews, and Rex Gibson. *Hamlet.* Cambridge: Cambridge University Press, 1994.

Shakespeare, William, Marilyn Bell, Elizabeth Dane, and John Dane. *King Henry V.* Cambridge: Cambridge University Press, 1993.

Shakespeare, William, and Rex Gibson, series ed. *Cambridge School Shakespeare.* Cambridge: Cambridge University Press, 1991–2008.

Shakespeare, William, John Jowett, William Montgomery, Gary Taylor, and Stanley Wells. *The Oxford Shakespeare: The Complete Works.* 2nd ed. Oxford: Clarendon Press, 2005.

Shakespeare, William, Barbara A. Mowat, and Paul Werstine. *The Tragedy of Othello, the Moor of Venice.* New Folger Library Shakespeare. New York: Washington Square Press, 1993.

Shakespeare, William, and Robert Ormsby. *Julius Caesar.* The Sourcebooks Shakespeare. Naperville, IL: Sourcebooks MediaFusion, 2006.

Shamburg, Christopher. *English Language Arts Units for Grades 9–12.* Eugene, OR: International Society for Technology in Education, 2008.

Sheltering Content for English Language Learners. ACCESS (Actively Connecting Content, English, Students, and Standards.) Brattleboro, VT: School for International Training, 2006.

Silverbush, Rhona, and Sami Plotkin. *Speak the Speech!: Shakespeare's Monologues Illuminated.* New York: Faber and Faber, 2002.

The American Heritage Dictionary of the English Language. 4th ed. Boston: Houghton Mifflin, 2000.

Theodosakis, Nikos, and Ian Jukes. *The Director in the Classroom: How Filmmaking Inspires Learning.* San Diego, CA: Tech4Learning Publishing, 2001.

Thomas, Dylan. "Do Not Go Gentle into That Good Night." *England in Literature.* Ed. Helen McDonnell, John Pfordresher, and Gladys V. Veidemanis. 7th ed. Glenview, IL: Scott, Foresman, 1987. 769–770.

Thomas, Lewis. *The Lives of a Cell: Notes of a Biology Watcher.* New York: Bantam Books, 1974.

Videopaper in the Classroom. 2008. Education Dept., Tufts U. 28 Sept. 08 <http://ase.tufts.edu/education/projects/projectVideopaper.asp>.

United States. National Endowment for the Arts. *To Read or Not To Read: A Question of National Consequence. Executive Summary.* Research Report No. 47. Washington: Office of Research and Analysis, 2007.

Wright, George T. "The Play of Phrase and Line." *Shakespeare: An Anthology of Criticism and Theory, 1945–2000.* Ed. Russ McDonald. Malden, MA: Blackwell Pub., 2004.

Index

Author

Mary Ellen Dakin, a National Board Certified Teacher, has taught English language arts since 1987 in both a private and a public secondary school. A fellowship at the Folger Shakespeare Library in 1994 sparked her passion for exploring innovative ways to teach Shakespeare's plays, and since that time she has presented workshops on teaching Shakespeare in cities throughout the country. From 2002 to 2006, she was a master teacher at the Folger Library's Teaching Shakespeare Institute. She was elected to the National Council of Teachers of English's Secondary Section Steering Committee in 2006. Her essays have appeared in *Shakespeare* magazine, the *Harvard Educational Review*, and *English Journal*.

Dakin's focus on adolescent literacy moved to the forefront of her practice after participating in the National Research Council's Panel on Learning and Instruction in 2001–02.

At Revere High School, Dakin teaches world literature, Advanced Placement English language and composition, and the Shakespeare elective.

This book was typeset in Palatino and Helvetica by Barbara Frazier.
Typeface used on the cover were Trajan and Handwriting–Dakota.
The book was printed on 50-lb. Williamsburg Offset paper by Versa Press, Inc.